Wine, Women and War: A Diary of Disillusionment

Anonymous

J. H. SEARS & COMPANY, Inc.

Publishers   *New York*

First Edition, November, 1926
Second Edition, November, 1926
Third Edition, December, 1926
Fourth Edition, December, 1926
Fifth Edition, January, 1927
Sixth Edition, January, 1927

MANUFACTURED COMPLETE BY THE
KINGSPORT PRESS
KINGSPORT, TENNESSEE
United States of America

Introduction

It is rarely an editor's fortune to discover a book deserving not only of publication, but of the widest reading, whose author, in its composition, had neither end in view, yet such happens to be the case with relation to the present work.

The existence of this diary of disillusionment was disclosed to me quite casually by its author, following an accidental encounter on a western train in the spring of 1926. Our friendship is of long standing, but, since 1918, our meetings have been rare, for our work is quite dissimilar, and while, in a way, our paths have paralleled, they have seldom converged.

In the course of our revival of old memories, quite naturally the talk finally turned upon my friend's adventures abroad during the period of the Great War. I had known something of his activities "over there" where, though trained as an artillery officer, he had been attached to "Intelligence," but nowise in detail. The anecdotes he recalled, however, as one by one the other occupants of the Club Car withdrew, and we were finally left alone with a drowsy porter, were so vividly illuminating that I expressed regret that he had not kept a journal during the period of his service. His reply was that he had, or, if not a journal, at least a detailed diary. He explained that the entries were made in a series of small black books in a half shorthand of his own devisement, but quite readily translatable.

My journalist's curiosity was aroused to the point of urging him to transcribe the diaries and let me read the resultant manuscript. His argument was that no one could conceivably have the slightest interest in the material. Finally, however, after an hour's persuasion he promised to make a running copy of the diaries, and, later, began the work with some zeal, a zeal that had evaporated, I may add, by the time the task was finished.

"There it is," he said, thrusting at me the parcel of manuscript, "do whatever you please with it."

My own amazement as I read those typed pages will be repeated, I am confident, on the part of everyone who reads those same pages transformed to make the present volume.

For here is one of the most remarkable books that the Great War has produced, a vivid, living thing; done without attempt at drama or at form by an honest man who possesses, unconsciously, an extraordinary literary facility. So far as one is aware, nothing like it has been produced in any country since the conflict, though why this is true is difficult to understand. Written with perfect candor for the eyes of its author only, it is published now without editing or emendations of any sort, save the devising of its title. This being the case, the necessity of its author's anonymity will be apparent to every reader. Authentic from the first word to the last, it is precisely what it appears to be—the undramatized record of the actions and reactions, recorded almost at the moment of their execution and perception, of one young American, who, given a part to play in the greatest drama the world has ever witnessed, played it through to the final curtain.

KARL EDWIN HARRIMAN.

NEW YORK,
AUGUST, 1926.

Contents

Wine, Women and War: A Diary of Disillusionment

August, 1917

Thur., 27th.—Teedle-de-um!

> "... *You'll never get rich,*
> *You son of a bitch,*
> *You're in the army na-ow!"*

Signed, sealed and delivered. "Candidate." 2nd. R.O.T.C. Ft. Sheridan.

November, 1917

Tues., 27th.—No more "walk my post in a military manner," keeping horses from committing nuisance. "Reposing special trust and confidence in my patriotism, valor, fidelity and abilities," W. Wilson, Esq., has this day appointed me 1st Lieut., Field Artillery, of his army. He's an optimist!

Wed., 28th.—Savings of a lifetime to the profiteers. Riding boots, whipcord breeches, calling cards, sterling silver identification tag, Sam Browne belt and other essentials of what commission calls "grade and position." Wonder if officers have to buy their own coffins.

Thur., 29th.—Getting used to being saluted. Losing the Uncle Tom feeling of "candidate." Occupied with size, shape and position of shoulder bars. Feel like a Knight of Pythias.

Fri., 30th.—Collecting equipment. Told to take a lot of soap—none in France.

December, 1917

Sat., 1st.—Official list of stuff to take. Only thing left out is firewood. Town full of still-damp officers—all buying. War is not hell for State Street.

Sat., 15th.—The old birds who say they "envy" us—who do they think they are kidding? Made will, fixed up life insurance, etc. All set.

Sun., 16th.—Off to N.Y. First farewells. The poor mothers! Glad *that's* over. Lucky beggars to training camps here. And they bellyache at not going overseas! Less boring over there, at that, maybe. Though I would like a hand in making wops into Americans.

Tues., 18th.—More buying. All sorts of patent gadgets. Chlorine for drinking water. Out to Governor's Island for field glasses. None to be had, thank God!

Wed., 19th.—G—— C—— bought a snakebite package. Must think he's going to Africa.

Thur., 20th.—Hoboken. Orders. Pictures, etc. Filled out second hundred thousandth questionnaire. Begins to look like war. Bought a large, expensive bag. Probably never see my trunks.

5

Fri., 21st.—Hard days, these, but worth living through for glimpse into S——'s sweet soul. Such calm steadfastness! The best of us weaklings beside the women. In heaven's debt now for the years I've had her, and no complaints if the loan is called.

Sat., 22nd.—S—— working like a dog—always with a smile. To-morrow's the day, and smiling not so easy.

Sun., 23rd.—Left S—— at 6 this morning. She the better man. God—what a moment! To ship with J——. Sailing postponed. But one farewell enough and then some. Hid ourselves until sure S—— and J—— were on train for home. Tried to "celebrate" at Biltmore. Wouldn't serve liquor to uniform. D—— worked his French and got address of place on 44th Street. Champagne in pitchers, and three members of French Mission. Sang the *Marseillaise* and *S.S.B.* R—— fell downstairs, and P—— cried on landlady's bosom until she cried, too, and her husband locked both in back room so they wouldn't ruin trade. Headwaiters of Biltmore, Sherry's and Delmonico's came in about one. More champagne. First time I was ever chummy with a headwaiter. Went to ship at daylight. F—— had to be carried.

Mon., 24th.—Sailing postponed again. H——'s wife down for usual good-bys. For their sake wish the damned boat would clear. Too awful. At night, party at Delmonico's, as guests of headwaiter. Lots of wine—good wine, not merely expensive, host said. Got back to ship somehow, though J—— had a private war with a couple of cops.

Tues., 25th.—Merry Xmas. Jolly day! Sailing still *mañana.* Very comfortable on boat. Except for uniforms and absence of ladies, no different from ordinary liner. Feel like Lord Nelson at Trafalgar, when a mast was shot away beside him. "Gentlemen, we're likely to die at any moment, but by the Lord, I would not be anywhere else for a thousand pounds!" No worry about U-boats. One of the stewards, on transports since the beginning, has never even seen a periscope. So glad I brought a life-preserver.

Wed., 26th.—Another reprieve. Thinking a lot of S——. So gentle—and so strong. "In case of death, forward to my wife," I write in flyleaf of this book. Though if I pass on in the next week or two it will be via water—no forwarding.

Thur., 27th.—Sailed at dawn. Only humor in the gloom furnished by J——'s dispatch-case, which his wife bought him for his orders. Wore it strapped around him, and ought to be as easily mislaid as a grand piano. But first thing he did on ship was to lose it. Secretly glad, I think.

Fri., 28th.—J—— gave me S——'s Christmas gift last night. Fellow I didn't know came in as I was reading it. When he learned the truth, he, too, dissolved. Later, we shook hands, and agreed we had nothing to be ashamed of. What a brave, sweet message it was. Valedictory to all the preparation. I shall keep it always. Soldiering doesn't end with war. It's a fight all the way, to the Honorable Discharge.

Sat., 29th.—Getting shaken down. Wonder if there's

any difference between the stuff the English put on their puddings and billposters' paste.

Sun., 30th.—Trying everything for H——'s home-sickness. Nothing works but whiskey. Prefer him homesick.

Mon., 31st.—At the speed we're making the war will be over before we get there. But nobody's urging the Captain to hurry.

January, 1918

Tues., 1st.—At anchor in Halifax, lately demolished by an explosion, and looking as dreary as we feel. Sub-zero weather. New year well started on its journey, which is more than we are. God knows how long we stay here. 2500 Chinese laborers came aboard to-day. Long days, though "Red Dog" and "Spit in the Ocean" help.

Wed., 2nd.—Room-mate, Lieut. M—— mysteriously taken ashore. Something serious the matter with him. Lucky stiff—he's merely going to die. Wrote long drool home. Wondering, like *tout le monde,* how long it's all going to last.

Thur., 3rd.—Having had our spirits thoroughly broken by three months at Sheridan, find it hard to assume mental attitude of honest-to-goodness officers. Such unwonted consideration! Colonels and Majors treat us almost like human beings. Sailed at 2 in blinding snowstorm, leading convoy. High winds and rough seas. Many seasick.

Fri., 4th.—My Jaeger blanket best thing I have. Wrapped in its soft folds, dream of days that are past, and sweeter days that may come again. A sort of link between this nightmare and the reasonable life behind. Read a poem in the S.E.P. by Grace Ellery Channing:

"From any woman to a soldier." More than wet the old lamps.

Sat., 5th.—Heavy going. Thick fog. Got a cold, settling in sinus, with nice fever. Feel lower than a snake's navel.

Sun., 6th.—Most of the crowd sick. R——, who's been very low, has got diarrhea now, which makes him a hundred per center. Seems silly to be writing a diary, here. We're a hell of a ways from land, yet.

Mon., 7th.—All the members of our gang wear without tarnish. Great fellows! No trip for anybody with jumpy nerves. The submarine isn't a painted devil to scare children. It's too damned real.

Tues., 8th.—J—— was telling to-night about a chap in N.Y. who was detailed to entertain the French Mission. One of them asked to go to a sporting house. So he led the way to Abercrombie & Fitch's. Wonder why I bought a trick mess kit there. We eat off perfectly good silver.

U.S. declared war on Britain to-night. Col. P——, O.C. ordered bar closed. Freddie, the bar steward, said the God damned ship belonged to his Britannic Majesty, George Rex, who took no orders from any blinking U.S. Colonel. Bar still open. All bets on Britain.

Wed., 9th.—On submarine watch. Spotted a periscope about 5 A.M. and sounded off. A bird—seagull or something—but everybody enjoyed the excitement except K——, who got bawled out for reporting without life belt. Cruiser joined us, blinking like a firefly.

Thur., 10th.—Slept without blankets. Excitement at noon by all ships reversing course for hour or two. Other ships then disappeared. No explanation.

Fri., 11th.—Sixteenth day from N.Y. Orders to sleep in clothes—danger zone. Most of gang solemnized occasion by getting boiled. Five ships now in convoy.

Sat., 12th.—Time filled with physical drills, French classes, cards, reading and drinking. My job is fire guard, on E deck, with cargo of T.N.T. under me, and two decks of Chinks above. My only weapon a cheerful smile, and the Chinese have a lot of rifles. If we ever have trouble, it will be good night. 4 pistols total U.S. armament aboard.

Sun., 13th.—Never knew there were so many different kinds of card games. Costs about five dollars to learn one. Haven't yet learned to shuffle, which troubles G—— more than a moral weakness. Chess a better game, the difficulty being the sort of man who likes it. Wrote S——. Hard to write intimately, with chilling thought of some dyspeptic censor cramping hand. Now in "extreme danger zone." Ship zig-zags continually. Blue lights. All noise muffled. Orders to sleep in clothes. These U-boats a damned *nuisance!*

Mon., 14th.—Saw first land about 6 A.M. Thrilled with couple of destroyers that came out of nowhere, scooted around, with a lot of blinking, and disappeared. All set to land about 2, but pilot boat went and got blown up. Anchored in roadstead until 1:30 A.M., with red flag on us, warning to look out for our T.N.T., I guess. Cabled home safe arrival, though long way from arrived yet. *

Pretty low—though it isn't the fear of what may be, so much as the certainty of a long separation from S—— and the children. And to think I brought this thing upon us of my own free will! But got to push on. Head up, however leaden the heart. Can see S——, that last moment in N.Y., with the loveliest eyes that ever opened on a beautiful soul. Can almost feel the touch of that cool firm hand. Gives me strength— and weakness, too. The miles between us are too real. Certainly the best friend God ever gave a man.

Tues., 15th.—Docked Liverpool 8 A.M. Grieved at orders—no London. Lined up on deck and divided three ways, Field Artillery, Heavies and Trench Mortars. The Heavy boys don't seem so downcast, but Mortars are disgusted.† Unloaded our own baggage. Jammed into cars. Left at 12. Got some lunch at 6. Arrived Southampton in rainstorm at 9:30. Marched to what they call a "rest" camp. My large and costly grip an albatross. Made mile to street car O.K. But mile at other end too much. Fingers straightened out and could hardly walk. Lost contact with column and wound up in midst of muddy plain, no lights visible—LOST! Then fell down in puddle and lost

*This cable was sent "Sans Origine." When it arrived the whole town, including a university president, put in weeks trying to find where the town of San Sorigine was.

†Legend had it that the incorrigibles of the African Discipline Battalions: military penal units—the Bat' d'Af.—were offered the privilege of service in the Trench Mortars—the "Suicide Club"; and that all accepted joyously. Hence the title: "Les Joyeux," and "Les Zephyrs."

bag, too. A swell night. No beds, no heat, no drinking water.

Wed., 16th.—More marching with that damned bag. Aboard boat for France at 6. Jammed with Australians. No place to sit, let alone lie down. Cold and sick.

Thur., 17th.—Arrived Havre 3 A.M. Ashore 8:30. Marched to another "rest" camp, 6 mi. up hill. Truck for baggage, thank God. Little boys, begging sous— all looking exactly like my own. Tents pitched in mud —no beds. The place is Senvic, a summer resort, they say. Not so good in January.

Fri., 18th.—Pulled out at 5, leaving Infantry boys behind. J—— full of commiseration. He's all up and at 'em. Expects to be slitting German throats in a week or two. * Probably right, as we'll have a long session of schools. Got orders for Saumur at station. Left at 9, after rescuing K—— from a debauch of *pommes frites.*

Sat., 19th.—After night "six months long" got *near* Paris, 6 A.M. Q.M.'s left us at Blois. No food en route except what we could buy. Got "ration issue" in morning, by looting freight car—canned goldfish, pickles and what not. Swell breakfast. Nearly everybody full of wine. Anybody craving a fight got it. Arrived 10 P.M. Trucks to ancient barracks. Quartered with one man, though room for regiment. Excellent

---

*After a month in command of a venereal detachment at Blois, J—— got a nice shiny desk managing Chinese labor, and, in sixteen months of France, never heard a gun fired in anger.

food, and women to take care of rooms. Feel like an officer again.

Sun., 20th.—Assigned 9th Section. Got baggage— *all* of it, *mirabile dictu!* Downtown for hot shower in *bains douches*—first since N.Y. Over to "Y" in old château belonging to Papal count who made his pile out of wine. Unlike corresponding American, who would be ashamed of it, this fellow's wall decorations all symbolic of grape, and legs of living-room table made from wine-press screws. Wrote S—— a lot of mush.

Mon., 21st.—5:45 reveille once more. Classes in Math. and *bridling.* "Revision of trigonometrical functions." Nobody even knew what they were. French amazement that we held commissions in artillery. Back home they're probably still measuring deflection with calibrated knuckles. The French know this isn't an Indian war. Equitation, etc. Ft. Sheridan, only more so. The French get their ideas of the U.S. from the movies. Think we were all born in the saddle.

Went on as Section Officer of Day at 10:30. Unpacked chair. They used to kid me for toting a chair to the Great War. Could sell it to-day for any price. No substitute for chairs. Nor for fires. Tried to start one, but our only stick wouldn't burn.

Tues., 22nd.—Lectures—and bicycle ride which nearly did me in. Not allowed to wear spurs in equitation, but required on bikes. It's a way they have in the army. The French, polite and efficient, but we're "candidates" still. Four-year-old morons at home—eight here, the only difference. More equitation. This was a cavalry school (founded by Napoleon, they say), so they're strong on the *caracole à gauche*, etc. Had a blooded bucking broncho to-day. Rőde his neck, but not thrown, thanks to presence of mind in half-strangling him. Thought I was pretty smart, but Chasseur d'Afrique in charge said: "Remembair to ride ze horse, ze horse must not ride you." I'm willing, but he ought to tip off the horse.

Magnificent here, even if it is not war. Cold and damp indoors, but spring outside. Country loveliest in France. Full of "cranneyed crag and storeyed ruin," and *le vin de Saumur* not hard to take. Get a great hate for the Boche. To think what he's done to this pleasant land and gentle people. The faces so sad—but so unfailingly cheerful. And so much black. Makes the throat ache, to go down a street.

The lights go out on me. Instead of writing down my thoughts, can only think them—dream of my girl's hand in mine . . . empty comfort.

Wed., 23rd.—Reveille again. I've certainly lost my taste for that tune! More equitation. And people say they "love" horses! No grooming here, but more riding. Maybe they haven't been told we came over for a war, not a circus. Drool on explosives by Capt. W——. Cold and lonesome. Wish to hell I'd picked a job like T——. He had some sense. *

Thur., 24th.—Thought when we left Sheridan, all booted and spurred, we were officers and gents. Hell!

---

*T—— started life as Captain in the Q.M., without wasting any time in training camps. Went to London, where his wife joined him. Had an important job, saw all the important people, and came home with a promotion.

We're in school again. No manure-piling or bed-making, but only because they don't trust us. Marched hither and yon, in "formation" for everything, even to weekly and obligatory bath. The *manège* a chamber of horrors. French cavalry knows no superior—and no wonder. Anybody who gets through this training ought to be superior. Extremely sore *en arrière*. Expect to be sorer. The war will end before I'm the kind of horseman they're set on making me. Full of curiosity about aforesaid war. Knew lots more at home than here. Nothing but *communiqués* less credible than most advertising.

Fri., 25th.—Passed test to-day taking apart and putting together breech of a 75, whole business in a bag, with sense of touch and copper penny only tools. Imagine doing that with our 3". But understand Washington is trying to "improve" the 75.

La Rochefoucauld's remark about generalities applies to American notion of money-grubbing French. In tobacco shop to-day where I bought briquet last week for 9 fr. 75. Old lady said she'd overcharged me, and handed back 1 fr. 50.

Newspapers full of peace talk—none whatever among the military. Not much talk of any sort—too busy. Exceedingly strict discipline. Every detail of life regulated. Like German prisoners I saw to-day. Stolidly docile—animal-like. Hard to believe they ever *think*. Therefore—good soldiers. Not brutes—automata, rather. Pitiful—a little nauseating.

Sat., 26th.—No fire ever been successfully built in our stove. But smoke from all other stoves in barracks comes in through our chimney. Can't breathe and fingers too numb to write with.

Unusually busy morning at equitation. Seven men thrown. One of them to hospital, en route, likely, to more permanent repose. *

Out in the country to-day with R—— and played with some children. Adorable, soft-voiced, and so polite. A grim pathos in their gentle ways. Everyone had somebody *à la guerre*. They get me. All my pay goes in *sous* to irresistible gamins who remind me, every one, of my own little lad. To a *pâtisserie* at D'Istrées, and sought oblivion in numerous bottles of Burgundy.

Sun., 27th.—The day of rest and melancholia. No word yet from home. Long talk with bunkie, M——. He is so lonesome and miserable I felt gay by contrast. To bed early. Nothing else to do.

Mon., 28th.—A lot of new arrivals—Captains, mostly. Pleasurable emotions in having rankers in guise of "new boys."

Great excitement to-day. Everybody with automobile experience called out, and bunch picked to go to tractor school somewhere. I among them. God knows what it means, but a gas engine has charms after these damned horses.

Poor M—— lower than ever. Panicky. Wonders if he hadn't better insult Col. D—— and get kicked into something besides Artillery. Can't see why first class

---

*After a long session in hospital at Angers, this man, B——, went up to the line as an observer, and while visiting an Infantry O.P., a German shell dropped the curtain on him.

shipping clerk should be wasted making rotten artillery-
man. Neither could anybody else—outside the army.
The army view is he got into F.A. by act of God, and
to take him out would be blasphemy.*

Tues., 29th.—Orders to proceed to Fontenay aux
Roses. Nobody knows where that is. But nobody
ever knows where anything is, so not surprised.

Wed., 30th.—Left Saumur 2:20. Maj. D——
down to see us off. Good fellow, now he's no longer
obliged to ride us. Destination: Paris. Fontenay, etc.,
somewhere in vicinity. Arrived 8 P.M. *La ville lumière*
in reverse English. Pitch black. No lights but *réverbères,* and they in blue. To Hôtel Edouard Sept. Took
stroll. Felt like emancipated slave. All but raped.
Zig-zig—nothing else but. More danger in French
skirts than Boche shells. But danger well advertised.
Nobody need fall unless he gets behind himself and
pushes. From the Opéra to the Etoile a million girls
all whispering: "Will you sleep wiz me?" C—— and
E——fell for the first ones they met.
    About 1 awakened by wail of sirens. Guns going
hell-bent by time I got to window, and colored lights
of defense planes high in sky. Flash of bursting shrapnel plainly visible. Bomb explosions muffled and distant at first, but one presently fell about a block away.
Terrific racket. No especial alarm among people.
Streets and roofs crowded with gapers. Funny to see

*M—— finally got with an outfit in the 3rd Division, where
he functioned in the Ammunition Train. Got a wound stripe
and a promotion—almost—and now subscribes to the Field
Artillery Journal.

wearers of *Médaille Militaire* (the only one that means
a damn) scuttle for shelter like rabbits when the *alerte* *
starts. Their contention that they're reasonable beings
sounds reasonable. But even air raids get tiresome.
Sleepy long before it was over, and back to bed. The
big city certainly did its stuff for our first visit.†

Thur., 31st.—Paris doesn't seem especially excited
about us. Its interest exclusively in our francs. Sam
Browne belts have no thrill for chambermaids, cabbies,
maquereaux, shopkeepers, etc. *Sales cochons!* Not
like down South, where a kid helped me carry bag half
a mile and saluted proudly, assuring me that between
"comrades" there was no silver for service. Paris shows
the *militaire* a hard, rouged face, and an open palm, all
too plainly itching.

Off to Fontenay aux Roses. Wrong town, of course.
Never heard of us. Back to Paris. Then to Creteil.
Finally, Camp de St. Maur. No cheers over quarters.
Cold and wet. To Vincennes for *confiture* and see what
Boche did to it other night. It was a plenty.

This camp strictly French. *Le Cours Pratique Ar-
tillerie Lourde Tracteur.* We the first Americans to

*The warning signal. Given in various ways, such as bang-
ing on an empty shell case, suspended from a tree. This had a
marked resemblance to the sounds given out by a railroad eating-
house before the advent of dining cars. The *alerte* in Paris,
against air raids, was given by sirens and the firemen, blowing their horns.
†Eighty-nine bombs were dropped in this raid, with 36 killed
and 192 wounded. From January to October, 1918, aircraft
dropped 228 bombs, with 206 killed and 392 injured: the long-
range guns fired 168 shells, killing 196 and wounding 417. Total
of "hits" was 396, with 402 killed and 889 injured, making the
total casualties of Paris 1211.

attend. Bum quarters, and especially rotten cans. But treated like adults. The C.O., Maj. C——, C.A.C., a peach. Looks like interesting work. Instructors automotive engineers who know their stuff.

Gassed all P.M. over future. Some think we'll go back to F.A. schools, some to new tractor schools, some attached to outfits. They say this such a new thing it constitutes entirely different branch of service. May not go back to Artillery at all. May even form a new corps, with different insignia—a crankshaft, maybe, instead of crossed guns. A haulage corps for heavy ordnance, officers mounted on baby Peugeots. More likely, though, we'll wind up in the dental corps, or be postmasters.

February, 1918

Fri., 1st.—New breakfast—frozen poached eggs. Cold as the devil. Got a stove and French soldier to run it, but no wood. Wish the home folks could see us now. No flags and clinking spurs here. *Pas militaire* this plotting cosine of pressure curve in 4 cycle 16 valve motor, and replacing compound fractured gudgeon pins. Overalls the *tenue.* French appallingly scientific. Our careless inexactness of speech. Too many words like "thingumbob" and "dewdab." Homesick as hell. Haven't heard from home in 42 days.

Sat., 2nd.—Reports of strikes in Austria, and hopes of early peace. Funny how notions change. Back home we drooled about "democracy" and "glory." Like Burgundy wine, that stuff doesn't stand a sea voyage. Most of the people whom the papers squeak about being "eager for the Front" about as eager for the small-pox.

Tremendously interesting work here. Learning true inwardness of gas engines, tractors, caterpillars, etc.— theory and practice. Knots, hitches, use of block and tackle, winches, cranes, "dead men," etc. Typical "recitation" is being given couple of 15-ton guns, and told to take them out of a pond and over a road full of shell-holes, through swamp, to determined position. May take couple of days floundering in mud, and half a dozen tractors to find "answer." Got about as much "romance" to it as hauling a busted street car out of Mad. Ave. tunnel. Dungarees the uniform, and no bugles.

Sun., 3rd.—Spent day in Paris. Trams crowded—mostly with widows and children.

Mon., 4th.—Put in morning on tractors and trying to pronounce "Panhard." Crazy about French instructors. Most of them 2nd Lieuts., but certainly know their hardware. After dinner over to Vincennes for bit of lushing. Got pleasantly jingled, but S—— passed out, and P—— disappeared entirely. About 11, couple of French sentries fetched him in. They'd had to gag him, so he wouldn't wake the whole place.

Tues., 5th.—This certainly not like Saumur. Gen. Petain visiting us to-day, and we were very apologetically requested to make *early* reveille—"a quarter to seven or seven"—so orderlies could police barracks for old boy's inspection. My God—*incroyable!* How we suffer!

Studying design of crank shafts and how to remove carbon more interesting than horse-shoeing and ballistics of manure. This course a real opportunity, and graduate of C.P.A.L.T. knows something. Whole idea new to our army. French say transport needs experts just as much as firing and orientation.

Awake or asleep, this life has all the privacy of w.k. goldfish. Hurried, regimented, always en masse and in plain view, all instincts of civilization violated. But one drifts with current, dreams incessantly, and somehow manages a sort of happiness.

We get wry smile out of "interesting" life we're

supposed to have. About as "interesting" as being behind a stockade in one of Mr. Ford's plants. War and
its thrills have stepped out of the office for a minute.
No thrills computing r.p.m. caused by 9° lag in exhaust
valves.

45 days, now, and no word from home. May all be
dead. *Maybe* better than what F—— got to-day.
First letter in two months, and news that wife had
died. All he could do was get drunk.

Wed., 6th.—Lecture on 155 G.P.F.* Remarkable
gun. Extreme mobility. Plate on one side of carriage: "Soignez vos freins." On other: "the well
aimed shot is the only one that's worth anything."
Hardly intelligible to American mind, which prefers
speed to accuracy any day.

Maneuvered 50 h.p. Renault, weighing 9 tons, all
over lot. Some bus!

Troubled with severe constipation, complicated by
acute homesickness. S—— J——, who isn't troubled
with anything, says two are part of same thing. Probably right. Sunny disposition and carbonized bowels
not buddies.

Thur., 7th.—Still laying down pill barrage, but enemy refuses to be dislodged. More lectures on internal
combustion theory—wish I could apply them to my
own! Sometimes the French irritate. They lay such
stress on non-essentials—such damned slaves to precedent. Exasperating!

---

*The Grande Porte Filleux, or 6″ long range rifle, designed
by Col. Filleux of the French Army. As admirable in its
class as the 75 mm. in its: and by the French, almost as
affectionately regarded.

Still waiting for news from home. If people over there would only realize what they can do with a fountain pen. Trivialities what we want. Reading ads. in home papers favorite diversion. A copy of *Vogue* went big. Commonplace things the only realities in a world of phantasmagoria. Morale O.K. Not a quitter or a grouch here, except T———, who's as yellow as his own Missouri mud.* But not a man who doesn't yearn for the end of it, and *home*. Lot of married men here, and that holy state not conducive to warlike spirit. No thought of home, though, until Boche completely *supprimé*. When that will be, *quién sabe?*

Much-touted German drive may never come off. Probably just feint, designed to scare Allies into negotiating peace. If the bluff's called, he may lay down his cards. Quit cold. Maybe end before summer. But no such notion officially. Extent of our preparations staggering. Tremendous lot of materiel delivered already. Heinie will never be able to stand against us. Troops rolling in steadily. And ideas with them. A lot to learn from the Allies, of course. But they can learn something from us. Organization our national middle name. Absorbing what's useful in foreign methods, but adapting and developing system strictly our own. Developing fast.

Just getting by, myself. Never graduate *cum laude*. Too damned technical. Can get a gun out of mud or grind valves, but plotting carburetion temperature curves—not there! Where do we go from here? Nobody knows.

---

*T——— later got with the ——nd Division, and was decorated twice.

Fri., 8th.—In quarters all A.M. with threatened mumps. Fear of quarantine. Examination in valve lag graphs. S—— grousing as usual. Say's he's here to learn how to run tractors—not build them. Nothing to do but go to bed. Light too poor for reading. Nothing to read, anyhow. Lie and mope, thinking how wonderful it would be to be back home and knowing that if and when we do get back, there will still be plenty of things to grouse over. That's the story—on and on—to the end of the book.

Sat., 9th.—To Big City for week-end. Dinner at Continental. Steak, f.f. pot., peas, dandelion salad, pudding and half bot. Burgundy—20 fr. Everything but cream, sugar and butter. Saw Rejane in "13th Chair" with rowdy audience, mostly fliers. Other boys busy elsewhere. Except M——, who spent evening in bath tub. Streets full of whores. Like gnats on July night. Paris most dangerous spot in war. R—— and E——, great swordsmen both, insist danger's overrated. French girls regularly inspected, and if you're careful, you'll be O.K., etc. Maybe—and then, maybe not.

Sun., 10th.—In Paris. Everything shut up. Christ, what a day! E—— full of virtue and a hang-over. Almost glad to get back to camp.

Mon., 11th.—Auto test. Lined up before strange cars and told to go to it. Great system! If you crank and *ne marche pas*, and you start tinkering with wiring, and go then to rear axle—*out!* Got to take it step by step. Diagnosis the thing. Mine a Delage, with horse-hair in needle-valve. J—— had distributor wires

crossed—mean, with almost a broken wrist as by-prod-
uct. Both got by.

After noon mess, out to country for driving test.
Poor M——, two French behind, with notebooks and
watches, given Peugeot and started up hill in sand.
Managed gear-shifting O.K., but at top, just as he was
going good, found a stalled *camion*. Slapped on brake
—no go—crashed. He's out! Didn't look at brakes
before starting—first thing to do in strange car. More
important to stop than start, they claim. M—— squealing all over place that he's driven cars for years, but
French adamant. He's through. De la R—— says:
"If you did that *au front*, you might be killed, which
would, of course, be of no special consequence. But you
would gum up the traffic, which would be serious."

Spent evening trying to learn bowline on bight from
all angles. S——'s everlasting yap about hard beds.
Everybody laughed at K—— when he first broke out
a nightcap, but he's been bid 50 fr. for it so far. Gay
life.

Tues., 12th.—Lecture on magnetos. Dope is two
more wks. of this. No news yet, from home. Hard to
be patient. So much can have happened. So powerless
to pierce the silence. Nothing much to write about.
Lectures, practical maneuvers in field, etc. Week-ends
in Paris, uneventful—even air raids. Raids here much
better. When a Boche gets chased out of Paris, he
drops all bombs he has left on us, there being an arsenal couple of hundred feet from our barracks. Been
ordered out at night several times. Getting to be a
damned nuisance—though it wouldn't be so nice if they
ever connected with that arsenal. Thank God for the
wine! If pacifists really want to end war, all they have

to do is end booze. Without it, everybody'd get so homesick they'd be useless. P—— dug up bottle of cognac, and had swell wrangle over Socialism, etc.

Wed., 13th.—Traction lectures and mech. man. in rain. Marvelous what edifice human brain has reared on law of lever. Feel like Archimedes! French very different from us. Been trying ten days to get couple of wooden horses for blackboards, out of French carpenter. Delivered to-day. American would have knocked them together in ten minutes. These all mortised and bolted—last forever. Means so out of proportion to purpose. Like sign over camp gate—work of art—ought to be in museum.

M—— got final orders to-night. Foul-mouthed little beast. S—— told him if his filthy tongue wagged again, he'd put wound stripes all over him. S—— no Puritan, but draws distinction between profanity and dirt. All with him. French say everybody swore lots more in '14 than now.

Thur., 14th.—Swell mess of "interrogation" on crank-shafts. Tractor work all aft. in mud. Sanctity of toil, etc.—blah! To restaurant in Bois de Vincennes with R—— and K—— for first class bender. Got lost coming back. Tried to break into arsenal, but prevented by "Rosalie" of French sentry at chest. Suggested mildly that next time somebody said "halt," I take him literally—he might be of nervous disposition.

Still no news from home. Everybody buried by this time, probably. Well, what can I do? *Je m'en fou.* That sounds like drunken writing, and it is.

Fri., 15th.—Spent all day hauling biggest gun in world out of pond with 2 tractors. Toss tons around like walnuts. Covered with mud. Brains and brawn both working full time. Whew! But what a grand and glorious feeling later! First letter from home—dated Dec. 29. Cold as the devil and fingers numb, but old heart on fire! Gosh, what notions at home about this show. W—— studying artillery. Maybe he'll enlist "when needed." Poor fish, he ought to be in the "Y." With his mathematical bean, he'd go big on triangulation and interior ballistics. But stuff about B—— makes me sick. Nothing but a God damned traitor. They shoot them here for less. Bolo, for instance. Playing the Boche game. Half the sad yarns you hear are made in Germany. If B—— thinks stories he hears are true, and the country's in danger, and all he does is stay home, wringing his fingers, he's just a dirty slacker—and those who aren't staying home will have long memories.*

Certainly knocks one in pit of stomach to hear complaints back home about gasoline restrictions, taxes, etc. Civilians here suffer privations Americans can't imagine, and always cheerful. Wish B—— could meet a lady (underscored) in Vincennes. Husband traded legs for Croix de Guerre. Little boy's feet stick through broken shoes. She tries to keep them alive by picking up odd jobs of washing. Her chief concern is for what she calls "the poor." Any able-bodied man who can be comfortable in U.S.A. has got an easy conscience. Don't envy him. B——'s dope all off about France being "bled white." Lot of frogs still on deck. And old J.B., despite feeding, financing and munitioning rest of world,

---

*B—— occupied himself with various aspects of finance and made a lot of money, notably in steel stocks. He now has a position of prominence in the community, and there is no evidence that the long memory of anyone ever operated to his disadvantage.

steadily increasing his wonderful army. The war will be won all right. But *we* won't win it. We'll merely help finish it sooner. Humility still our cue. Not muddling as much as claimed. Blunders, of course. But my guess no worse than what the Allies went through at beginning—or Germans, either.

Smoked last of M———'s cigars. Each one a sort of hecatomb to memory. Fellows carrying their precious letters around, reading them over and over. Heigho! Maybe I wouldn't like to see that little Lt. in the Home Guards and his Red Cross sister, and their adorable mother! It's an ache, sometimes, to get home and prove how much she is to me. And I know that if and when I do get home, I'll be the same God damned crab I was when I went away. *C'est la vie.*

Sat., 16th.—Coldest day yet. Ice everywhere. Lectures all day. Fingers too numb to hold anything but a bottle. To Paris, P.M. Walked streets on tight rope between common sense and dear delightful women. Fled like St. Anthony back to hotel. Found M———, nothing on but B.V.D's, and couple of ten-minute female eggs, much at home. Awful shock, because M———'s virtue one illusion left in cruel world. He tried to explain, but I said there was nothing to explain—be human like the rest of us. He nearly blew up. Turned out that R——— and E——— had brought the two hookers into adjoining room, leaving them for some reason, and they wandered into our room. Poor M——— knowing no French, and just turning in, was helpless. Chased them out and M——— and I went to bed.

Sun., 17th.—Early this morning, knock on door and one of the girls asking where Monsieur R——— was. She said both their boy friends had skipped, and they were hungry. So I went in, nothing on but pyjamas, and ordered up breakfast. Explained that R—— and E—— were not *sauvages Americains*, but had probably just stepped out for a prophylactic. While we were eating, bang! bang! on door, and mgr. of hotel was demanding we all clear out—such behavior not permitted in respectable place, etc. Appearances against us, but M—— offered to push his fat Portuguese face into his back collar-button, and he beat it.*

Parted from ladies and took in Invalides with M——. Not same thrill at Bonaparte's tomb I got ten years ago. Seem to feel differently about military men now—especially Generals. Makes me realize how much gilt has chipped off war's picture-frame. M—— quoted Grant: "never was a good war or a bad peace." That would be treason at home. Nice thing about being here is you can be treasonable in safety.

Met M—— J——. All dressed up. Capt. Judge Advocate's Dept. Has car, travels all over country—going to Italy next month. Important as hell. M——, who got 2nd Lieutenancy F.A., after six months training camps, can't see justice of it. Says he's worked like machine and stabled like horse. Funny, though, M—— J—— probably wishes he was "in thick of it," "where men are men," etc., and writes back home cursing his desk job.

Back to camp to find letter from A——. Stuck at

*Found out afterward that what the manager was really mad about was the fact that the two girls were unlicensed vendors—cutting in under the regular *concessionnaires* who were supplied by the *concierge*.

Saumur. Thinks he's got indeterminate sentence, and wishes he was with us.*

Another barracks row. S—— picked on A——. Wanted to start another Civil War and kill all Southerners. Long, cockeyed argument on cause, origin and consequences of Rebellion. A—— snored all through it. Then an air raid. Have them every moonlit night now. Lights out, and Archies going full blast. Machine guns aloft plainly audible. A—— awoke, glanced out of window, cursed racket, and fell snoring again. Hard to keep excited, even over air raids.

Mon., 18th.—Lectures. Supposed to be taking short course toward diplomas as trouble-shooters. French seem to think we're here for life. Sweat blood calculating coefficient of rolling friction and plotting isothermic curves. Difference between French and ourselves. Do small things infinitely well. Much more precise in planning. Thorough where we're superficial. But we amaze them the way we dig in. Moved a big howitzer through swamp in 4 hrs. other day. French student officers took a couple of days. We have more ingenuity, more open minds and greater initiative. They find us dumb at mathematics. We find them impractical, wasting time terribly on non-essentials. Humor and exasperation on both sides. Anyway, we're learning a lot—and so are they. Fair exchange.

Learned to-day we leave here Mar. 1. Assigned to outfits, probably Nat'l Guard, and in action shortly. Some fully equipped and fairly well trained. The

*A——, after serving in the Ambulance and winning the Croix de Guerre, came home, joined the army, and after months of schools, here and abroad, did garrison duty for the balance of the war.

"Real Thing" not so far off. S—— confident he'll be
pushing daisies within a fortnight, but thanks the *au
Delà* his education nearly over. Says he'd rather die
than suffer another "interrogation." Well—war, or
recruiting labor gangs in Madagascar—got to take it
as it comes.

Sent home some money to-day, to apply on dear old
mortgage. First time in my life I've been able to save
anything.

Tues., 19th.—Lecture on torque, etc. Dug gun-pits
all P.M. One letter in 9 wks—at that one more than most
of boys have had. B—— dished up some more of his
sewage, but little reptile piped down when S—— came
in. Latter a muscular Christian who says his prayers
on his knees.

Wed., 20th.—Out to country for maneuvers. Expected regular Q.M. lunch. Found tables, with linen
and cutlery, in court of quaint old castle. Eggs, wine,
fruits, coffee, salad and cold meats. Also nuts and figs.
China to eat from, and men to wait on us. Me for the
French army in next war.

De la R—— told anecdote of Von Krohn, "attaché-
pirate" at Madrid. Crossing France from St. Sebas-
tian to Geneva, "in true Boche fashion concentrated on
matter of nourishment." Dining car swamped. When
he asked for bill, dining-car steward said: "Keep your
money and your regret for French cooking. I will give
you credit—until the Day of Revenge."

The sort of stuff we're doing: "A tractor weighing
5741 kilos, of which 3428 is on rear axle and 2493 on
front. Distance between axles, 3.20 meters. On rear
of tractor is crane, projecting 2.96 meters. What load
may be carried on crane without blocking up rear of

car, assuming safe maximum load of 5 tons per axle, and allowing 30% factor of safety?

What torque is developed by 24 H.P. motor at 1200 R.P.M.?

In motor firing 1-3-4-2 cylinders 1 and 4 misfire. What is trouble?

Explain how to time magneto with 25% fixed advance.

Does exhaust valve open at high dead center? If not, explain why.

What is magneto speed of 6 cyl. engine at 1800 R.P.M.?

S—— wants this one put on his monument, back in Seattle: "Top of carburetor float chamber having been punctured, is repaired by soldering plate, .4 mm thick, on it. Plate weighs 5 grams. Diameter of float chamber is 65 mm. Diameter of needle valve, 7 mm. Sp. grav. of petrol, .072. Ratio lever-arms actuating needle valve, 2-1. How much will float have to be moved to compensate for washer? *Answer:* .85 mm. Discovered, Feb. 20, 1918, by J—— S——. R.I.P."

Dreamed so vividly last night of the children—touching B——'s soft cheeks. Weakness! Mustn't be always looking backward toward the west. But hard to keep those gentle voices out of the ears, and those countless little scenes burned in memory—forgotten gestures, phrases, incidents of a past so far away. If we ever get home, war-worn and heroic, full of lies but sure of listeners, veterans of the Great Adventure—ah, me!

Learned that B—— H—— got himself transferred from overseas duty to Des Moines. Not sure I envy him.

Papers full of "German Offensive." Boche seems encouraged by Russian situation. But Maximalism not yet understood. It yields to Germans arms, but I think German people will yet yield to it. Militarily, Germans can hold out long time yet. Cling to faith German *people* will wake up. Meanwhile, these God damned problems!

Thur., 21st.—H—— S—— in trouble again. Girl complained to C.O. he'd "run off with shoes and 40 fr." *Qu'ils sont sauvages, les Américains!*
God-awful exams in traction.

Fri., 22nd.—Latrines working overtime on rumors of what happens to us next. Rainy and cold. Sort of day devil does best business in *le cafard*.
P—— hatched great scheme. No street-women for him. Too dangerous. Going to spend week-ends with *petite amie*. Safer and much cheaper.*

Sat., 23rd.—To Paris. Met M—— C——, 2nd Lieut. Q.M.C., buying tinware. Very comfortable in beautiful old apartment in Latin Quarter. Squeezing every ounce of drama out of situation. Talks of being "bored" with Paris, wanting to go to Front, etc. Old stuff. At that, not a *camoufleur*. *Poseur*, rather.†
Saw E—— J——. Dead to shame. Desk job in Red Cross, fat salary, motor car, and traveling expenses. Contemptuous of men in line. Amazing how many young able-bodies in Croix Rouge and "Y." Wear uniforms. Even hang titles on themselves. That husky *embusqué* O—— G—— referred to in society columns at home as "Colonel."

*P—— got his the second week.
†M—— C—— later got some sort of staff job, and had portrait painted, bandeau on arm, with background of smoke clouds, broken caissons, dying horses, etc. Also decorated, and promoted, of course.

E—— J—— having "time of his life," he said. And
B—— having such an "interesting" time in Washington
—sweating over 4 Min. Men, probably. On other hand,
D—— R—— turned down for army because of flat
feet (also cold, he says) joined French Red Cross, and
been in really hot sectors for months, got to be identi-
fied with fellows like J—— and G——. Not fair. Resent anybody's not suffering, somehow—person or pocket.
Envy, probably.

Found E—— at hotel, primed for large evening.
Nose slightly damp, myself. Fell in with couple of turf-
riders who led way to *maison d'amour*. Old dame on
stairs, counting—a throw-back to the knitters of the
guillotine. Indescribable naïveté of girls. Little wine
and lot of laughter. Approaching a state of mind like
the ancient Greeks had. Little stress on morals, as
such. Squeeze as much fun out of the dry old orange
of life as you can. The idea of the "bad shot"—after
all, a fall from high purpose is only a fall—one miss in
the everlasting game of shooting at the narrow target
of righteousness. Leaves no scar on the soul. Pick up
and start over. Why not? Better philosophy, maybe,
than what grew in gloomy attics of Plymouth Rock.
Badness and goodness hard to tell apart these days.
Standing on one's head, rather. So many "bad" so
surely merit heaven: so many "good" such swine. To
bed 2:30. R—— checked in 3:30, more than usually
drunk.

Sun., 24th.—Called on G—— T——. Sort of over-
cultured effeminate American colony so fertile in. Made
me feel bad words, and ashamed when I spoke them.
Picked up F—— R—— and couple of tarts, off duty.
Traded lunch for some excellent conversation. Hard

life these girls lead—no illusions—but they get their fun out of it. Back to dreary hole at St. Maur.

Mon., 25th.—Gunnery exam. G.P.F. lectures. Out for night maneuvers. 4 guns—15 tons each—position in forest. No lights. Wheels mired to hubs. Great stuff! Got job of phone corporal. Worked all night. Full moon, but windy. No Gothas. Back to barracks 7:30. Everybody crabby.

Tues., 26th.—Lecture at 9—changing tires! Good God! Off in trucks 20 mi. to Mt. Griffon. Gun emplacements—last of Marne defense—made in '14 and never used. Bored with gunnery. Views, ideas—small coin of imagination so much more precious. Tedious trip back. Uniform agreement that anyone joining up for this stuff was an ass. Curious how quickly we've taken on the fed-up feeling of the people here. Not much glamour left. Parlor warriors and steam-heated publicists back home have it all. About as much glamour to soldiering, so far, as collecting garbage.

Wed., 27th.—Lecture on Ford car. We think it marvel of cheapness—the French, a marvel of mechanical ingenuity. Lavish care on their flivvers. Talked to *poilu*—9 yrs. in U.S., lately butler at B——'s in Cleveland.

To Fontenay with R—— for "collation," *petits pains, confiture,* and *quelque chose à boire.*

Thur., 28th.—Reveille, 5:30. To Mt. Griffon with guns. Rain. All guns emplaced by 4—some job. Inspected by *gros légumes.* Then took them out—more of a job. Removing *cingalis* a fright. Bed at 12, cold, wet and tired, but proud of good job. Capstan hauling, most of it—slept without rocking.

March, 1918

Fri., 1st.—Like last day of school. Valedictories, inspirational talks, and usual crap. M—— and P—— came home from Fontenay very tight. Hard to keep matter private. Capt. R—— thought he ought to report them. S—— said he'd break his neck if he did. That ass, R——, awful thing to have no sense of humor —going to prefer charges now against S—— for insulting him. If R—— lasts out this war, will be a General.

Caterpillar maneuvers most of day. The way those tanks go in and out of shell-holes—marvelous! Like riding loop the loop.

Sat., 2nd.—Saturday night—and about the only *militaire* in this town not out ranging after the wild women! Another letter from home. That makes No. 1, No. 14, and No. 12. K——, after ten wks, got 24 in one bunch. Must be nothing but veterinaries working in P.O. A trench helmet being sent me. Ought to arrive about August.

Funny ideas at home about number of troops we have ready. Never think of baggage, equipment, supplies, transport, etc., necessary. Doing damned well, I think. One of these days Jerry Hun is going to learn something to his disadvantage. Yanks hate war. Crab incessantly. Anxious to go home, so all for hurry-up in Kultur-extermination. French joyful over prospects, and Germans massing their dirtiest players—the "butchers"—for us. When it reaches the rough-and-tumble, there'll be some startled Jerries. We're good imitators. Fritz will see some stuff that'll make him think he's been to the stockyards.

So H—— J—— is "working like a fiend" at Great Lakes. Glad he's in it—for E's sake. Always nice to see a wife believing her husband's a hero.

Saw M—— D——. Capt. Judge Adv. Dept. Free as a bird. Full of envy for him.

No orders yet. Original plan of brigading us with French at Front, been discarded. Dope now, we go Heavy Artillery units as instructors. Anyhow, if it is not action, it is not, thank God, more schools!

In the loneliness and tedium of the specific task here, one forgets the splendor of the whole. Then comes an eloquent word from S——, that she has *not* forgotten. The flesh is exceedingly weak. But when I think of her, who smiles and smiles when it is not easy, I'm ashamed of being low. Three months, now, since we parted, and her gentle spirit is closer to me than ever. Miles are long, but soul speaks to soul across them.

Sun., 3rd.—Cold, wet day. No coal in camp. Lights worse than usual. Sat around bickering. Announced another prophecy—my last. Said I'd had a vision during night, and that war would end on June 26. S—— insisted he'd had same flash. Agreed that 26th was day. Everybody weak-minded enough to believe *anything.*

Mon., 4th.—End of C.P.A.L.T. Trunks packed. Relieved to find I'd passed—well down. E—— the drunken bum—No. 20. So much for virtue. One third of course flunked out. Poor M—— among them. Sent back to Saumur. Such an amiable, generous, upright soul, who worked so hard. Tried to get him through. But French very jealous of this school. No go. Dinner to French officers. Heavy going, at first, but good wine and plenty of it, and Entente finally established. One of them had little boy, 4 yrs old. Got friendly with him. His home, up north, completely sacked by Germans. "I suppose they carted off everything?" I said. "No," he answered, with a little smile. "They took very little—the French had already been there." There's a good "atrocity" story.

In to Paris, all pleasantly *allumé*.

Tues., 5th.—Gang breaks up. First separation for F—— and H——.*

Met M—— D—— and M—— J—— again. Their captaincies and plush jobs in Paris, by contrast with humble lieutenancy in mud-hogs, further confirmation of suspicion that I'm damned fool. Neither wasted any time in training camp.

Buried about three fourths of my equipment to-day at American Express. A *musette* for shoulder and dictionary in pocket, all one needs. Silly, the stuff we took over—soap, folding table, trick lanterns, mess kits, campaign hats—*two* of them, and they're forbidden here! Haven't used any sheets yet, and still on first cake of soap. Wonder how I failed to bring my book on "Diseases of Horse."

Streets a sea of slush. Getting around at night, with no lights, a dirty process. Grand day to be pushing off

*They lived next door to each other at home. Went to training camp together, crossed together, and a month or so after this, again found themselves together in the artillery center of Limoges.

for Bordeaux, where it's green, there's sunshine, butter, sugar, and no air raids. I'm to be "loaned" to Heavy Artillery brigade, as instructor. What outfit, or for how long, don't know.

Looks as if Boche meant to clean up Russia and have final go at Allies before we get in. Job may be bigger than he thinks. Bolsheviks won't fight with guns, but bears with tongue and pen. Going to give Hun a lot of trouble, my bet. Silly to talk of Russians as "traitors." Well-meaning hicks who've blown out the gas, that's all. They'll make trouble for the Kaiser before they're through. Next time he stubs his toe, his people will begin to think. Then we can reserve berths for home.

Great stuff—diagnosing future. Asked a Frenchman when war would end, and he said: "This year, *sans doubte.*" And when I asked why, he said: "Because it is the fourth year." Probably as good a reason as any.

Saw Irvin Cobb for moment. Just back from British front. Asked about German drive. He said it would never come off—they were bluffing. British all ready, and would smash anything before it got started. He seemed positive, and I was greatly cheered.*

Began "Private Gaspard" (René Benjamin) best war book I've read. 7:30 train for Bordeaux. No beds. Jangled all night with Frenchman over danger of night air.

Wed., 6th.—Arrived 6:30. Chapon Fin for breakfast, and "Y" for information. Tram to Camp de Souge. Got wrong one, of course. Finally reached St. Medard.

*The drive started seventeen days later, and British 5th Army, at least, did all its smashing in reverse English.

Then 4 mi. afoot to camp, where I tried to present my orders to a Maj. Miller, as directed. Couldn't. Nobody'd ever heard of him. Sat around, waiting for something to happen. Finally got attached to —th F.A. Rest of gang straggled in toward evening. Shared shanty with H—— B——, good egg. Have stove, and orderly, fine upstanding Mormon from Idaho. A perfect soldier and an equalitarian. Respects himself and us, impartially. Strict discipline in business hours, but privately, we talk as man to man.

Two Nat'l Guard Regiments here. From Idaho, Washington and Utah. Splendid fellows. Enormous camp, full of all nations and floating on sand. Cold nights and nippy mornings, but June when sun comes out, with soft fragrance of pines in air.

Called up before Colonel, and asked my specialty. Told him I knew practically everything about gas engines and tractors. So was assigned to telephones and signaling.

Nothing much to do yet, but sit around and bicker. Mess run by French concessionnaires. Very formal. Stuff like that seems chief occupation of American generals.

Thur., 7th.—Drool by Col. Y——. A 22 blank, they say. Spends his time chasing waitresses: Gen. H—— all out for formalities. Put on Guard Mount worthy of West Point. M——, H——, and others of our crowd moved on to Libourne. Went off singing the Song of the Casual—"Where Do We Go from Here?"

Hard to concentrate on simple problems of soldiering. Mind persists in wandering off to why's and wherefore's. Whole business an apotheosis of the practical, the definite and the ponderable. Other things there were before. Other things there will be again.

Just now—ballistics, squads left, get on with it. So
much talk about making world safe for democracy. But
when men come in from route-march, fagged, hungry,
and some one asks "what the holy hell did we come
to this for?" and the answer is "to free the slaves!"
—oaths, catcalls. We knew, once, why we came. We've
forgotten. Minds are colorless—protection against
thinking. Be a machine—the only happiness. What
rot is written of soldier psychology! Half propaganda,
half sentimental lies. Fake letter printed in magazine
from some bird supposed to be here. "The great peace
which came over him." "Consciousness of service, etc."
The newcomers have some of that. Seem to think it's
somehow fine and brave to sleep in mud—despite comfort. Old campaigners different. One here—14 yrs.
Regular Army. Goes to bed like lady in beauty parlor.
Nuts about cleanliness. Enlisted men pretty well
rubbed down, too. Toted rifles and scrubbed harness too
long to have any more illusions about soldiering than an
office boy has about cleaning gobboons.

And all the squawk about "slackers." Too damned
much altruism for the other fellow. No especial virtue
in being here. Most of us here because we were afraid
to stay home—afraid of our women. It's the women
who've made all the wars in history.

But the draft-evader—he's not playing fair. De-
faulted on the social contract, and ought to be made to
pay up. Funny, he and "Conscientious Objector" unknown in France.

So J—— C——'s a Major! Like to be one myself.
But I'd hate being an ass and wear long ears for insignia. *

*J—— C—— never saw service with troops, at home or
abroad, but was very bitter about "slacking."

Fri., 8th.—Camp full of Chinese. Amazing fellows. Cheerfulness itself. Immune to any effort to make them work. As hod-carriers, each one solemnly picks up one brick.

Assigned Hdqtrs. Co. Lecture on projectiles. Poor old brain reels with mathematics. Job of censoring enlisted men's letters. Full of humor, pathos and inspiration. Three classes: (1) To best girl. Magnifying hardship. Full of vainglory and heroics. (2) To boy friend. Nonchalant, sophisticated, bold comments on wine and women. Spent a lot of time with both, apparently. Contemptuous of war and danger. Hard guy. (3) To mother. Usually brief. Laborious explanations and apologies for not writing oftener. Mostly truthful. No pretense of hiding homesickness. And a certain brusque tenderness that's hard on censor's eyes. One lad, apparently having allotted 1-3 his pay to his mother, fearful that she'd save it for him. Insisted over and over she must spend it on herself. Hardships glossed over, and "we won't go up for months yet."

Splendid spirit of carry on. Feel I know these men. And proud of it. No complaints—food, quarters, or officers. Most seem studying French, and express liking for native. Find him genial, helpful chap, with sense of humor like their own. This in contrast to officers, who mostly ignore the language, and feel only tolerant disdain for native.

Great system—this army! After exhaustive education in tractors, and finding nothing I know less about, they make me regimental radio officer. A lot of good taxpayers' money being wasted.

Wish I was with motors. Misuse of materiel, due to ignorance and carelessness, appalling. Hate to see good machinery mistreated.

Subtle antagonism between N.G. officers and us of Reserve. Attached to regiments, here, not assigned. Rather out in cold. Ought to be used to that by this time.

News from home that C—— C—— a Major. Not so envious. The lower the rank, the more fun. Be Sergeant, next war. No manual labor, no responsibility.

Also news my little Lt. In the Home Guards merits promotion for improvement in management of bladder. He gets Croix de Guerre with 5 palms for dist. service in use of puckering string.

W—— W—— killed. Good kid. Too bad.

Sat., 9th.—Took Battalion out for 2 hr. hike. Maj. F—— suggested I "go easy with boys." He's druggist back in home town. Thinking of post-war business. That's the weakness of the Nat'l Guard. Too many personal relations.

Stood retreat in sand ankle deep. As I made right about for salute, feet gave way, and sat down. Undignified and "prejudicial to discipline." Everybody laughed, for which sergeant, an old timer, gave them hell.

Sun., 10th.—No mail. When I'm old and feeble, sitting by fire telling lies to grandchildren, the postman will bring me the letters sent to me in France in 1918.*

Summer weather. Fine hot bath. Drowsed away day, speculating on end of war. Seems long way off. Have a hunch that Jerry will make offers toward end of summer, perhaps what he holds in West for free hand

*One letter, mailed in France in August, 1918, arrived Sept., 1919.

in East. England will probably oppose that. But France wants peace without demanding too much. U.S. will have deciding voice.

Not afraid of semi-draw. The war, alone, holds German Empire together. The extraneous menace removed, the whole fabric, if it doesn't disintegrate, ought to take on a cast far from military and imperialistic. Cling to faith in common people. In the end, they'll settle her fate—and ours. Regardless of the length of the war, or its outcome, Kaiserism done for. Feel sure of that.

Mon., 11th.—Officer of the Day. In dastard plot to ruin me, H—— B—— got himself into race riot. But got him out without casualties. Radio work in afternoon. Nothing to do—@ $6 a day. Poor taxpayers! Check of men's quarters at 10. Everything O.K. Line of light, however, under door to sergeant's room. Only snores when I kicked on door. Persisted, though, and it opened to sheepish sergeant and three corporals. Lecture on evils of gambling, especially poker, infractions of discipline, and promise to bust them all in morning. Then to bed and forgot it. First thing officer learns is large number of things advisable to forget.

Tues., 12th.—Attended balloon ascension with D—— A——. Wanted me to join him, but Maj. C.O. said nix. Just as well satisfied. He goes up 1500 meters, attached to mother earth by cable thickness of lead pencil. If it breaks, there is a parachute—which sometimes works. All then well if you don't land in tree or in front of Paris express. D—— a dour cuss. More disgusted with army than most. In Nat'l Guard for years, in Utah outfit that really worked. Knew more gunnery than most regulars.   After bouncing all over France, wound up here.   Wouldn't let him near guns. Made him balloon observer—which work makes him sick to his stomach, more ways than one.   Lives in hope the consequences will descend upon Col. E——'s head —literally.

Wed., 13th.—Visit from Sec'y Baker.   Poked fingers in breech blocks and made usual helpless remarks of layman.   Looked about as uncomfortable as he probably was.

Gen. Pershing with him.   Had honor of saluting him. Seemed more interested in state of my buttons than soul. Generals get that way.

H—— has funny story about buttons.   Seems the English have always been great button shiners.   But this a scientific war, and shiny buttons too good a target.   So orders out that for first time in history of British Empire, buttons go unshined.   Whereupon, morale promptly shot to pieces.   Panic-stricken, they go back to button-shining—except for the Guards. They such good soldiers that whether they shine, shave or anything else, they're still good.   Dull buttons now practically equal to V.C.

Had yawp to-day from Maj. O—— of Staff, gingering up morale.   "Don't talk peace.   Don't think it, etc.   War our only business now."   But doesn't *some one* have to do some thinking about peace?   Win the war sounds good.   What's it *mean?*   What is "peace"? When Hindenburg hands over his sword, and movie operators get the scene for Pathé weekly?   When Heinie beats his pip-squeaks into ploughshares and begins work on the south 80?   It'll be a hell of a peace if it's done in the historic manner.   Terms reading like the survey of a suburban lot—Germany deeded so many hectares, N. by N.W. along left bank of creek running S. by S.E. of N. Section of W. township, etc., etc. Peace treaties in past always made by professionals. Why not give amateurs a chance? Whatever the decision, it means living arrangements for world for long time to come.

A bas all those outworn terms of nationalism. New world. Needs new kind of peace. Maunderings about "victory" not only silly but dangerous. Tragic to defeat Germany without achieving ends for which we fight. That not impossible, if politicians allowed to control. We're not here for revenge or punishment, nor to satisfy pride or avarice of any nation or class.

All those "afraid it will be over before they can get in" located somewhere west of Hoboken. Quick call for the wagon if Frenchman said that. Over here, flush has left purple dawn of war—pewter skies. Interesting, I haven't yet heard *Marseillaise* played or sung by French. "Sorrow too deep for tears."

Learned to-day G—— T—— telephone officer of his regiment.*

Thur., 14th.—"Absolutely nothing to write about" —phrase appearing on half the letters I censor. Formations, lectures, more lectures, bickers, etc. Watched Mormons handle their new G.P.F's. French method of removing trail spade carefully worked out. Takes several men. But Yanks strong boys! One took a crowbar. Got spade off in fraction of time it would take French. But—he smashed it! Well—what the hell.

---

*We put in many hours together learning the buzzer code, before going to training camp. Also learned wigwag. Might just as well have learned to shoot an arquebus.

We'll get another, etc. Perfect example of national temperaments.

Fri., 15th.—Order out all officers have to stand reveille. Bitter wails of downtrodden. H—— B—— a marvel. Dress like fireman myself, and have to run for it, leaving him in bed. But he hasn't been late yet.

Learned that A—— submarined. That makes third of liners crossed on now on bottom. Nice of them to wait till I debark.

Sat., 16th.—Got a copy of *New Republic*. Pacifist leanings. Most of army has, too. War spirit in inverse ratio to proximity to war. Quickest way to end it, put all journalists and politicians under arms. Leave peace arrangements to soldiers, under rank of Lieut. Make talkers fight and fighters talk.

In struggle for victory, danger of forgetting what we want it for. No outworn formula of territory, treaties and crowns. War of ideas. Victory only if ours prevails. Victory if Germans conquer half the world—and see light. Defeat, if she's smashed and we go down in reaction with her.

Too much political discussion based on assumption that nations are constant factor. Always changing. Germany can't be democratized from without. Got to come from within. Real hope of world lies with children—his and ours. Unless they understand each other, work together, etc., all this war complete waste.

Aim of war not to destroy Germans—great people—but make them good citizens of free world. Mr. Wilson sees this. Several laps ahead of the Metternich-Talleyrand school of thought.

Sun., 17th.—Left N.Y. 12 wks. ago. Thoughts of

certain sweet voices—and the curse of memory. D——
found bottle of champagne. With that, and old guessing game of when war will end, and tying knots, got
through day. What a life to be heroic about!

. *Mon., 18th.*—Box of candy from home. Impossible
to express emotions! Rumor traveled fast. D——
barged in, saying he smelt it up in his balloon. Had a
rage on. Crew went off for mess at noon, leaving him a
mile or so in air. M—— to hospital with diphtheria.

Censored letter last night. Hard work—not because
of poor light, either.

My dear little boy:
I hope you are well, and keep well till daddy
comes home, be a good boy and daddy will bring
you something real nice. I want to see you so bad
I do not know what to do, I just want to give you
a "big big" Bear Hug. You know, like daddy
used to do. I will close now, and come back to
you as soon as I can. I hope before long. Bye,
bye, Honey, till daddy comes home. Your Lov-
ing Father.
P.S.
Write daddy a letter and tell me how much
you love me—also what you would like to have.*

Tues., 19th.—All day road march with guns. Rain.
Bawled out by Adj. for missing reveille Sunday.
Everybody a little touchy. Been cooped up together too
long. At supper K—— and D—— sounded off bitterly. Subject: Eastern *vs.* Western football. Pleasant
change from guessing end of war.

---

* Writer of this fell and was crushed between caisson and
limber. Died in hospital same day.

Wed., 20th.—Wondered how it would be to kill H—— as he slept. Tired of his face. Woke him up and told him scheme. Didn't seem surprised. Said he'd often thought same about me. Agreed we needed change. Have to wangle an evening in Bordeaux.

Thur., 21st.—Lecture on audion bulbs and amplifiers. D—— claims to understand it, but he's all alone. Marvelous, what they're doing with wireless. Set up couple of telephones, hundred yards apart. Could hear fairly well. Frenchman told of capturing German officer with blankbooks full of conversations that had gone on in French phones opposite for couple of months. For signaling to planes, though, only the panel system so far. But damned few planes, anyhow.

Ordered to take battalion out for "singing." Marched them out into country and solved problem by turning it over to top sergeant. When in doubt, there's always the t.s. He was near mutiny.

Fri., 22nd.—D—— called up for idling. Defense that he wasn't any different from rest of army. May be work *au feu*, but precious little here. Extreme ingenuity evading little work there is. Most everybody learned the army game.

Just when we decided war had been called on account of rain, long awaited German offensive bursts out. Got first news at radio station. Came from Nauen. Only got snatches. That fellow there sends too damned fast! Evidently, big show on.

Sat., 23rd.—Drive on, all right. The big thought, here, but know little. Get communiqués from Paris and Nauen, but nothing in them. Curtain of censorship has

settled abruptly. Wonder why. Idea seems to be that
for both sides this the last hand in game. Boche throwing everything in pot, win or lose. His last chance, and
seems to admit it. Rumors of great successes, but
French say that means nothing. In their own great offensive in Champagne, took lot of prisoners and terrain,
but lost battle. German losses must be terrific. Inade-
quate artillery preparation and troops in close formation
obliged to halt and cut wire with clippers. British machine guns must have slaughtered them! Concentra-
tion apparently not yet developed. When it does—
wow! Can't last as long as Verdun, though similar
otherwise. Two months should see decision. May be
home for Christmas after all. D——, however, points
out we've been having "decisive" battles since beginning. Damned pessimist!   · .

Rumor of big German gun bombarding Paris from
75 mi. Ridiculous! Nobody here believes it.* D——
and S—— argued half the night about it. S——, as
usual, full of cockeyed theories.

Sun., 24th.—Certainly hard life here! Music with
meals, by band of —th F.A.—a peach. Great mess.
6 fr. a day. Artichokes, etc. Lots of officers sneak off
to battery messes—want cakes and maple syrup, etc.

Except for that damned bugle sounding off every
minute, and breaking ice on water bucket in morning,
nothing to complain of. Do plenty, though. One of
our games, going through motions of packing. Every
other day, G—— fixes up his trunk to go home.† Droll
to think of home now, just when big push is launched.
Crisis like this, though, more endurable than when noth-

*This was Big Bertha's best day—21 shells.
†G——died of the flu in Brest.

ing is doing. If the Boche fails, end ought to come quickly. Then the waiting for ships, repatriation, etc. Probably go to Idaho and do strike duty, or guard Mexican border couple of years before muster-out.

Mon., 25th.—New General commanding brigade. Met him this A.M. and properly bawled out for salute. Didn't take thirty minutes for whole camp to know there was new hand on bridle. Snappy guy, but everybody likes idea. Brigade been getting sloppy. Like West Pointers, now. Even H—— gets up 30 secs. sooner.

Wild German *communiqués*, but no Allied news. Ticklish time. Whole camp in wild flutter, first over the Boche, and second, General M——.

Put in afternoon erecting aerials. Very hot and enervating, despite Gen. M——.

Tues., 26th.—Rumor of big German victory near Peronne. Learned that letter home to Dr. F—— used for recruiting, etc. Kidded by S—— and other experts. Sentiments expressed so much nobler than those felt. 99% of stuff about this life is bunk. Honest-to-God soldier hasn't yet appeared in print. Too drab, dull, disgruntled and cynical. More of real thing in Kipling's "Boots" than a thousand "Rendezvous with Death."

7 months to-day since I put on King's Coat. Took 10 o'clock check. Rotten Nat'l Guard discipline. Inevitable, with men and officers so chummy. S—— sneaks down to barracks to play cards. Always regretting he got a commission. Gen. M—— has a job on his hands, with all that and politics underneath. Col. Y—— slated to get the gate.

Wed., 27th.—Heard from **R**——. Still at Saumur, instructing.

Fall of German mark indicates increasing odds against her as betting proposition. Looks as if the curtain about to fall. Even if checked in this push, Boche may dig in and trust to diplomacy and defeatist propaganda to get better terms. The German people must be fed up with promises. When Allies attack, ought to go through like stone through tissue paper hoop. Germans haven't failed yet, by long shot, but in ticklish position. Caught between reënforced wings of French and British, may get squashed.

Thur., 28th.—*Rien à signaler.*

Fri., 29th.—French version of place to which, they say, even kings walk afoot, is mere hole in ground, over which operator squats, balancing on heels. Not comfortable, though possessing certain physiologic advantages. **D**—— **A**—— found all ours *complet* this A.M., so wandered on until in precincts sacred to Gen. **M**——. Astonished and delighted to find August Personage had had a little stool built for himself. **D**—— torn by conflicting emotions. But no time for delay. Emerging from tabernacle, horrified to encounter Gen. himself. Doesn't know that it's anything but coincidence, but this afternoon permanently assigned to balloons.

Heard from **M**—— **C**——. In Paris, en route to London—then HOME. Envy the deadliest of the sins!

H—— **B**—— at locked horns with Maj. **W**——. All my money on **B**——.

Brief caustic talk from Gen. **M**—— on discipline. Every neck feels ax already. Something like panic in officers' quarters. Badly needed.

Lights out and finish with candle. Incidents in letters from home—tiny spots of color in a twilight fabric.

Sat., 30th.—Road hike. Fell out with D——. Seen by Colonel. D—— not alarmed. Says he's got too much on the bastard—knows all his women! Orders out to-day for permanent assignment of some of us to regiments, and more travel for rest. Firing-critique at 11. H—— B—— as usual bluffed way through. He'll be C. in C. if war lasts long enough. J—— S—— all ready to flunk, but wasn't called. Disappointed. Hoping for demotion. Wants to be back in ranks.

Sun., 31st.—Easter. Peace on earth, good will, etc. Rained all day. Apparently breathing space before second German effort. Everybody anxious. Feeling great things impend. Silence from Nauen.

April, 1918

Mon., 1st.—"Y" Sec'y bounced. Had it coming—no sense. Got men to picture-show, and slipped prayers over on them. Walked out. Nearly broke up place. New man, different. Ex-army. Lost arm in Philippines. Advertised prayer-meeting for yesterday—no movies. Filled the house! Some men want religion, some want shows—nobody wants them mixed.

Letter from G.H.Q., wrongly addressed, under date Mar. 10, ordering transfer to liaison service, dependent on consent of C.O. to release.

Tues., 2nd.—Saw Col. Y——. No objections.

Watched M.C. captain doing squads east—awful mess. Finally got men in hopeless tangle. Had to dismiss them. Came over to where we were snickering: "It may interest you to know that I'm one of the best God damned obstetricians in the U.S."

Wed., 3rd.—Orders out. Me for Limoges, instructor in artillery center there.

Lecture to enlisted men. One fellow asked embarrassing questions. Had him up to quarters. Proved to be civil engineer in civil life. Told him if he tried making a monkey of me again I'd put him on K.P. for life. Saw the point and we're friends. Tutoring me, privately.

Col. Y—— S.C.D'd. Poor devil. New ultimatum
from Gen. M——. More necks to fall.

Great Picardy battle halted. Lot of fighting yet, but
Boche never so close to winning as last week. On down
grade now, and ought to slip fast.

Thur., 4th.—Nothing stirring. *C'est la fourbi—la.*
H——offered 200 fr. for chair. No business. H.Q.
company all on range as fire guards. Momentary leis-
ure. But calm before storm. New C.O. man and soldier. Things beginning to pop. He has no liking for
Nat'l Gd. system. These regiments soon be unrecog-
nisable. More than one amateur officer back in civil life
shortly. O.R.C. men coming into their own. Nothing
asked of enlisted men that Reserve officers don't know.
Discipline certainly ground in at training camps. Good
O.R.C. men are *very* good. Free from faction-spirit
that wrecks N.G. regiments. Gen. M—— knows it.
Dropped registration shell last night, stating expecta-
tions, and adding: "Any man who does not feel himself
competent to be an efficient artillery officer should at
once resign or apply for transfer to a more suitable
branch of the service." Beginning to dawn on lot of
men that Decoration Day Parades aren't much "training." Even veterans of the Keystone War look glum.

Fri., 5th.—Idiotic prejudice that keeps good men out
of Q.M. Feeling back home is—put best at front: anybody will do for rest of it. Over here, it's—anybody
can fight, but chase the morons out of the Q.M. so pay
won't get muddled up, baggage lost, grub be rotten, or
supplies missing. Many brilliant Regulars in Q.M.
now. Ludendorf himself Q.M. Gen'l.

Night thoughts: Embarkation. Placid seas—no

U-boats, Statue of Liberty. The pier. Crowds. Overseas caps. The accolade. Swagger up the Avenue.
20th Century. The diner—silver and white linen.
Eager queries of strangers. Heart palpitating. Engle-
wood. Smoke clouds. Quick search through jostling
crowds of station. Familiar voice . . . dream worlds
much pleasanter than one we live in!

Sat., 6th.—The "dog robber." Chops kindling,
shakes down stove, sweeps, makes beds, runs errands.
Work voluntary and gets about $4 apiece out of us.
Most men tickled to get job, first because they get out
of much drilling, second, because of money, third, because of gossip they pick up around officers' quarters.
Other men profess to despise orderlies. Misguided dem-
ocrats back home wrathful because dear boys shine officers' boots, etc. All wrong. No compulsion or servility
involved. Always more applicants than jobs.

Spent morning firing 75's. French instruction in
grenade throwing. Got hooked for guard mount, but
bribed L—— to take it. Caught truck with D——
A—— for Bordeaux. Town full of Yanks and M.P.'s.
No army's morals ever watched over like ours. Went
to shop for picture postals. D—— ran through stock,
throwing out smutty ones. Old French woman in tears
at that. All Americans she said seemed to think smut
and France same word. Insisted on our taking decent
ones free.

Ran into Col. Y—— slinking down side street. Poor
devil. Busted—no job. Afraid to go home, probably.
Got to fix up some sort of lie, first. Dinner at Comédie.
Innumerable bottles of *Macon*. Talk, talk, talk.
D—— a philosopher. Just able to stagger to truck.
D—— passed out. Close second myself. Hell of a
ride.

Sun., 7th.—Extremely low. Stomach *révolté.* What a morning! Couldn't even hold water down. Sherman must have been a drinker.

Soldiers—funny animals. Yap at stiff discipline, but soft officer gets nowhere. Hate being trained, but proud when they are. Superb material in Nat'l Guard. But hard to be good officer when men come from home town. Whole A.E.F. needs overhauling, and getting it. Too many jealousies and distinctions between Reg., N.G., and O.R.C.

Too much "war to bitter end—Destroy Germany" talk. Give them only two choices: German peace or obliteration. That keeps war going. Significant that most of German propaganda money in France was spent buying out most vicious *anti*-German papers. Our bitter-enders play directly into Junker hands. German people just about ready to quit. Great danger is our safe and sound jingoes in high place won't give the chance. Wilson is the boy. Incomparably, *the* statesman of the time. Vacillating, at times, but far-seeing. Germany can certainly thank God for him.

Bicker with H——. Subject: death. Merits of passing out on some shell-swept hill, etc., not appalling. Human failures and weaknesses blotted out—forgotten —in mirage of heroism. Tender recollections for those behind, and pride—not such a bad heritage. Dead idols the best sort. *Nihil nisi bonum*, etc.

Mon., 8th.—All A.M. at observing station. G.P.F. firing.

French have invented new cooling liquid. Can't be frozen, but eats out radiators. Everybody knows it except G.Q.G. They'll find out in twenty-thirty years. All armies alike. Typical British example in 9.2. Cast

into carriage are directions for recoil fluid—not used for
two years back. British guns for next hundred probably still have same directions on them.

Attended G.C.M. Pathetic prisoner, in under 92nd
A.W., threatening to kill an officer and God knows what.
Appalling indictment. What really happened was, kid
got tight, and at retreat, raised rifle and said (referring
to Lt. F——): "Here's where I pick me off one o' them
birds." Another soldier testified he "couldn't never have
hit him, his gun was wobbling so." Obviously, just a
drunken joke. But the guard-house lawyers yapped
back and forth, and finally one of the Court said: "Oh,
hell, let's give him life and go to bed." Gave him
twenty years. Poor kid collapsed. So did I, almost.

Tues., 9th.—Summoned Bat. Hdqtrs. and ordered to
give "lecture" on transmissions and lubrication. Half
the men at lecture were the regimental band. Keen interest in transmissions—not!

Orders from Adj. to proceed to Paris, reporting Chief
Liaison Officer. No idea what next, except maybe at-
tached some French divisional H.Q. O.K. with me.
Had enough of co-tangents and little Alpha.

Greatest thing here the "Y." Certainly helps morale.
Wise helpfulness of personnel. Great enthusiasm in letters of men.

Editorial in N.Y. paper suggesting we take note of
recent events in Russia. Good God! The fact that we
persistently *haven't* is shown by number of extra German divisions on Western Front. Three times they've
asked for re-statement of Allied aims, and consent to negotiations on basis of no annexations and no indemnities.
We aren't frank with Russians—nor with ourselves.
Wilson is right. Beside him, T.R. is a noisy small boy.

Wed., 10th.—Packed. Sad at leaving H——. Good lad. To lecture by French Mission. Half the fellows absent—explanation: Guard Mount. "Very beautiful ceremony," said one Frenchman, disgustedly. "Ver' beautiful. But I question if you will win ze war wiz it." Some of our fat-head generals care more about snappy saluting than accurate gunnery. Other armies the same, probably. That's why wars take so long to get fought.

Thur., 11th.—To Bordeaux on truck. Strolled around town. Saw first Yank *blessés* being evacuated from station. To bed with singular emotions. Apprehensive. Army life makes for dependence on the crowd. Lonesome. First time since leaving home I've been *alone.* Not a human voice to be heard here. Stillness gets on nerves. Half wish I was back in barracks. Slept badly—not used to real beds.

Fri., 12th.—To station. Saw number of refugees from war zone. Piteous. All aged and infirm, many scarce able to walk. Very poor. One old woman, in rags, tottering along on home-made crutches, assisted, almost carried, by young *poilu.* Tenderness of helpers for these unhappy derelicts most striking. Sight of these feeble old creatures, after lifetime of toil, reduced to this, filled me with great loathing for war. Sudden gust of hate for swine who had loosed such a dreadful thing on the world. Then—recalled day I left home, and that grotesque assembly of poor old men and women at Union Station, bound for some institution. Infirm, minds half gone, herded along by stolid policeman. Equally pitiful sight.

To poor, war and peace, all one. Merely suffer more

dramatically, more suddenly, under guns than under crushing weight of "peaceful" industrialism. The dispossessed, the broken bodies, the numbed minds, in peace as in war—and fewer friendly hands to help.

What is there in life to make so many people afraid of death? Surely there can be nothing beyond to surpass in pain what civilization has provided for so many here on earth.

The same sorrowful picture again and again on station platforms en route to Paris. Many young women— and little children. One pair, little boy about four, leading little sister by the hand through crowd, guarding her from the jostle of the unthinking, comforting her when she wept . . .

Reached Paris, 8:30. Heavy trunks handled by female porters. *Pourboire* rather over schedule—small tribute to *les dames merveilleuse de France.* Porter on train also a woman—marvel of gayety and industry— three sons *au front.* It's such things fill one with detestation for the filthy madness of war, and the Boche. They probably have the same hate for it in Germany.

To Continental. Overpowering sense of luxury in white sheets and bath tub. Electric lights. Chairs. Soft carpets. Turned in, and Gothas arrived simultaneously. No sense worrying. But unpleasant—like lightning. You see a flash out of corner of your eye, there's a crash, and windows try to climb out of frames. You speculate on penetrability of masonry, and try to calculate speed of falling bodies. Rattle of machine guns. You wish they'd cut out the racket and let you sleep. Stop counting bombs, and listen to clock chiming. Eleven. Extra loud wail of siren announces new esquadrille. Boom! Clup! Clup! Rat-tat-tat-tat! Well—insurance all paid for. Draw your knees up.

Turn over. Air raids a nuisance—like submarines. But they do, or they don't. Next thing you know, it's morning.

Sat., 13th.—Made toilette, taking more time than all toilettes of previous month combined. Reported to Maj. H——. First question: did I speak French? Tried me out. No cheers, but seemed satisfied. Men wanted at front, he said, but temporarily to report to Maj. L—— at Ministère de la Guerre.

Put in afternoon digging through files and ledgers. Maj. L—— handles bills for material we buy from French. A job to curl hair of a C.P.A. After six months hippology, firing data, F.A.D.R., ballistics, rolling friction, knots, bends and hitches, the buzzer code, and audion bulbs, I'm a God damned *bookkeeper! Merde!*

Sun., 14th.—To Voisin's for lunch with B——. 56 fr. Up in Ferris Wheel. Too much like balloons for pleasure. Wandering through dark streets. Ever-present women. So mysterious and seductive in darkness. Whispering refrain—*se coucher*, etc. A fellow's got to hang on to himself here. Not many do.

Paris filled with inflammatory publications. French consent to shooting an occasional editor, but at least they *think*. Gluttonous for *ideas*.

Feel like Tomlinson's ghost, wandering through space. Floating brain more disastrous in military life than floating kidney. Wear blinders and believe censorship the voice of God. Mustn't talk peace for fear enemy will think you want it. Everybody scared of saying what he thinks. Only talk worth listening to is drunken talk. Only certainty that what everybody believes isn't so.

Cartoon of *poilu* in trench, head bowed. One of his pals is saying: *"Son fils est mort sur le champ d'honneur."* *"Quel âge?"* asks a second. *"Deux jours,"* replies the first.

Story in *Cri de Paris:* Lady, following custom of protecting windows' against breakage during bombings, by pasting strips of paper on them, called in Picasso to devise arrangements worthy of modern art. "The result was so beautiful, so significant, so terrifying, that some children who were passing by, were seized with a sort of frenzy and never stopped throwing stones until not a single window was left intact."

Mon., 15th.—Office at 9—too early! To Méditerranée with papers. Errand-boy duty all A.M. Lunched with F—— masquerading this time as Maj. Judge Adv. Dept.*

Ran into J—— C——.† Infantry. Going up shortly. Never looked better in his life.

Dinner with M—— at his apartment in Passy.

Tues., 16th.—Spent morning checking bills. Gossip around Ministere that war situation is excellent. My French not so good, but a little wine helps. Bottle better than dictionary. Slang growing under the ears. Current salutation: "Morning, old top. D'you live in the *axis?*" Reference to fact that there is no deflection to Big Bertha, and a ruler on map of Paris takes in most of hits. Another phrase, meaning something like to crab your own act, is "upset the flower pots." Refers

---

*F—— is a well known poet—the "Anne Knish" of the famous "*Spectric*" hoax.

†Killed in action. Argonne, Oct. 14, 1918.

to shell dropped in garden of German embassy. Fascinating to see language grow this way.

All afternoon collecting receipts. Military *elan*—zero. Maj. L—— nice chap, but hell of a soldier. So am I.

Saw M—— C—— in his tinware office, and dinner at his flat. D—— R—— there. Specializing in *chansons de guerre*. Some very ancient. All obscene. Very droll one, beginning: "I belong to a society to which all males from eighteen to sixty are admitted." Old stuff in time of Condé. Cracked bottle of what M—— thought was Burgundy, but proved to be Marc Bourgogne—re-distilled lees, 99% proof.

Streets full of tarts. Hard battle, but managed to get home safe.

Wed., 17th.—All morning at commissary, standing in line purchasing misc. cargo jam, crackers, bacon and stick candy for Maj. L——. Took it all to Ritz in taxi. Swell job for *militaire* who knows The Army Horse in Sickness and Disease, with degree from C.P.A. L.T.

Afternoon in office. Doubtless very valuable to Cause Sacré, but about as military as Montgomery Ward. Busy carrying documents—hell, just plain *bills*—between Trocadero and Place Bastile. Excellent exercise and great way to see Paris. But Boy Scout on bike could do it better.

Dined with D——. Soft spring night, and the call of the wild. Adventure with fat old dame, who warned of "bad" girls who used cocaine.

Thur., 18th.—Maj. L——'s boy friend, ambulance driver, just got commission. Takes my place. No longer A.D.C. to flour barrels. Probably go now to some provincial town and buy manure. Or go in *cuvettes* business. Join the Marines and see the world. They have nothing on me. Only thing left is go to baker-school and play in the band.

Busy Bertha still booming. Its chief objection—suddenness. Bang! Glass in windows goes out in fine spray, and cobblestones try to crawl over one another. Doesn't do much damage, though. Supposed to wreck Parisian morale. Doesn't. *Parigot* refuses even to get mad about it. His chief wrath seems to be against newspapers for calling it "Bertha" when there are so many nice French girls of that name. The journalistic effort to be rancorous because a church was impiously shot up on Easter only makes for chuckles. The Frenchman insists on being reasonable.

Many offices have pools on number of minutes between shots. Le Ministere, yesterday, sounded like an auction. Everybody shouting numbers. *Faites vos jeux, messieurs.* Great people. The Boche certainly wasting time with that gun.

Saw L—— C—— in his Croix Rouge outfit. Looked like milk-fed pullet, recently under faucet. Also F—— G——, devil-may-care buccaneer, who goes A.W.O.L. and flies into Paris.

Such changes in men! Some good. Some not so good. Wonder what it'll mean later. The wage-slave who's learned the trick of command—will he go home with some of the bloom rubbed off his docility?

L—— B——. So free from cant and twaddle. Doesn't shy at a new idea. Has vision. (That word's greasy from over-use.)

Fri., 19th.—Moved to pension, kept by ex-empress,

Mlle. G——. Room next to Rev. W——, Red Crosser. Good fellow. Practically all French here. No English spoken. 13 fr. meals inc. Hard to talk French to respectable people. With hack drivers, waiters or *filles de joie*, go big. Dumb as potato in polite society.

First occasion to use wristlets mother knitted for trench wear. Incredibly cold.

Understand Shelley's "mania for liberty." The evanescent thrills that a band could evoke, the *sursum corda* in the jangle of spurs—all gone. As routinous and drab as being a shipping clerk in a packing house. "Over here" the same as being in a coal famine or a plague of meningitis. Life's a matter of contrast. All the thrill, now, would be in peace.

The individual's eternal compromise with the community. In peace he gives little, in war he gives all. An intelligent man ought to be resigned to that. But intelligence only part of us. A cat likes cleanliness. Logically, a cat should like water. But cats laugh at logic. The worst crime—to be dishonest with one's self . . . and the commonest.

Rev. W—— so pathetically anxious to know how to live in what he calls "the field." Enough camping-out junk with him to stock a depot. Always cheery and bright—so *damned* cheery—and takes cold baths.

Sat., 20th.—Butter and sugar for breakfast—*systéme* "D." To Guignolle in evening with M—— and D——, both well lit. In seat ahead was British navy fellow— stiff with gold braid. M—— suddenly leaned forward. "Admiral!" Then following dialogue:

Britisher (monocle in eye—rather testy): "Well?"
M—— (very feelingly): "I just *love* the British navy."

B. (grateful): "Oh, indeed—thanks."
    (Pause)
M——(more feelingly, with another tap on shoulder): "Admiral."
B. (slightly bored): "Yes?"
M—— "*And* the French army."
B. (very bored): "Oh, yes—quite so."
    (Long pause)
M—— "Admiral."
B. (excessively bored): "Well?"
M—— "I just *love* the British army!"
B. "Eh? Oh—thanks, awfully."
    (Long pause)
M——(tapping shoulder): "Admiral!"
B.: "Eh?"
M——: "*And* the French navy."
B. (almost frantic): "Quite right, sir, quite right."
    (Long pause, followed by tap on shoulder, this time by new character, D——)
D—— "Admiral!"
B. (enormously bored): "Well, sir?"
D——: "I just *love* the American army."
B. "Does you credit, I'm sure."
    (Pause)
D——: "Admiral!"
B.: "Eh?"
D——: "*And* the Swiss navy."
    (Curtain)

The part of the "admiral" was played by Admiral Wemyss, British C. in C.

Sun., 21st.—Awakened by parson, wanting me to go to church with him. Far from well, and gave him first lesson in morning-after etiquette. Shocked but grateful.

Routed out later by D—— and K——, and away to Fontainebleau. Difficulty in getting on train, F. being in Zone des Armées. No time to get passes. D—— presented sentry with receipted bill from N.Y. Yale Club. Blue stamp did the work.

Cold and rain, of course. Who called this "sunny" France? D—— charming. Full of rare humor. All gods' gifts and unaffected. Missed train back. Sat in station watching troop trains. French *poilu* apathetic now. War become a trade. Night at F. Talking books till late. D—— rather disdainful of American letters.

Mon., 22nd.—To Paris at 9. Assigned to desk under Lt. B—— at Ave. Montaigne. Nice old duck, but *pas militaire.* Saw F—— J——. Has hung accent on his name and carries calling cards.

Went to Olympia Varieties with B——. Lobby and aisles swarming with easy women—any price but all cash. Nice, misty, moonlit night—fine for raid. Hope not. Such a bore going down to *cave.* More growth of slang. Used to say *"A la gare"* for "Beat it!"—"Get th' hell outen here:" now it's *"A la cave."*

Tues., 23rd.—More clerking—not too arduous. Only bad feature of this military life, the war.

Never really make war, on German pattern, till we accept paramount importance of State. Complete submersion of individual. Dictatorial, irresponsible gov't essential to success. Bitter truth for liberty-lovers to swallow. To hell with free speech, etc. Here's a comforting fact, though. So hard and painful for individualist democracies to make war, that war won't be popular when all world goes democratic.

Irony of our "making world safe for democracy."
So many of our people don't believe in it. But Wilson
does. Our entry in war probably prolonged it. "Negotiated" peace been possible all along. Left to themselves, France and England might have consented to
territorial adjustments and indemnities.

Development of H. G. Wells significant. Personal
grief in loss of son, but sees beyond personal to grief
of blundering world. Used to burble like worst Middle
Western editorial-writer—now apostle of new order.

The fantastic French! Lewis Carroll would have
been at home here. Impossible to untangle Gallic politics. Emma Goldman type "radical" is Royalist.
Hard-shelled conservative who wonders "what things
are coming to" is Socialist. Clemenceau was Irrecon-
cilable in '14, his paper suppressed. Man who put him
where he is, Daudet, publishes *l'Action Française* de-
voted to restoration of Bourbons. People talk of "revolution" *après la guerre*—meaning Royalist restoration.
Tout le monde reads, thinks, talks politics. Number of
piquant little papers legion. Our front-page murder
stuff, etc., buried in back under *"dernière heure."* Front
page given up to something like disquisition on Sanjak
of Novibazar.

Paris a writer's paradise. Appearance of new book
almost as important as *communiqué*. Intellectually,
Frenchman superior to corresponding class among us.
Indefatigable reader. This applies to gentler species.
Her head has more uses than support for millinery.
Especially the *demi vierge*. Even streetwalker reads
De Musset and *Revue de Deux Mondes*.

Free love an institution, sanctioned if not approved.
In process, mere animalism receded into background.
Men really *love* their mistresses. Living with woman

without benefit of clergy infinitely more than moments of carnality. *Demi-mondaine*, trained to please in all things, cultivates mind as well as finger nails. Result —amazingly charming personalities.

Air raid to-night. The parson's first. Nearly burst with emotion. Hilarious descent to cellar by entire *pension*—half bore, half picnic. Joined by everybody from street. A cake and bottle of wine discovered; and gayety reigned. Americans—new to raids—go out to watch barrage. French shrug shoulders, mention "imbeciles" and skip for cellar.

Several American girls here. Nursing, Red Cross, etc. What S—— would be doing if she didn't have job with next generation. A treat to talk to them. Intelligent—so much more subtle than most men.

Wed., 24th.—Bawled out by Lt. B—— for not reporting last night. He'll have office doing Guard Mount before he's through. Put in busy morning on errands, licking stamps, etc. Getting splendid insight into office end of war. Difference between line soldier and M. LeBureau, difference between wolf and woolly lamb. Latter clean, sweet and pretty, but love him not. Too soft.

Great battle taking up third phase to-day. Renewed suspense. Boche probably smash harder than ever. The last gasp, I think—though nobody agrees. The war can't continue much longer. Possible to endure poverty, suffering and death indefinitely—but not boredom. If Germans fail again, then the Allied counter-push—and *le berloque!* If we suffer from intolerable stupidity of existence, Germans must suffer even more. We've got to quit soon, or go mad.

When this *deuil* is over I'll destroy these pages of

drip. It will cramp conversation if the truth of these dreary days is there in my own handwriting.

Busy afternoon, and over dinner hour on important duty—lettering signs. My spurs helped a lot!

Thur., 25th.—Purchased riding crop to match spurs. Essential to my work. So glad I studied hippology. Saw B——, shifty-eyed rascal. In Y.M.C.A. "*'y à moyen se coucher avec*," the tarts say that stands for.

Took French lesson. Learned that no foreigner can ever learn to pronounce "huit." Dinner at *pension*. Charmed with sweet little C—— G——,* whose mamma has her eye on me as likely *milliardaire* to be plucked.

Fri., 26th.—Spent A.M. at commissary and similar heavy work. Bad attack of *cafard*.

Letter from S——. After six weeks C.O. venereal detachment, made prison officer, special charge cleaning latrines. Then to Tours for Staff duty. More men than needed, but can't get away. Got new daughter, two months old. Hopes to get home for her début. Cheering assurance that if war ends to-morrow at least a year needed to get us back. Signs himself "Chief of the Rear Hounds."

RECOLLECTIONS—A.E.F.

When this cruel war is over and we've laid aside our hates,
When we've crossed the bounding billow to our loved United
    States,
When I sleep in thin pyjamas, not in sweater, socks and pants,
I will think about this billet where I froze in Sunny France.

*C—— was caught, some months later, pinching stuff from the boarders' dressers.

When I sit all snug and cozy, and it isn't any dream,
That I hear the radiator hissing merrily with steam,
When the house is warm and comfy, here's an idea I advance:
I'll forgive the heating systems that are all the vogue in France.

When I watch an open fire eating up the seasoned logs,
I'll recall the snappy sticks fresh out from sodden Gallic bogs.
When I hear the fire crackle as I watch it jump and dance,
I'll forget the smoking fireplace that I froze beside in France.

Arising in the morning from a decent Christian bed,
With teeth that do not chatter till they loosen in my head,
I'll slip into a shower bath and think there is a chance,
That I'll laugh about the ladies' bath I fumbled there in France.

I'll go into my toilet room and find it always neat,
Warm and odorless and cleanly, with a polished oaken seat,
Where the pipes are never frozen, then the budding poet grants
He will shiver when he thinks about the icy cans in France.

I'll slip into my bed at night beneath a quilted spread,
That tucks in at the bottom while it reaches to my head.
Whether woman helps me warm it, or I sleep alone, perchance,
I'll never miss the liver pad I froze beneath in France.

Each morning when I'm shaving, and the running water steams,
I'll think of freezing shaves abroad as odd fantastic dreams.
But when I see a chamber pot, there isn't any chance,
I'll forget the mug of amber ice beneath my bed in France.

Sat., 27th.—Met W——, pleasant Texan, on remount duty, who'd seen no horses. Told about bunch of all-star cowboys from Pendleton, Oregon—cavalry outfit that got dismounted as soon as they hit. France, and now guarding railroads somewhere. 6-day bike riders probably all in cavalry.

Letter from S—— B——. Reg't Surgeon, —rd Inf. On Marne salient: "One wonders as you look at our men going through those bloody wheat fields, what they may be thinking about. If a man gets hit, they say something about 'those German bastards' and keep on. Somebody told them to go out and get the Hun—and that's what they are doing. I've planned a lot for after the war. I shall visit you first, study colloid chemistry next, and get married, *right*, when a miracle occurs." *

Anecdote picked up in *Oui:* "When the eyes are specifically turned toward the battle, the name of Napoleon is often heard in the Senate. Whoever has strategic ideas does not hesitate to evoke the authority of the Great Man. When M. Briand was President of the Council, a senator vehemently reproached him for not being master of the situation. At the end of the argument he put his two fists on the tribune, and in a terrible voice demanded: 'Do you know what Napoleon would do in your place?' 'Yes,' replied M. Briand, 'He would entreat you to shut up.' "

Letter from P—— H——, lovable scamp. With —th F.A.: "Of all the God damn wars I ever fought in this is the worst and also the last. Pull out to-morrow for the dear old Front. Certainly hope they send me to a very active sector, as I would hate to be resting when other men are fighting hard. Was made general prisoner for five wks, third day after getting here, due to my inability to keep up with my organization in the Battle of Bordeaux. Shot one of the old timers for wearing that green Texas guard duty badge."

Letter from T—— G——. Up in line with —th F.A. Reg't'l Tel. Officer: "Best part of my work is working and living with small detail of enlisted men, all of whom I picked and trained. They are fine, full of courage, and cheerful, and not one of them hasn't

---

*He did all three, in the order named. And with cumulative success.

already done work worthy of a citation. My family doesn't know from me that I'm forward, so be discreet when writing home."

Made me think of British Tommy, with 32 wounds in him, who wrote home: "Top hole and feeling fine." Also, by contrast, with letter from enlisted man at Souge, who described rain of machine gun bullets on his dug-out as making noise like a kid running a stick along a picket fence. Five hundred miles from the nearest machine gun!

Sun., 28th.—On duty in office. No duty, but somebody had to be on. Hauled out for wild ride around town with Maj. H——. No idea what it was all about. Told I was going out with shipping-board party. Then told I wasn't.

Squad of Yanks in drug-store in Loire-et-Cher. Sergeant made speech. No results. Hunted among pillboxes. Some made display of bellies with shamelessness showing deplorable effects of Continental spirit upon American modesty. Finally druggist had inspiration. Gathered together all he knew of English. "Ah—water closet, very much, *hein?*" Yanks cheered. What they wanted was castor oil.

Another bit. Young embassy secretary assisted, minus wife, at official dinner. Returning home, wife asked how Mme. X looked. "Oh, very décolleté," he said. "And Mme. Y.?" "Even more décolleté." "And Mme. Z.?" "*Je ne me suis pas permis* to look under the table!"

Mon., 29th.—Usual infantile business all A.M. Come to conclusion nobody in army has anything but infantile business. Three men for every job. But war infantile business, anyhow. Back of lines, certainly.

Lunch with M—— D——. Long talk on problem of sex morals. Everybody's got it. His resolve to stand tight for wife's sake. Wonder if she'd appreciate it. Or think him queer. Sometimes think men can arrive at more delicate moral standards than women. Certainly, no man ever gets as low as a low woman.

Tues., 30th.—Rec'd trench helmet. Very useful in Paris. Orders for X——. Farewell chat with Mme. V——. She misses her husband so. Charming—not quite charming enough. Don't like this married stuff. Got a moral streak on. M—— responsible, I guess.

Dined with L—— and some girls from home. E—— among them. Simply ravishing! Reaction from easier women overpowering. So intelligent and sympathetic and *clean*. Fell for her 100%. Wish my daughter would grow up like that. Oh—cuckoo! *

---

*Seen her since. Certainly must have been cuckoo! But we got that way. A *decent* girl knocked us off our pins.

May, 1918

Wed., 1st.—Left for X——. Sad at going. Such nice people in *pension*. Some English mechanics on train—half drunk, wholly unattractive. None of charm of French. Some day they'll have a revolution in England. They've got some of the most attractive people in the world—and some of the least. They need averaging.

Arrived 4:45. Town jammed, but got hole in Hôtel de la Paix—ironic name. Lonesome, but felt better on bumping into K——, C——, and bunch from C.P.A. L.T. Big artillery center here, and old gang still taking courses, though attached to C.A.C. outfits. Stroll *en ville*, and turned in early. Beautiful weather and climate. My official title now *"Officier Américain de Liaison, aux soins le Général Commandant le ——me Région de l'armée Française."*

Thur., 2nd.—Reported to Capt. R—— at Etat Major. Not a Frenchman here, from General down, who speaks any English. R—— pleasant but heavy. No military training, but takes his rank seriously. Formal presentation to Col. B——, Chief of Staff. Thick-mustachioed bandit, a hard egg. Sound as to head. Body not so good. Most of French that way—crocks. Met Capt. DeM——. Charming. Presented to M. le Général C——, kindly old fellow, putting on no dog. Shock, after American generals.

First job, negotiating lease of field from Frenchman, for artillery purposes. American method, decide what you want, ask "how much?" and come across or get out. French work differently. Visited field, Frenchman and I discussed syndicalism and war aims for ten minutes, while Americans fidgeted. From that into mutual congratulations on the Alliance. All sorts of topics canvassed. Then back to house, where he served up some extra-special Burgundy. More conversation on this and that . . . and to-morrow we'll go on with matter. "Wasted" time, doubtless, but to-morrow we'll settle it, every blade of grass itemized. Done American fashion, owner would get sore, and we'd have to resort to condemnation.

French difficult to handle if habit of thought not understood. Gentle manners conceal stout will. Unfailing sense of humor solves many difficulties. Deputy, in Chamber, complained bitterly other day that he had received many letters from constituents complaining they had found bits of foreign matter in their government-monopoly tobacco. "Ingrates!" cried the Président du Conseil, leaping to his feet. "The foreign matter of which you speak was *tobacco!*"

Current anecdote: Three interned officers, Briton, Frenchman and German, taking walk in Switzerland. Lost. Night fell and it was cold. Found a little cabin, just big enough for one. Briton went in.first, but came out immediately. French tried it, murmuring of squeamish Englishman. He, too, quickly emerged. German went in. Minutes elapsed and he did not reappear. Then out rushed "well known and wholly undomesticated animal."

Fri., 3rd.—Further dicker on lease. Reported to

Gen. D——, lately C.A.C. Colonel. Very upstage with star. Looks like Keystone Comedy cop.

Saw bunch German prisoners. Ferocity, bestiality, dreadful *purposiveness* with which we endow ensemble so completely lacking in individual. Man for man, as attractive as any one knows. Device of partisan journals to photograph Hun just emerging from a week in line—preferably a repulsive one. Then say this is enemy "type." Lies. These prisoners notable in physique and intelligent in appearance.

The mighty problem. Nations fight for "territory." How can individual envisage such abstraction vividly enough to offer life for it? Easy solution that Boche fights because he knows no better, and because he must. But what of us?

Why *do* men fight? Not individually, but in groups? First months of war, comprehensible. Novelty. Exaltation. Rhetoric is real. But when words no longer mean anything? When life's a dirty rag, better thrown away than kept? Talk with B——, Frenchman who spent three yrs. in Germany as prisoner. Some idea of agony Germans going through. What makes them stick it?

First idea that this might be last crack of Boche, given way to universal pessimism. Rumors of Papal peace effort derided. No great divergence of opinion among French as to what they want. Alsace? They call that "blague." The sentiment end of it, that is. They want Alsace because it's full of iron, and been Germany's greatest single asset. Above all else, they want insurance against another war.

Understand Wilson—better than British do. Want to make peace whenever Germans will let them. But no trusting latter. *"Une race à part."* Tragedy of it that German hasn't shown himself fit to be trusted. When things are sour, he's all for sweet reasonability. But with a victory—more frothing at the mouth about "force" and the filthy thing he calls his German god.

Looks as if Almighty had wearied of human life, and given devil *carte blanche* to destroy it. The twilight of "civilization." Must be mirth in hell at dreadful mess we've made of things. The war over now, as far as gain for either side concerned. The square-head knows the game is up. But he goes on. We give him no alternative. How can we? The dreadful circle has no break. The pillars of life in the Western world may go down in the crazy madness of the German Hercules.

No end in sight. And life, as it was, quite apart and finished, gone irrevocably, no less than in Death itself. Moments when one feels happiest conjunction of planets would be one's self and some kindly shell. The future an arid waste—reason asks if living worth its penalty.

Live by the day the motto, here. Forgetful of past, heedless of future. Soft beds, full bellies, acme of spiritual satisfaction. *Avant la guerre* a previous incarnation. Tragedies at home less vivid than sorrows of Cheops. And *apres la guerre*—guesswork. Who cares whether he can play a golden lyre within the pearly gates?

Never such bleak despair. Everywhere. With all the price paid, we are advancing nothing. World no better when we're through. At best, not so bad as it might have been, otherwise. Fighting for change of heart in Germany, and while we fight, change cannot come—what a paradox!

What tangled feelings! Everybody has them, but nobody voices them—unless he's drunk.

- - - -

Sat., 4th.—Rabelais not an author in France—he's a state of mind! Not sure Frenchman isn't healthier-minded than we are. Difficult to learn language. One thing to "speak it." Very much another to *understand* it—in all its nuances and *tournure de phrase.*

Sun., 5th.—Small, but powerful body of opinion in England actively hostile to ideals for which we are officially fighting. Not so obvious, but same forces in France. "Democracy" anathema to both. Ironic that Trotzky picks the radical Clemenceau and his "jingo" ministry for special condemnation. Nothing like responsibility to conservatize the radical!

Is great new step in human government coming from the sad travail of Russia? Unless Western Allies comprehend significance of Bolshevism, they'll not only never lick Germany, but will have internal trouble themselves. *This* war is ending, but there may be a worse one ahead.

Seeing French, English, Swiss and German papers, all shades of opinion, realize extreme parochialism of our own. Some intelligent interest in international politics may be one item on credit side of our being in war. We're too important a part of the world not to know something about it.

Given membership card in Cercle de l'Union. Quaint old club. Well equipped with roulette wheels, chemin de fer outfits, etc. Idea being that since men will gamble, best to have them do it at club. Rake-off goes into paintings and rare enamels. Marvelous collection. Gambling *supprimé* during war, however.

Mon., 6th.—Busy at caserne. Ironies of war. Lt. B—— (French) wounded in first few hours, first battle

of Marne. "Wound" not much—lost a finger—but he's
a piano player!

Raining hard and quite cold. Amorous little waitress
from Amiens. *Saperlipopette!* The fruit one can have
for the picking! No peace in the war with old lady
Nature.

Tues., 7th.—Still negotiating with Monsieur F——
over lease of his fields. Prospects bright. Got most of
grass counted. But I'll be a drunkard before he's
through with me!

To caserne. Ridden by stuffed shirts in eagles and
oak leaves.

Wed., 8th.—Bleak, rainy morning. Got "medaille de
charrion." Very Catholic town of X—— celebrating
Feast of Ascension. Afternoon off. Walk with Capt.
DeM——. Delightful gentleman, antiquarian and
archæologist of repute. Written considerably. Filled
with lore of region. Son killed at Verdun.

Visited Cathedral. Service profoundly affecting.
Such a place like a burning glass, focusing all the tragedy of war to a point. The lame, the halt, the women in
black, the little children, frequently quite alone, pray-
ing . . . one wonders, sometimes, to What? It rains
in Germany, too, and sad-eyed children pray in German
churches. But what man, not God, began, man will
have to finish. Doubt if he knows how.

Gen. Maurice's letter to Parliament. Think Lloyd
George ministry will fall as result. His strength wan-
ing, largely due to support by such Tories as Milner,
Curzon, Carson and Northcliffe. Coalition gov't possible once. No longer. Tory gov't could make war.

Many doubting it can make peace. Asquith may return. Upheaval in British politics certain.

Serious military crime of Maurice—going out of channels. Same as Col. Repington. Both attacking secret diplomacy—same as Wilson. Same battle, sub rosa, in France, with Clemenceau and Austrian dossier.

Significant that court was held behind closed doors. Growing effort everywhere to drag diplomacy out into light. Also, per contra, to retain old methods. On outcome of this struggle depends outcome of war—much more than any battle.

Curious that visiting representatives of American labor more *jusqu'au boutiste* than French labor. Latter urge conciliation and immediate pourparlers with German labor. Americans oppose it. French think we pledge our last dollar and "last drop of blood" too gaily, never expecting to have bluff called.

French labor in minority here. Condemned bitterly by press. Puerile to talk of conferring with German Social-Democrats as long as they are so submissive to Pan-Germanists. Holding out olive branch to mad dog, etc.

Bitter-enders just as surely leading to long war and ultimate self-destruction. They strengthen German gov't in contention it is fighting in self-defense. Talk of signing peace treaty in Berlin, sheer idiocy.

Criminal, of course, to give any idea we aren't all out for victory. Got to come fast—with all we have. But Europe needs our fresh ideals more than our army. If we'd had a man in Russia like Brand Whitlock, things might be different now. British envoy seemed to dominate. Announced in so many words Allies could not recognize government of "Socialists." Russians did not and do not love Germany the more, but us the less. Exclusively our own fault.

While we dream over dreadfulness of such things as *Lusitania*, busy Boche goes about his propaganda. Trotzky once ran a newspaper in N.Y. The bitterest Bolsheviks learned their class hatred in sweat shops of East Side. They know—or think they know—the U.S. Derision for our expressed purpose in fighting for Democracy and oppressed peoples.

Fri., 10th.—To Cusaix with E——. Dined with him, and movie show. Punk. To low dive for beer. Character on screen so like S——. Made me homesick as hell.

Sat., 11th.—Reported to Gen. D——. On job with Sgt. D—— and interpreter. Worst thing on earth, half-Americanized Frenchman. All worst qualities of both. Preoccupied with sex. Enough of that around without talking about it all the time. All my Anglo-Saxonism to fore. Probably, though, nothing but a beer-hangover working out. Dinner with K—— and opera, *"Si j'etais Roi."* Arabian nights era—chorus synchronized. Scenery, early Pleistocene. Tenor slipped fast when out of range. But soprano reminiscent of M—— M——. Rest of show didn't matter.

Sun., 12th.—Letter from home that our house sold for taxes. Felt like hero of "Way Down East." Taking advantage of absence to do dirty trick like that makes me see red. I'll meet that son of a bitch some day! Lawyers here say not to worry. But it's hell to be four thousand miles away engaged in saving your God damned country and have some greasy slacker steal your

house from you. Some day I hope to have a visit with
that bird!*

Long talk with M—— over woman-question. Both-
ers him a lot. Immense regard for F——. Feels he
couldn't go back and face her if he slipped here. Ob-
stinate cuss, and may get through. But battle of bats a
hard one. Question hard to settle, and many casualties.
All sorts of defenses—ethics, æsthetics, and plain cold
feet. These damned wisps of flesh, flitting, whispering,
along streets at twilight, worse than microbes.

M—— insists same thing, going on at home. Lives in
terror of snake in grass (male) there. B——'s caustic
comment. Calls it gratuitous worry.

I'm a swell prophet! Instead of Lloyd George down
and out, he's back with vindication. But unrest and interrogation continues. Question of conservative and efficient gov't as opposed to democratic and "defeatist"
gov't not yet settled. After all, isn't that what the
whole damned war's about?

Asked Capt. DeM—— why he did clerk's work at
Etat when he could be retired. Silent for a moment,
tears in eyes. "Son gave his life: *he* could do no less
than give his time." Then, sadly, "*Ah, la guerre—c'est
dur.*" Heard more *hate* in ten minutes at home than
I've heard in all France.

Letter from J——. Asks if I recall his early enthusiasm for *la vie militaire*. Do, but don't hold it against
him. Same way, myself, once. Says the minute the
war's over the speed with which he resumes civvies will
make a Spad on the wing look like a study in fruit life.
You and me, both, J——!

*Haven't had it yet, and never expect to, now.

Sun., 12th.—Day of rest. The worst sort.

Mon., 13th.—Everybody here sore over story of my house and tax shark. But nobody surprised. The soldier expects to get it in the neck.

Sprightly conversations of Angele, the waitress, bright spots in weary days. Written me off for anything but talk, and does her hunting elsewhere.

21 weeks since that morning I bolted breakfast, kissed my best girl casually, and beat it, as if for the 8:24 to town. Pretending cheerfulness. S——, scurrying around, eating at lunch counters to save money to buy things for me. What a person! Gilding the base metal which I am, the columbine around the rotted stump. Her picture before me. Portrait of a Beautiful Woman. Beauty of ensemble and harmony. Beauty in cut granite. Beauty of strength, of dignity, of soundness all the way through. Beauty of the rose, the precious stone. The scintillant, breath-taking loveliness which stuns the vision now and then, can wither and die overnight. S——'s sort remains, firm in its hold under the revealing sunshine of morning as in the gentle charity of the twilight.

The *uncertainty* of this sentence the thing that hurts. A date for the end—even five years or twenty—would make it more endurable. But this endless necessity of forgetting yesterday, of ignoring to-morrow, of conquering hope and stilling regret. Life lives on anticipation. When there isn't any . . .

When big offensive started, great talk of "this is the end." No more of that. Even to think peace held evidence of weak mind. No more prophecies. Shrug of the shoulders and "God knows." Had to revise significance of June 26. No peace, but insist it'll be big day, somehow.

World's in mess, and doesn't know how to get out. Germany licked—no question. Raw materials shut off, and she'd die. But leaders astute. Halted in West, they'll dig in on defense. Then wait for Allied weariness and compromise. This all dependent on success in keeping own people in line. Revolution may break suddenly. When it does, it'll move fast.

Wilson's demands, paradoxically, an obstacle to peace. Allies have more sympathy for dominant German. Any liberation of German people will necessitate corresponding liberation of allied peoples. Complications in this "making world safe for democracy."

German leaders won't quit—dassn't. Hang on, dickering—that's their game. Unless spark of revolution reaches tinder which I think awaits it, and is fanned by some measure of sympathy from more democratic elements of Allies, we'll have to go on to a knockout.

At show to-night, charming damsel took fancy to me. Began with sly pokes in back. Not long before I was holding hands. Unmaidenly to extent of kissing me, and sat in my lap. No extenuation except youth—just three years. Suppose when I get home, J—— will be having callers.

Tues., 14th.—Busy days. *Rapport* at the Etat Major. Then the jobs. *Item:* Engineers want camions which French don't want to give up. I get them. *Item:* Complaints about fast driving of our chauffeurs. Investigate. *Item:* Civilians seen around town with American cigarettes. Lies. No Frenchman would smoke American cigarettes. Anyhow, what the hell. *Item:* Signal Corps reports lumber for R.R. construction not

delivered. Visit Service de Bois, and weep. *Item:*
French recognize *la maison de tolerance.* We don't.
French madames consider sacred rights interfered with
when we post M.P.'s at their houses. Business ruined.
Girls starving. Etc. *Trés grave!* Col. B—— pulls
whiskers. My job to square things. Can't. Nobody
can. Trouble remains. Always will be trouble as long
as there are women. *Item:* Entertainment at *Foyer du
Soldat* of 43rd Regt. General O—— invites me. Therefore I go. Sit with Mme. O—— and daughters. Show
starts at 8, ends at 1. Too long to sit in one place. But
being Officier de Liaison, I sit. *Et ainsi de suite.* Diplo-
matic fireman, pinch-hitter, always on tap. Not very
exciting. Certainly not war. But bed is good and had
lobster for lunch. One should worry.

Wrote letters home. Thoughts camouflaged and interesting descriptions of things that never happened.
The real ones go here.

His Majesty, the American soldier. Fine lad. Well
disciplined, not so much from necessity as choice. Quick,
keen, and when edges are smoothed, gets on well with
natives. They like him as much as they dislike his officers. Astonishingly well behaved. In town near here
men put on honor two months ago. No M.P.'s yet.

Americanization process. Draft men, of foreign
blood, scattered through all units. Located Italian,
speaking French, in —th. Protested when ordered
for duty as interpreter. Didn't want to speak French
for fear people might think him not Amurrican.

Acquaintance growing up among different regions of
U.S. Oregon reg't and outfit from Boston on same ship.
Mass. boys at first dubious of "wild" Westerners—
which had highest percentage of collége men and generally *bien élevé* of any outfit I've seen. Most refrac-

tory bunch yet encountered, from Alabama. Pistol toters. G.O. ruled rods out. After that, all scrapping Marquis of Queensberry, and several good lickings helped. Negro troops—*salutingest* crowd! Very smart, but need extra-strong officers. Liquor their undoing. Something of problem in land of wine. As to alcohol generally, more drunks around Highwood Saturday nights in old days, than around one of our cantonments here in entire month. Light wines and watery beer O.K. Whiskey, champagne, etc., forbidden. No difficulty for officers, though.

Everybody studying woman problem. Frenchman gives it considerable attention. One reason, maybe, the position of women. In two classes—those who produce children and run establishment, from kitchen to cash-register; and all the rest. Our idea of relation between sexes beyond French comprehension. He may "love" a woman, and write sonnets to her; for most part looks on her as pretty low order of animal life. Our platonic feelings, result of coeducation and sports, unknown here. Our "morality" called hypocrisy— which much of it is. If Frenchman has mistress, presents her to friends. Polygamous. Sees no reason for not having one respectable female with knack for cuisine and good dressing; and around corner another, not so respectable, with flare for other matters. Loves them both, in fashion we can't understand. System has much to recommend it. But going to change. Sex relations now based on intellectual, moral and economic subordination of women. French women getting interested in "rights."

Against Gallic viewpoint, forgotten strains of ancestry and environment protest. Can't help resenting idea that highest form of entertainment for visiting fireman is a woman. But admire French candor. Less smutty-minded than we, despite impression given by comic papers. Less furtive snickering over *double entendre*. Fact is, we'd benefit by French acceptance of physiologic fact: and they could use a touch of our idealism with regard to women.

Americans may gain new independence out of this experience. Those who began by blushing at candor with which Gaul of both sexes goes about processes of excrementation, may return to U.S. converted to sensible notion that distended bladder less pleasing in sight of Lord than reasonable, natural, and comfortable figure of man against convenient if only nominally sheltering tree. If it jolts Puritan tradition to that extent, this war will not have been in vain.

In personal habits the French, generally, are filthy. Even upper classes content with plumbing primitiveness unknown to us. Cuisine unsurpassed, but table manners atrocious. In management of knife and fork, Yank doughboy a grand duke beside a *poilu*.

Home papers still referring to "Sammies." How the boys hate that word! Never use it and won't answer to it. No objection to "Yank," but generally refers to self as "Amurrican."

Wed., 15th.—To Cusaix for lecture on mech. maneuvers. Jolly mess with 59th C.A.C. Charming fellows. Enlisted man who wouldn't keep policed. Turned over to men with curry brushes. To Naxon. Smashed differential and towed to Pierre Buffière Messed with C—— and hospitable officers of town.

H—— L—— having proved wash-out as B.C. is retired to Line of Communications. Not quite bad enough to send home.

Droll attitude of people at home, giving up everything because they can't bear to be happy when the dear
boys are suffering over here.   Will they refuse to be
happy rest of their lives because many millions of fellow humans still living in degradation and misery?
A.E.F. well content if home folks get all fun out of life
possible.   Average *militaire* better pleased to know his
people happy than hear they're having nervous pros-
tration from too much war-work.

Some of my letters censored. No idea why. No
secrets revealed—don't know any.   Maybe they've got
an inspector on me, and G.C.M. shortly, with dismissal
from army. Let us pray!

Folks at home think they have hero in family. Make
me out a knight in shining armor, sort of Arrow Collar
boy in O.D.   Expected to write romantic fiction.

Sometimes, there are sounds—cadence of marching
men, rumble of gun-limbers over the cobbles, the roll of
the drums in *Sambre et Meuse*—for about thirty seconds
feel heroic as hell. Seldom longer.

Bone-headed diplomacy of Allies!   London *Globe*
says: "A big organization is being formed in Germany
in order to place first in the peace negotiations the question of raw materials.   Let all the Allied nations agree
that in order to punish the Germans for their abomi-
nable crimes, they will not renew commercial relations
with their enemies until two years after the war."   That
sort of stuff ought to stiffen the Boche backbone!

And speech by Mr. T——.   Never agreed with anything he ever said before, so not surprised to keep record
intact. All for war to bitter end, etc.   But no intimation as to what "end" is. Idea seems to be: "Let's get
to end, and when we're there, decide where the end is."
Tiring—that sort of race.

Kindly folk at home evidently getting after lads in Washington bomb-proofs. Poor J—— C——. Instead of being picked on, he ought to be medalled. Public benefactor for not coming over here. He might be a B.C.—and that would be murder. Way these damned fools talk, you'd think any ass could do supply work, but only supermen fight. We need few more supermen in S.O.S.* Too many wet fuses in it now.

Black Jack knows it. Lots of men, like S——, who could fight and want to, kept at desks. Lots of unsung heroes like him, with no medals or wound-stripes, except what they pick up in the cafés. And these smart cracks about "ground" aviators. Who the hell do they think takes care of planes, feeds the men, pays them, etc?

C—— M——, in Washington, trying to get into "active" service. Most of the casuals been trying that for months. Some of the boys from Souge just turned up here for course in radio telegraphy. As a war, this is a grand Graduate School.

Thur., 16th—Got some white bread for Lt. DeC——'s wife—stomach won't go French war bread. But palate objects to ours. *Fade*, he explained.

Fri., 17th.—To Perigueux—shades of Cyrano! Tense expectancy and much talk about new German drive. May break any minute. French very anxious. Hot. First fly of season. K—— F—— happiest man in army. Bounced from 59th and made postmaster—used to work in P.O. in Montana.

*Service of Supply. Originally called Service of the Rear but changed because "the rear" means the latrines, and those in the rear were sensitive.

Sat., 18th.—So hard to write truthful letters. What *is* truth? One, like John Reed, sees regiment—bunch of bored, diseased, commonplace kids. Another, a company of knights. Don't see with eyes alone. "Web of life of mingled yarn, of good and ill together." Shimmers in the light. What one sees bright and colorful, somber and knotted to man beside him. State of bowels has good deal to do with it.

Extraordinarily hot, with sun beating down on dust of streets until whiteness almost incandescent. Sick of flannel shirts, choke collars and puttees—army life. Like the British Tommy: " 'Taint the shells, 'taint the mud: it's the bein' damned abaht all the damned while that damns me!"

Those singular folk—the Irish of France (their representative in the Chamber is named Jean Hennessy!)—*les gens de Midi.* Mixed blood and wild—tameless. Full of troubled, futile surgings—a little tragic, not a little humorous. Typical anecdote in Paris paper: *"Oh, CE MIDI! Toulouse. Beaucoup de monde au café. Soudain, on entend un renflement de moteur. Un avion passe dans le ciel bleu. Un consommateur sort, regard attentivement le grand oiseau, puis rentrant dans la cave, il dit d' un ton tout à fait rassurant: 'C'est un des nôtres.' "*

Men from Midi who staged mutinies early in war, and last year. Always in trouble insulting their officers, but get most of the medals for bravery. Also supply most of the politicians and journalists. Singular people—anti-war when war is on: bellicose in peace. The Midi gave birth to I.W.W. and invented *sabotage*—word originated in silk mills of Lyons. Difficult, very—never tiresome.

Discussing arms with DeM——. It was curving of

sword blade that changed whole course of history. Mah-
rattas of India found secret first. As conquerors, passed
it on to Saracens. With it, latter almost able to subdue
Europe. Charles Martel stopped them—not far from
here—only because he learned secret, too. Before it,
men pecked at each other like gamecocks. Afterward,
a strong man could split his enemy, helmeted and
armored, right through to saddle. The shearing cut.
Then—gunpowder and quantity production.

X—— makes one feel relativity of "time." Occupied by British, under Black Prince, 34 years. Not a
trace left. Wonder how long Black Jack will stay?
Change comes so slowly. "Street of the Butchers,"
meat shops exclusively, owned and operated by five
families, intermarried since 13th century. Wealthy, but
still live in filth of ancient houses, carrying on business in ancient way. Splendid modern villas in country, but for bulk of year live and work in 13th century.
Characteristic of French—incredibly slow to change.

Wearing a mustache. Doubts as to beauty. But
they're custom of country—almost *de rigueur*.

Humor of France its salvation. If Chamber becomes
unruly, the President puts on his hat, as signal for
cloture. In recent crisis, chamber in uproar, situation
serious. President reached for hat. Horrors! Not to
be found. Fortunately, one of members had his. President clapped it on. Proved three or four sizes too large.
Chamber gave one look and dissolved in laughter.
Crisis averted!

Letter from S——. What magnificent isolation!
How many pigs on farm, health of infants, high cost
of living, etc. Still in world most of us left so long ago.
Quite happy. Prefer her candid apathy to hysteria of
others. Why should she be troubled? She had not

social consciousness *avant la guerre*. Why now? She's
honest. And doesn't pretend that B—— is "doing his
bit" as farmer. Like that best of all. Things are
simple. That some should go, and B—— stay, nothing
to her. Just happened. That ends it. War hasn't
"come to them." Hope it doesn't. If I get killed, same
regret as if run over by taxi.

Poor C——. Things must be hard for her. So typical
of absurdity of whole German game. Hostile to all
that German victory would mean, sympathy for all
ideals we're fighting for, but feels the call of blood.
Ready to offer life for ideas she despises, ready to com-
mit intellectual suicide for *Kultur* . . . Germania herself. They'll make *her* suffer because the beast in man
got loose in Belgium.

Pitiable spectacle of some of our best clergy trying
to write foot-note to words of Christ anent forgiveness
of enemies. Church cutting sorry figure in this business. Incredible puerility of "Jesus never knowing
Germans." Don't seem to grasp utter sterility of hate.
God knows I shan't love word "German" after this.
But that's weakness. Pray the Ruler of things that
children be spared it. Damned be he who tries to carry
venom that has rotted entrails of this generation into
as-yet sweet lives of the next!

News of K—— and thought of me. The great compensation in this. Friendships. Grow fast but strong.
All things that mattered, *autrefois*, minus here. Live
frankly. Everything on table. No pose. The *real* revealed. Pleasant to think of reunions we'll have, some
day. Worth everything they may have cost. *

Letter from D—— R——. No superior for felicity

*There have been few: and those, not very satisfactory.
Somehow, we seem to have reverted to what we were before.

of expression. And with a sympathy, a sweetness of understanding that endows all he writes with the charm of his personality.

Those letters home! Breathes there the man with soul so dead he would not tamper with the truth to make a good yarn better? Comes an Ohio newspaper with letter printed in it, written by one of boys now with 59th. He's having a lot of trouble with that letter. Most of it memorized by brother officers. T—— promises to set it to music!

So F—— E——'s married—to a flier. Problem may not be a permanent one. Ha! Ha!—as enlisted men always put in letters.

Sun., 19th.—Lunched with D—— and mistress— charming girl he wants to marry. She firm against it. Urged me to secure one, during duty in Limoges, on sanitary grounds. Very earnest about perils in promiscuity. Angry at *les Américains* for being treated as "loose woman" because of relations with D——.

Lonesome dinner, with none but A—— for company. She willing to extend company beyond serving dinner. Willing enough, myself—but scared. This God damned plague of women! Wish I were *old!*

Mon., 20th.—Pathetic Bohemians, from U.S. Enlisted in fine fervor of idealism, and find themselves in French army. Want to get in ours. Red tape in way. Nothing army hates so much as idealist.

Tues., 21st.—This not Germany, nor exactly "suffering." But damned sick of fare, just the same. Three meatless days a week. To-night—potato soup, and tiny fish, largely cartilage. Three or four peas, with

skins of carrots.   And ancient, wrinkled apple, slightly
decayed.   Tempted to join army mess, with oatmeal,
bacon, milk, butter, jam, pie, sugar, etc.   But hours
and distance don't square with job at Etat.

Not very busy.   R—— adequate for most of work.
Only odd jobs of erranding left over.

Read splendid article in *S.E.P.* on imminent dissolution of German power.   Greatly set up—only to discover issue was dated Sept. 17, 1917.   Suppose they'll
be printing same sort of articles when I'm retired for
old age.

Pleasant doctrine of darkness before dawn, etc.
Worse it looks, better it must be.   No sense to that, but
comforting.   German offensive hanging over us.   Don't
think it will be successful.   Then—if all-but-mythical
German "people" ever going to assert themselves—will
be the time.   If morale behind lines ever taints army,
end will come fast.   Fritz may awake from his delusion
over night.

L'Humanité—Socialist sheet—most interesting.   May
be cracked in its economics, but at least trying to see
beyond next week—which is more than any of our God
damned governments do.

Representative of Manchester *Guardian* chased out
of France—probably for suggesting we spend a few
minutes thinking about what we're fighting for.   Northcliffe all for more Prussianism.

Only country to-day which is unit, is Germany—
through fear and repression only.   In all the others,
lion and lamb march together against common national
foe.   But remove foe, and two will fly apart as before
—maybe further apart than ever.   Going to be a lot of
private wars when this one is wound up.

Wed., 22nd.—Never want to see an *egg* again—long as I live!

What rot goes into this book! Passing emotions, half-baked thoughts, tosh. And when all pages filled —the fire. Of all foolish things, keeping a diary the foolishest.

Life's a play—not without interest, but in need of the blue pencil. Whatever is, is wrong. Occasionally, though—humorous. That saves it. Ugly. Comedy in wrong places. Stupid in plot. Action slow. Always promising—never fulfilling. Brought into it on false pretenses. Why the hell do we try so hard to stay? Take the resolution to do or die—and do neither. What a lonesome thing—the human soul. What a musty attic full of shadow-shapes it lives in.

Droll to think of *plunging* into war—like into cold bath. None of our crowd even got their toes wet, yet. Or will, for some time. G.H.Q.'s idea to be thorough in training—thrifty souls, they don't want to waste ammunition.

Big hospital here—2000 beds, located in Haviland china factory. Delay in getting started—waiting for china to come from U.S. Just arrived. All marked: "Haviland-Limoges."

"Limogé," in French slang, means "on the shelf." Used to bury their benzined generals here. Now they bury us.

A lot of officers who came over with troops have been S.C.D'd and offered choice of resignation or transfer to non-combatant arms. Enough officers now to pick and choose. Bunch of C.A.C. fellows, Nat'l Guard, just arrived. Welcomed with exam. in math. Lot of them, including two Majors, plucked.

Flaming heart and stout hands not enough for fight-

ing men—not in artillery. Lot of bullet-proof jobs getting filled by brave souls with sub-caliber brains. Town
full of them. Odd jobs. Some just hanging around.
Probably here for duration. Sore as boils at first, but
six months will reduce anybody to complete irresponsi-
bility. Take what comes and to hell with it.

Marvels never cease. Saw Gen. K——, next to
Pershing biggest man in A.E.F. *Polite*—to *me!* And
to-morrow le Général C—— giving lunch to Gen.
D——. Nothing lower than Colonels—except myself.
Getting like lad who wrote home he "didn't notice
avions now no more than a flock of crows." Got to sug-
gest to provost marshal he keep junior officers off streets.
Save space for me and generals.

Just read, in *Lit. Digest*, eulogy of Liebknecht—
"heroism tried and found true." On next page, denun-
ciation of pacifists and defeatists in our midst. What's
crime in an American is glorious in a German. Why the
hell can't we fight a decent war without drooling hypocrisy all the time? Let's lick the Boche the way we
started out to do, and admit he can be a traitor to his
cause, or believe in it, same as we. Christ, the stuff
that's published! It's certainly a cockeyed world just
now.

Thur., 23rd.—Sick of inaction and vegetable diet.
Notion of getting in tanks. Plenty of excitement, anyhow. But thought of another school makes me shudder.
K—— says I haven't even scratched surface. He's been
in nine so far, and no job yet. War's gotten too damned
educated!

Fri., 24th.—Family effort to make little tin god out
me. Nausea. Too many eggs, maybe. Or too much
vin rouge.

Sat., 25th.—First half of morning polishing boots, second half fixing office typewriter. Gen. C——'s de luxe luncheon. After coffee, Gen. D—— made oration, in "French." All the Frenchmen attention to the last word. Great applause. When it was over, Col. G—— dragged me out to garden and fell on my neck. Said I was *"de la maison"* and he could relieve himself. Tears of joy on his furrowed cheeks. Gen. D——, poor fish, actually believes he got away with it.

After lunch, Col. S—— (American) sprang this one: "Why is Germany like Holland?" *Ans.:* "Because it is a low-lying country damned on all sides." Insisted I translate it to M. le Général. Latter listened with utmost politeness. Explained that it was non-translatable *calembour*, and that he would materially aid the Entente and l'Union Sacrée by laughing when I did. He did—heartily. Later inquired if perhaps Col. S——had not perhaps had a trifle too much wine.

Against good manners and tact of French, *gaucherie* and excessive self-confidence of some Americans show to sorry advantage. We need a few hundred years more of civilization to make us understand that etiquette is not mere effeminacy, and that skyscrapers, bath-tubs, quick lunch counters and express elevators do not in themselves justify our belief that we are a superior race.

Dined with R—— T——. Charming. Asked why, at his age, he had come over. Answered simply that with all the fine young blood going, he didn't think an old crock like himself had right to stay home; and that while he cherished no particular illusions as to his own usefulness, felt that possibly his going might influence younger men to do likewise. Probably no service flag on his house—he's merely running a hospital—but merits admiration, and has mine. Living in discomfort,

working hard and usefully, far from home and frankly
homesick, and all without compulsion or tooting of
horns.

So many men at home think their whole duty in "buying" Liberty Bonds. K—— says *service* is measured by
degree of sacrifice involved. Probably hurt fellows like
B—— more to lose a per cent or two on their money,
than their lives. They're the real heroes.

The very strength Germany now showing, proof of
her end. Like a match, just before it goes out, will
flare into last blaze of light. No reserves. The last
desperate hazard. No more trench warfare. No slow
retreat backward to the Rhine. Probably not end before snow. But impossible to believe in another winter
of war.

Capt. DeM—— would not attend to-day's function.
Anniversary of son's death—*tué sur le champ d'honneur.*
Not hate for Germans. Only rather dulled and
apathetic hate of war, a wonderment that a just God
could let such things be. "A clean lad—so fond of
books and pictures . . . and of me. We were very good
friends. A volunteer . . . I—I suppose there are many
such days as this in Germany, too. *C'est triste!*" To-
morrow, his cheery self again, full of jokes and a smile
for everyone. Not to-day.

Sun., 26th.—Met Judge Ben Lindsay, and most
charming wife. Surprised to find him quite conservative. Simple, naïve, not a trace of side.

Mon., 27th.—Morning with K—— and Lindsays.
Latter over here on one of the regular "investigation"
tours. Not a "cultured" man, not, probably, a broad
man. Sympathies not as liberal as to be expected, nor
especially well-informed. Disappointed when he men-

tioned as good representatives of U.S., in eyes of Europe, Taft, Root and Lodge. Not that he admired the views of these men, but that he accepted their preëminence without much thought. In short, an active man, rather sketchy outside his line. Struck fire, now and then, with contempt for staff "colonels" of Red Cross. Frank, too, about organized charity, and such institutions as Rockefeller Foundation, "The Charity Trust." Very curious about French politics, of which he knew nothing. Much interest in so-called "labor" delegation.

This, a curious affair. Origin obscure—backstairs social politics in Washington, etc. Usual *"cherchez la femme."* Delegation strange enough in itself. Comprised few labor people, male and female, capitalists, railway men, society folk, authors, editors, God knows what. Only thing in common a limitless ignorance of European affairs.

Noised about they represented American labor. So welcomed by French labor. Luncheon at *Bourse de Travail*, with vast amount of platitudinous bunk by Americans—last drop of blood, last dollar, etc.—which ceased to interest radical French some years ago. Their reply so brutal French press did not print it.

French disgusted and shocked by American speeches, which not only betrayed no evidence of sympathy with labor or liberalism, but no evidence of intellectual capacity of any sort.

Thing spread. Radicals answered reprovingly with howl from conservatives. Americans, in perfect daze, taken from labor conferences to tea with Clemenceau, from meetings with railway workers to Palais Bourbon. Finally split up themselves. Capitalists shook Daudet's hand and yelled *"jusqu'au bout."* The horny-handed sons of Gompers, finding the C.G.T. as far removed from them as Debs from Taft, went to movies. And the ladies went shopping.

Didn't end there. Entanglements with British labor. Letter from Branting—one of Europe's *real* statesmen —followed. There was the abortive attack on Lloyd George—the Manchester *Guardian* incident . . . for several weeks Europe was more or less by the ears.

The net result—a feeling of deep disappointment among liberals here for the utter lack of sympathy or understanding on the part of Americans, a suspicion that Wilson does not really speak for the nation, and a strengthening of the element of reaction which we are professedly hostile to.

What Europe is looking for is not hyperbole and rhetoric, but sound, reasoned thinking as to how to end the war so that aftermath may not be as bad as war itself. Not much interested in phrases. Whereas U.S. is worrying about "pacifists," England and France are wondering if there isn't even more peril in the chauvinist. No desire to have for German Junkerism, French or English variety substituted. European political thought years in advance of ours.

Curious murmur outside, like rustle of branches in wind. Clatter of many feet on cobbles. Street black with sorry picture. Refugees, pattering wearily along toward their barracks. Small children, leading still smaller ones. The very old, trying awkwardly to help each other. Pitiful vestiges of homes—dingy little bags, an extra hat, a pair of shoes, a bird cage, one old woman leading three small dogs. And then . . . clump, clump, clump—company of soldiers, 60 lbs. apiece on their backs, steps dragging. So, on this street, all day long, and all night, too. Dirty war. Never a band. No flags. Just hanging on. Dreaming that to-morrow *la guerre va finir.* Keeping matter of fact, laughing, in a stubborn denial that there is a shadow over life.

Some say that it's "business as usual," and the French their ordinary insouciant selves. But few see them off parade. A proud breed, which does its weeping in private. *La vie intime* not seen by the journalist with two weeks between steamers.

Hard for us to understand French. They *will* prefer perfume to soap-and-water. They would rather talk than make money—though they *do* like money. Art is a vital thing, and contentment the *summum bonum.* And to enjoy life, as it passes, a solemn obligation. His readiness to lay down his life against the German not due to any love for democracy, but because the thought of the latter intruding on his calm with awful notions of *efficiency* is worse than any fear of death.

Frenchman called insincere. Not that, but politeness veils a vast reserve. Slow to offer real friendship. But when he does, it is very real. So false, that stagey, Parisian post-card notion of him. Has his faults but, characteristically, knows them better than we know ours.

Tues., 28th.—Big German drive launched, with gains.

DeM—— told amazing story of Russian mutiny at La Courtine. Early in war Russians sent couple of brigades to France. At the revolution, these mysteriously went Bolshevik. French put them at La Courtine, where they raised hell. Kicked out officers. Elected soviets. Arguments all night whether drill next day or not. Sometimes yes. Sometimes no. Officers all drunk. French emissary found C.O. in epaulets and boots, playing leap-frog with orderlies. Pie-throwing contests. Got to bullets. Such a nuisance, finally, for

French towns around, French troops sent. Pitched battle fought. 8000 rounds fired by Russians—no casualties. DeM—— kept diary of whole affair. Last entry: "To-day, last of Russians moved out—first Americans move in. God preserve us."

Wed., 29th.—Bad news from war. Breach between Rheims and Soissons widening.

Spent evening with Capt. DeM——. His real interest in life, "amusement of an old maniac," he calls it—enamels. Wife and daughters away, his youngest boy, of charming manners and quick humor, did the honors. Showed me his treasures, pictures, books, etc., above all, his war-interrupted life's work, a catalog of fine enamels of Europe, gathering dust, while he slaved all day at clerk's job. Talked on everything from Wagnerian music to the groined arch. Then a bottle of Curaçao, and a little talk of the other son, *mort pour la patrie.* Showed me the picture, with Croix de Guerre and silver star, and the brass plate, with the citation on it. Also, other pictures of the lad, before the war. Parted late, I with feeling that in this captain in the armies of France, sometime antiquary, and dreamer of ancient beauties, there dwelt as sweet and gentle a soul as I would encounter in this life.

Thur., 30th.—Ticklish days. Soissons fallen. Rheims next. More, too. Excitement of Etat Major. Much head-shaking as communiqués come in. Some one ventured hope they'd be stopped by the Vesle. B—— spat on floor. *"Voilà—le Vesle."* Situation grave. Still—German attack designed, using all lessons learned in March, to draw reserves of Foch. Ludendorf thought sentimental importance of Rheims would force French to fight for it. Foch has refused to fall in with these

ideas. Preferred to hold lines thinly, and give way—
retaining reserves for the day which will come—*le jour
du riposte.*

Few agree, but persist in conviction we're in *"le
dernier quart d'heure."* 200,000 Yanks to-day worth
2,000,000 to-morrow.

Americans, despite blurbs in home press, not yet succeeded in revolutionizing art of war. Splendid troops,
all agree, but still have number of things to learn. Some
stories of recent actions not wholly in accord with facts.
The Yank, potentially, has no superior, while Fritz is
a low, dog-like creature, devoid of aught but superficial
cunning. Despite all our hopes, he declines to run away
in terror. His tendency, these days, all the other way.

58th C.A.C. arrived. Rented bakery for them, etc.
Earned citation for mollifying French lady whose
chickens run over by U.S. truck. Didn't get it.

Fri., 31st.—Endangered reputation by sitting in café
with de la R——, *"amie"* and sister. Americans can't
understand it, but de la R—— extremely refined and
fastidious—too much so for furtiveness of sidewalks.
His philosophy that no young man can live satisfac-
torily alone. Ergo . . .

To movie with K——, and through "la rue des Filles
de Notre Dame"—ironic name for abode of the lost.
When a woman has come to end of road of public love,
ugly and diseased, but still in ring, takes habitation
here. Proscribed territory for *soldats Américains.* A
nightmare. Just as it was in 13th cent., with sewage
running down drain in center, as odorous as swill barrel,
fat, sweating creatures hanging over doorways, struggling to contrive enticement with sorry wreck of wrinkled flesh and broken, yellow teeth. Makes one think
of François Villon. *"Où sont?"* etc.

June, 1918

Sat., *1st.*—Bad news. Depressing to look at map. Too hot to eat. First cherries. *"Clafoutie"* (sp?)—national dish of the Limousin.

Sun., *2nd.*—*Cafard*—bad! Restless as cat. Futility of writing letters. What sparkles off pen, lifeless on arrival. Events give lie to everything. Raving—this stuff. Shorthand. Torrents of words rush in out of darkness. Can't get them down. Don't—dare. Names. People—what's left of them. Corpses. Fragments. And places—Soissons, Villers Cotteret, Château Thierry. Wish I were there. Wish Anastasia'd cut thread to my sorry tale. But why wish? Here I am. Here I rot. Quit struggling. Take it as it comes. Only way to keep sane.

Meaningless words, these. But full of meaning—once. What matter? None to read.

Mon., *3rd.*—Lunch, Cercle de l'Union. Perfection of alcoholic arrangements. *Allumé.* Just right. Nobody agreeing with my war guesses. Dined with K——
and T——. More drink—American style, this time. Picked up couple of *filles* (non-professional). Park bench stuff.

Tues., *4th.*—In the doldrums—miserable. And first class hang-over. Saw B—— about transfer to tanks.

Said no chance, and called me Quixotic ass besides. Stay where you're put. Army gospel, all right—but hard to get used to.

John Reed interned. Rose Stokes got ten years. Widely approved, no doubt. And by same people who want things safe for democracy. *Some* honest people, though. Capt. R—— considers democracy "unsuccessful." What the hell's he here for?

According to American press, we're "paying debt to Lafayette," and "restoring Alsace." French yawn politely at both ideas. They find us *young*.

Maybe, when German's licked, there'll be another war. Bolshevism, with which the simple mujik appears to have made monkey of himself, not going to be disposed of by calling it names. Maybe it's not disease, but symptom. Jail-sentences and hangings won't kill spirit of change, of all colors from bomb-throwing red to nut-sundae Socialists. Dislike of *have-nots* for *haves* —can't settle it by merely saying it isn't nice.

Curious notion that "peace" means dawning of era of brotherly love. Good old quarrelsome process of readjustment and evolution going to take up march again. Ungentle people will strike and break things. And soap-headed legislators will still try to settle everything with more laws.

New regiment here. Officers expectant of Front in week or so. Great progress so far. Two Lieutenants now Paymasters. One Captain mess officer for life. One Major simply relieved from duty. Lot of others will see Front only via movies. Efficiency exams. daily, and heads falling. First quiz was in logarithms and all who flunked bounced out of artillery. Others still have months of school and range practice before they go into action.

So this is "the war to end war." What rot! If we
can end this one so it won't be a hatchery for another
in our lives, we'll be lucky.

Cheerful news from R——. Hoped I'd be sent to
Front, as promised. But French gov't has officially requested that as the value of a liaison officer is so largely
personal, we refrain from transfers. Good God—it's a
life sentence!

Still a line officer and wear crossed guns. What a
joke! But got nothing on G—— C——, commissioned
in Infantry, and now billeting officer. What's use of
struggling? Take it as it comes. Got a safe job, and
comfortable. "Doing my bit," etc., etc. I'm lucky,
and a damned fool to squawk about it.

Unnerving—the letters from home about the children.
Questions—which is better, a picture, memories, an
ideal—or papa at the head of the table? Answering
tempts to ways that are soft. Yet even shining road to
glory may be selfish. So hard to be truthful—impossible, perhaps. One evades—even on paper. A live
father—or a dead hero? Is the answer this side of
heaven?

S—— has good line: "Compulsion without conversion
never was successful." Ought to be tacked up in editorial rooms. Do folk who gabble about "imposing our
will," etc., want to maintain garrisons of a couple of
million in Germany for the rest of time? Do they think
the capture of Berlin would change the German heart?

Amazing fallacy of "punishing" Germany. What
can *we* do that circumstances won't do, automatically?
Only an idea can conquer. That's all life leaves behind.

And the "teaching a lesson" nonsense. Was Wilhelm
deterred by the fate of Napoleon? Will future *Kriegs-*
herren be frightened by his? Nix.

Great question now—how much the club, how much the velvet glove. Both necessary. Wilson, alone, seems to realize it—wherein his greatness.

"Right to choose its government applies to weak nations as well as strong." Rabbit has "rights," too—but what does tiger care? World working toward unity. May take million years, but must come. Inevitably, little states must lose identity in larger. We sentimentalize over Belgium and Serbia—not over Mexico: and magazine article on our course in San Domingo officially suppressed. Hand of evolution not to be stayed. Don't know whether Germany will swallow Russia, or other way to. But bound to be swallowing. Nationality not immutable or eternal.

Amazing bulletin on news stands: *"Alerte à New York!"* Everybody rushing inland. Must give London and Paris chuckle.

"Revanchism" of France. Does not exist. D——
said to-day: "You and British will hate the German long after we have forgotten there was a war. That is our great weakness." *

Worth mentioning that in six weeks close association with members of Etat Major, not once heard dirty story or what could be called vulgar innuendo. For simple, kindly, cordial gentility this group of *blessés* not to be surpassed.

In expressing ennui for French insistence upon sex, fall into pitfall of generalization. After all, it's insistence common to mankind. The Frenchman frank: we tend to let thoughts dribble out in indecency. Preference for French method.

Wed., 5th.—Singular communication rec'd by Gen. C——.

*Not often that a prophecy proves quite so perfectly wrong!

*"Mon général: "Cette lettre est confidenciel,
aussi je panse que vous ne la monterez à personne.
Je suis habitant de C..., à quatre kilomètre et
mon mari, le nommé Joseph B... est caporal de
l'auxiliaire au dépôt. Il est certe bien gentil, mais
les necessités m'ont obligé à modifier mon train de
vie. L'alocation ne suffit pas: Joseph (c'est mon
mari) ne gagne rien. J'ai pris un ami, mais je
suis resté malgré ça honnête. Pensez, j'ai été
élevée au couvent de Saint-Jacques, rue Denizot, et
j'ai guardé mes principes. Mais si je fais ca, c'est
par nécessités et pas par vices. Cet ami me donne
de quoi tenir mon ménage et élevé mes deux en-
fants.*

*"Aussi, vous comprenderez ça, je ne voudrai pas
que Joseph s'en aperçoive. Aussi, comme vous ête
gentil et que vous comprenais les chose, je vous
demanderais de le renvoyer plus loin, mais surtout
pas au feu, car je l'aimes bien et ne vouderai pas
qu'il lui arrives quelque chose. Vous avez com-
pris? Plus loin pour que je fasse mes affaire tran-
quilles.*

"Veuillez, etc." *

---

*(Translation) Sir: This letter is confidential, so I hope you
will not show it to anyone. I live at C——, about four kilo-
meters from here, and my husband, Joseph B—— is corporal
of auxiliaries at the depot. He is a splendid chap, but necessity has forced me to change my method of life. His allotment
is not sufficient; and Joseph (that is my husband) is earning
nothing. I have acquired a friend, though I have remained a
good woman none the less. Understand, I was brought up in
the convent of St. Jacques, Rue Denizot, and I have remained
faithful to my principles. What I have done has been perforce and not through weakness. This friend gives me the
wherewithal to maintain my home and bring up my two children.
So, you see, I wouldn't want Joseph to know about this. So,

Tea with B—— *en famille. On ne parle pas l'Anglais.* Amazing people. Have faculty of keeping war going full blast, without losing interest in things of spirit. Cultured—without offensive snobbery so often associated with word *chez nous.*

Bit flushed with wine; fell in with couple of *poules.* One, charming. Stage set for trouble. But imagination interfered. To kiss her lips—and think them another's. Trying to breathe life into rag doll. Odd, when one so homesick, yearning for touch of woman, and one has it—more homesick still!

Thur., 6th.—All leaves revoked. Further inquiries into tanks. One question asked of applicants: "Are you absolutely fearless?" Who but an idiot is that? Requirements surprisingly stiff. At least one year's military experience, and knowledge of a lot of things. More schools! Insignia—pleasing thought—a wreath!

To Gen. C——'s for Gen. D——'s party call. Busy —few bi-linguists present.

Cartoon of Wilhelm II, looking at himself in mirror, and appearing very put out. "And to think it should be Clemenceau who is called 'The Tiger!'"

Growth of slang. *"Mandoline"*—delicious.

Item worth recording: Yanks used to say: "This God damned war." Then: "This damned war." Now: "This doggone war." Can't even be bitter about it any more.

French impression of *"Les Sammies."* "One sees

since you are kind and understand things, I would ask you to send him further away, not, of course, to the Front, because I love him dearly and wouldn't want anything to happen to him. Do you understand? Just far enough so that I can live without worrying.

them everywhere, in doorways, in the villages, along
the roads, in the fields, a rapidly growing multitude,
well-disciplined, silent, hard-working, coming we know
not from where nor how. The felt hat, negligently
thrust on the head, the soft khaki shirt, pockets bulging
with note-books.* The frame so well set up one would
believe them wearing corsets, clear-eyed—a curious com-
posite of priest and cowboy. When we first saw them,
we cried: 'What handsome fellows!' And immediately:
'What intelligent heads!' Most striking is the voluntary application of each one to his appointed task. They
are learning war with a religious fervor. Discipline is
remarkable. That the most democratic nation in the
world should have been able to endow its army with
such discipline is the most striking psychological phenomenon of the war. And those of German blood—
are they in the A.E.F.? You would astonish an American officer with such a question. He would reply:
'Why not?' "

Most characteristic pose of American soldier—lying
on roadside, chewing grass, and wrangling about bat-
ting averages.

Combination of Yank "take a chance" carelessness,
and German gas, responsible for 85% of casualties so
far.

T—— says that at first big Ypres gas attack there
was ex-professor of chemistry from McGill among Canadians. He recognized chlorine, and told everybody
to saturate handkerchiefs by means everybody has handy,
and hold it against nose. Example spread, and day
saved.

Looks as if German effort would continue all summer. Practically everybody believes it will take a big

*Bull Durham and "papers!"

offensive next year, with **A.E.F.** as prime factor, to give
the knockout.

Don't think so. From what little filters through
from other side of Rhine, Boche pretty badly off. Allies not much better. Nothing published and little said,
but biggest problem, right now, is to keep their own
people in line until we can get going. France thoroughly fed up. England, apparently, even more so.
Simply going mad.

This the last promise the German people will swallow. When they quit, they'll quit with a bang, with
every man of them trying to get aboard the band wagon.

Not a war, any more—an endurance contest.

Fri., 7th.—Hear from Front that roads are thick with
Yanks moving into line. Old man Ludendorf going to
have to hurry some.

Sat., 8th.—Received copy first installment of serial in
P—— Magazine. K—— saw it on table. Wanted to
know if I read that sort of trash. Delighted to assure
him I didn't—I *wrote* it!

Wangled leave for Tours, R—— helping, and left
on 12:14. Alone in compartment with especially dirty
poilu, who invited me to join him in his lunch of *singe*.
Waved a big knife when I declined. Thought better of
it and joined him. Observed that all *officiers Américains* were rich . . . extreme simplicity of slitting my
throat. Crazy—admitted it himself. Four years *au
feu.* Trifles like life and death—*c'fait rien.* Been *en
perm*—A.W.O.L. His C.O. a son of a bitch, who might
try putting him *en boîte.* He'd shoot the *costaud* if he
tried that. Get him in the first advance. More about
American riches and feasibility of helping self to mine.

Not so very amusing. Had to talk fast. Admitted feasibility, but pointed out it would hardly be *gentil*. And *all* Frenchmen, even those *complètement fou*, were *gentil*. He laughed at that—"*c'est vrai, mon vieux*," and sheathed knife. But it was long ride. Glad when we reached Châteauroux.

Arrived Tours 9:30. Found J—— and C—— installed in mansion, with shower bath, piano, billiard table, and superlative cook. Both pleaded for no revelations at home of hardships under which they were fighting war. Also lovely garden.

Met W—— L——, extremely attractive. Now a Major. Right in midst of *les huiles*. Don't like staff atmosphere much. Too much gossip. T—— C——, Major of Ordnance cruelly critical of R—— E——, who had gotten Engineers Captaincy without arduous preliminaries of training camp. E—— different from most in that he's homesick and admits it.

Saw H—— B——. Major, Judge Adv. Hoped war would last two more years, and Germans punished, so no one would ever again, etc., etc. Implication that after this war, world's going to be as sweet as new-mown hay.

Saw D—— B——. Red Cross Admiral, or something. Voice still quavers. Says only reason he's not bold, bad soldier is lack of weight. Must be true. Has shrunk three sizes. Also wearing mustache. Looks like two bits of frayed and water-soaked clothesline. Think I'll remove mine.

D—— S—— commanding Red Cross here. Doing great work and very popular. Asked for *Mr. S——*. Ratty-faced little man in Sam Browne and puttees, corrected me. Should have said *Capt. S——*. Personally, I'd *like* to be called *Mister* again.

Met disabled British staff officer. Name is Chesterton—cousin to G.K.—but his job managing English female labor companies, always called Capt. WAACS. Wears red band of staff on cap. Some one asked how he dared venture near Front with such a target on him. Replied that red band meant safety—Germans always hang anybody who kills British staff officer!

J—— working hard and doing well. Office job. Wants to be with troops. Pulling wires toward gas service, newly organized, Col. Fries at head. Given up all hope of ever seeing Infantry again.

G—— C——, whose wife wrote him she heard he was being sent home for inefficiency, is Chief Billeting Officer. French say he's done remarkable work. Expects transfer to Gen. Staff. Like J——, no hope of line work. Organizing genius, with attractive personality—and shrewd understanding of army game. Ought to go far.*

Every man at H.Q., S.O.S., seeking transfer to something else. Some yap about yearning for Front, but C—— says that's mostly camouflage. Tours a perfect hotbed of wirepulling and gossip, with everyone all out for promotion.

Like general offices of a railroad. Barracks transformed into office buildings. Thousands of clerks. Fact that all the job transporting million men overseas, with equipment from matches to locomotives, done by rank amateurs, makes accomplishment marvelous.

New services starting up every day, and scramble for men intense. Like college town, with every frat rushing newcomer. All sorts of jobs going begging.

*Went over as Capt. of Infantry. Wound up Lt. Col., H.Q. First Army, and been accumulating millions ever since.

Met C——. Over here as civilian, under Adj. Gen., developing personnel system. Huge waste in human materiel, hitherto. Says he couldn't do thing if he had rank less than General.

Sentimentality our greatest obstacle so far. Germans began classification of men when they began army. British only last year. Getting business-like, now. Individual may prefer medals to typewriters and a bayonet to a fountain pen. But we're fighting a most practical enemy. Striking attitudes won't do.

Met W—— H——. Commissioned Capt. F.A. Came over on *Tuscania*. Submarined. 6 wks. in England. Finally wound up here, assistant Provost Marshal General. Hasn't seen a gun.

Met Maj. Alan Pinkerton, C.O. Dep't Criminal Investigations. About snappiest man I've seen in army. Asked some questions. Then offered job—choice of London or Paris. Took both, immediately. Plain clothes —ways that are dark—feel like Nick Carter already! But J——'s probably right. Nothing will happen.

Rec'd H—— J——'s article on naval station. About as lively as *indicateur de chemîns de fer*. Accurate and comprehensive, but less space to hearts of pals than contents of his ditty bag.

Sun., 9th.—Out to flying field. Too windy to go up. Café and club. Constant talk of personalities. A totally new aspect of army life.

Mon., 10th.—Saw everybody in world. Topped off by getting tight on Vouvray. On loose. Wild party. Fascinating mistress of dive. Provocative but unassailable. Famous, they say. Standing wager up of 2000 fr. that no man can overcome her.

Tues., 11th.—Left Tours at noon, not so good as to head. Arrived beautiful, hilly Angoulême at 4. First town without Yanks! Left at 6. Conversation with Frenchman from Limoges. Most entertaining, on pictures and books, philosophy of living well. Thoughtful chap, though in our sense, uneducated. His feeling for his children. Idea that when work of day was done, a man ought to retire to contemplation of the good, the true and the beautiful. Made me think what long way we Americans have to go yet. Not surprising that so many develop notion of getting place "somewhere in France" and settling down after this is finished. They've come under spell of this old and finished land, and the harsh, raw adolescence of their own repels a little.

Arrived Limoges at 10, tired but with curious feeling of coming "home."

Wed., 12th.—Back to work. To movie with B——. Sight of Pullman on screen wrecked show for me.

Thur., 13th.—Saw Maj. C—— *re* transfer to tanks. Lunch with enlisted medic., just over. What greenhorns the newcomers seem!

This silly, teeth-grinding, fist-smiting rage at the Hun. Can't exterminate him, unless we do as Shaw suggests—slaughter his women. He'll be with us after war. Got to *do* something with him. Resolving to hate him permanently, just nonsense. Got to go on—even after peace. Just beginning, really.

Most talk nowadays just "overweening impulse to jump on thing that's scared us in dark, to break it with our hands, grind it into ground with our boots, tear ourselves away—and wake up."

French morale undermined? Yes and no. *Les*

grand grognards—mais ils marchent quand meme. Exasperated, weary, but *jusqu'au bout*, still.

Curious that most anathemized man to-day is quiet dreamer Nietzsche. They say words accomplish nothing —but nothing ever done save as consequence of words. Men of dreams, men of action. Each to his last. Got to have both.

That duality in every man. The heart a laboratory. The sea to be seen in a drop of water.

So hot to-day and air so dead. Hardly breathe. Plodding around dusty streets, in fierce sun, makes backwardness of Spain understandable.

Curious peeps into sub-cellars of human soul. Mail censor dug up bit worthy of Havelock Ellis. Some fellow, writing home to wife, begged her to put on silk stockings and finest underwear, wear for a few days, and then—send to him.

And another. Young soldier, writing to girl, says: "Try not to yield to temptation. Keep *it* sacred. (Etc., etc.) But if you find you must give *it*, don't give *it* to anybody but George."

How thin and tawdry that word Democracy has been worn. Yet it remains the Word. *Must.* After the Germans—others. In our midst as well as abroad. The war that never ends.

Countless stories of trench life. So little of the rest of it. Who runs post offices? Who the hospitals and shops? Who knows anything of the hard-working M.P's? Not one in ten *fights*.

The Town Major. When you arrive at some desolate town at 3 A.M. in driving rain, and the patient T.M. meets you with his map, and marches you, smooth as silk, to a billet with a fire in it—great lad. But Colonel may find rat or two in bed, and T.M. lucky to miss jail.

When troops move out, claims for damages settled, irate feelings assuaged, billets cleaned.

G—— W—— always scheming to get back to regiment. Fat chance. Too damned good as T.M. No promotion, of course. T.M.'s never get that.

Chief firing artillery is doing here is firing weak minds out of it. Grand process of shake-down. Took Fritz forty years, so mustn't be impatient of our progress.

Fri., 14th.—Ford car arrived, Sgt. McG—— driving. Thinks he's Barney Oldfield and the Ford a flying coffin. Fixed up vocabulary for Capt. DeM——. "Right," "left," "stop" "go ahead," etc. No use. He *will* get them mixed.

Sat., 15th.—Maj. F—— and remount detail from —th F.A. in. Learned that H—— P—— doing month's regimental for drunk and disorderly. No shock to me.

Sun., 16th.—Austrian offensive launched.

Out with F——, K—— and gang last night. All very low. Fell in with woman and little girl, and sister —Marcelle. B—— much taken, but no French. Called on liaison officer for service. Played John Alden for him, and arranged matters. Home alone. Met little *dactylo.* Promenade to Pont Neuf. Shame to crack fragile crockery like that. So took her home—intact. Damn fool—she'll fall to-morrow.

Unpleasant twist of French character. Have no regard and little knowledge of anyone but selves. Frankly contemptuous of British army. Despise Belgians no less than Portuguese. Hate German, but not very violently, recognizing in him soldier almost as good as selves. For us, amiable tolerance, though think we've been taking

hell of a time to make good on promises. Think we're
smart kids in some ways, but never amount to much
in military way.

Whatever is theirs, is the best. Limoges not much.
Not even main-line town. Dirty, squalid, no architec-
tural beauty. But to hear Limousin, you'd think Thos.
Cook ought to feature it.

K—— ran across following picture of casual officers:
"It is the consciousness of belonging that straightens the
back and fires the eye. Take these young fellows who
mope around unattached in various odds and ends of reserves, training courses and the·like. They have no
officers permanently in leadership to whom they can look
for orders, but are only temporarily detained and feel
in consequence much like new boys unwillingly in
school." Those at the Front probably don't suffer as
much mentally, as the poor fish who have been lost in
the rear, or for whom no real job is ready, and who kill
time all day in bunk fatigue. Nothing worse than being unnecessary.

Number of base hospitals here. Lots of American
girls. Good many no choice but virginity. Plenty,
though with face and figure that proves French *fille* has
nothing on U.S. variety.

Six months since I've seen children. Probably forgotten me. Lucky if they have.

Mon., 17th.—At rapport, tried to explain mechanism
of Ford car. Couldn't do it in English, let alone French.
So argued about *maisons de tolérance* some more.

Tues., 18th.—To caserne. Gen. D—— getting
jealous. Thinks I ought to be on his staff, not French.
God forbid!

Visited one M. Biot, getting cement for La Courtine, and found him my companion of train from Angoulême! Combination of business man and student, rarely found among us.

Dined Café de Paris. Encountered Marcelle. *Très passioné*. Rendezvous with B—— for 10, in park. She failed to show up. Got locked in park. Had to climb palings!

Wed., 19th.—Lots of talk, for centuries, about free love. In Europe, *fait accompli*. *Maybe* youth and beauty that won't fall, but damned few. Axiomatic that any woman, whatever her position, ready for business until she proves contrary. Sex-morality badly jarred in France. Worse in England, they say. What must it be in Germany! Strange, but large proportion of sex stuff going on, non-commercial. The Yank, healthy, amiable, moneyed, and with lure of novelty, can have anything he wants. No more surprise at infidelity of wives with husbands *au front*, maids with thirst for new experience, or old eggs hungry for arms of virile American. Surprising thing anybody pays out cash to street walkers when free berries are there for anybody with basket.

Yank not going so big as he did, though. Asked Marcelle how things had gone with B——. She seemed not so pleased. "All *les Américains* are like that," she said irritably. "Animals! So *cold*—scarcely ten minutes . . . no caresses—no love." But when I commiserated, drooping eyes, and "I am sure *you* are not like that." Business of closing ranks with her sweet-scented person. It's a hard war!

Four more of the old battery blew in to-day, including the stool-pigeon, B——. That makes about a dozen here, and thrice as many more scattered around France. Luckier than most, I guess.

T—— very low. Been running mess for couple of months, nothing to do but wrangle with cooks, heard from home that he's supposed to have got himself a cushy job in the Q.M. In fit of rage, put in application for tanks. Application returned to-day with notation by C.O. "Transfer not approved. Doing excellent work where he is." What's the use!

Bawled out by Gen. D——. "You should have your coat buttoned when reporting to the General Commanding." And he should have a part in a Fatty Arbuckle show!

Thur., 20th.—Boche attack halted at Rheims. Office all day. Out with T——. Thimblebelly—noisy on vermouth cassis. Gentle little Loulette—so pathetic. The street life so *dur*, so *dégoutant*. Good family up north—wiped out—everything gone. Made me proposition. Much cheaper than living in hotel—and pleasanter. Guarantees faithfulness. Needn't pay anything. All she wants is home. Sidestepped. Told her I had no money. Wanted to know when I got paid. Said the first. Urged me to consider matter until then. As sweet a child as I ever met.

Fri., 21st.—Office routine. Hell of a life for a hero. R—— untroubled. Seems to think he's doing something. Out on town with F—— and B——. All pleasantly tight.

Sat., 22nd.—Official *déjeuner* at Cercle. Beaucoup vin. R—— unearthed bottle of gin, and gave French first cocktail. *Sipped* it—commenting on *taste.* 6

months' service brisque sewed on coat. Hell of a lot of
"serving" I've done. Hate to wear same insignia as
those actually in war. But orders is orders.

Things *rigolo* do happen. Had box of senna and figs
in room. Discovered this morning it had been emptied.
No sign of chambermaid all day. Another tragedy of
the sugar shortage. Unhappy woman must have had a
busy time!

Easy to spot newcomers. Such offensive drinkers.
Old timers don't try to put away all the wine in one
sitting. More to be had. Quieter, more polite—manners of native affected even roughest. Salute on entering store, know how to behave when funeral passes,
etc. Know the map. Know also that damsel who stops
you on street and invites you to spend night with her,
not necessarily telling truth when she says she's daughter of marquis and wife of colonel—nor necessarily lying, either!

American girls ought to be grateful not born French.
French girl has status valuable pedigreed dog. Anglo-
Saxon idea of love *n'existe pas* in France. Frenchman
talks more and knows less about it than anybody in
world. Women either mistresses or wives. Loves and
respects wife, and very pleasant in home life—but always like man with faithful setter at his feet.

Knows nothing of chivalry. In American movie comedy, man starts off with bride, she loaded down like
donkey with trunks, etc. All Americans in audience
laughed—no French.

We're different—not superior. Toss-up. We treat
wives better, he treats mistresses better. Never talked
to French *fille de plaisir* in intimacy of couple of beers,
without her expressing herself shocked at harshness, bru-
tality, even, of Americans. Purely animal, shamefaced

in fashion she can't understand.   Admits she'd have none
of us, except for our money.

If we treated wives as he treats mistresses, and vice
versa, better world all round.   He could do with little
of our idealism for women.   We could certainly trade
our Puritanism for more candid Hellenism of French.
Sure the French woman, after first shock, would enjoy
being considered something more than flesh.   And even
our most upright ladies might like occasional descent
from altar on which their men insist on enshrining them.

American bewildered by *dames des trottoirs*.   Despite
loose morals, seems to want same deference he'd show
lady at home.   She being for sale, he assumes everything goes.   Also bewildered by her gentleness, complete candor and seeming lack of guile.

Promiscuity of A.E.F. may have advantages from
standpoint of future conjugal happiness at home.   Anglo-Saxon may pick up few pointers in art of love.

Very educational process.   Those fresh from Hoboken
at first furtive, full of consciousness of sin.   Quickly get
humorous about it.   Six months enough to Gallicize
most Yanks.

Be-spectacled "investigators" of A.E.F. come to two
conclusions.   (1) Drifting toward hell fire.   (2) Pure
as driven snow.   Why not appoint commission to "investigate" and see if sun is shining?   With life a tedious
and doubtful thing at best, with values standing on ears,
death a subject for jokes, life forgotten, moral values
old wives' tale, who cares for consequences?   Empty
cup—to-morrow under ground.   Squeeze fruit of experience to last drop.   If dregs be bitter—to hell with
it!

Plenty of sediment in the glittering bubbles.   Certainly a mixed drink world's getting now.   Lot of lads

wounded—with no stripes. The spirochete gets more than bullets. A blessing, sometimes—bullets. Quick death and glory better than long, unlovely rotting.

Aviators—pique imagination. Most honored by public, most detested by other services. To Infantry, Artillery a home for loafers, tolerated because occasionally useful. But flyers—anathema. Cocky, loose-living rakes, who don't work—won't even salute.

Not always sorrow when somebody goes West. B—— crashed after bringing down *nth* plane. Citation, etc. "Pure young life extinguished," etc. V——'s comment: "Damned lucky for his wife he got it." "Much is writ in the purple testament of bleeding war." Knots and broken threads under the damask.

J—— had lunch with R——. Latter very low. Being sent home for venereal infection. Shot himself on way to train.*

Danger, in these things, that one forget the beauty, the essential splendor in the whole business. For there *is* splendor in man's readiness to venture all, not for principle, which often he does not have, but simply because he dares.

Fatalism. Free will. What is it? What moves us —individuals—makes us do what we do? Do *we* do— or is it a force outside ourselves? Chance. The hero, *ordered* to the feat of daring that wins his cross. There to receive order because drafted. Drafted because Wilson decreed draft. Wilson, because . . . is there an ultimate Power setting it all in motion? Coral atoms, mindless, without will, building up earth, not knowing why. And the philosopher—great argument about it

*In a quiet Connecticut valley there is a granite headstone over what is left of R——, and on it our equivalent *for "tomb sur le champ d'honneur."*

and about—forever coming out the same door wherein he went.

Thoughts of children and the *beau geste*. And thoughts of mirror. Hair thinning—beginning to gray. G—— probably right. The blood cooling. No lightning-smiters, we. Ajax was a *boy*.

Sun., 23rd.—Encountered amorous Loulette. Attentions beginning to fatigue. Her proposition renewed. A home and fidelity guaranteed for 300 francs a month. Economic aspects of plan emphasized.

Life sometimes seems a strait-jacket—the only free people, the dead. Probably coincide with bilious attacks. Field for scientific research.

Sat around barracks arguing about getting to Front. In letters home, every man hot for fray. No poses here. All dread thought of going home without taste of "action." Sight of wounded makes for reflection. A *taste* would be enough. Anyhow, to stay or go—no choice. Half a dozen T.B.'s arrived to-day from Front. Probably on way home. G—— one of them.*

"Victory," according to press, to be march down Unter den Linden, T.R. in front, and Boche all with rings through noses. I think it's war within war. With Germany licked, only one battle out of many been won. Nonsense of punishing Germany with economic boycott. What good would that do? Victorious only if we can make Germany faithful ally in cause she now battles against.

Germany's got to be crushed by force of arms. O.K.

---

*A "T.B." is a "Throw Back"—officer returned to S.O.S. having been found wanting as combat officer. If punk enough, sent back to States. G—— now holds commission as Colonel in the Reserve, and very active in military affairs.

But merely military victory incidental to ancient struggle of People for supremacy. That struggle won't end with this peace, any more than Constitution made men free and equal.

Vengeance? Punishment? Bombing Berlin? What'll that get us? And we've got to get *something*. Agony of this four years must not be wasted. Thank God for Wilson!

So N—— J—— gets home every night. If some over here could do that, their future lives would be happier. Man was not made to live alone—and in large numbers, doesn't. The full price of this God damned war won't be paid for many generations.

Poor E—— W——! His death the sort every soldier fears. Not much glory in having a tree fall on you.

Among jokes played hereabouts, one of "leaves." Officially, get one every 4 months. But Hun always staging drives, and leaves canceled.

Droll letter about horns Mrs. F—— putting on her husband. Adultery seems to be summer sport at home. Having seen F—— in Paris, think Mrs. F—— entitled to some fun. Sympathy wasted on faithless wives' husbands. Most of them doing fairly well by selves. Sympathy for wives. They'll get theirs later.

Soirée at B——'s. Find speaking French, in good society, full of pitfalls. B—— asked if I didn't think sister resembled him. Agreed, but *"plus grosse."* Grammatically sound, but happens to mean pregnant! Being single, that constitutes a *gaffe*.

Card issued by G.H.Q., Paris: "Venereal disease is prevalent among the public women who will accost you on the street. If patriotism, morality and personal hygiene do not prevent you from associating with such women, prophylactic stations are open at the following places." Patriotism, etc., helpless against Mlle. Nature.

Place jammed with Yanks, and more coming. Not long before U.S. weight will be felt. And then—good night, Wilhelm. All the Boche prisoners talk about it. Haven't a prayer, now, and know it. They say the conviction is beginning to percolate through their army, despite strenuous official efforts to prevent it.

Mon., 24th.—Came up to us quietly, as we were seated on café terrace—a little old woman in frayed and rusty black. Caught her eye and she burst into laughter. "Ah, but it is droll, m'sieu. One is fortunate who can carry all one has like this—" Held up tattered relic of handbag. "*V'là—regardez:*" With quick gesture, snapped it open. It was quite empty. Nodded her head, chuckling. "Jacques—*sur la Marne.* Pierre —*torpillé.* And Jean—*chasseur d'Afrique,* 246th—a citation with palm, *oui, tué à Verdun.* And Emile— one would have thought that of five, one would remain, *n'est-ce pas?*" She nodded pensively. "*Eh b'en*—one did. Le p'tit André, ah, *le pauvre—mobilizé* in a shell factory. *Chut!* There was a fire . . . *vous comprenez, m'sieu? C'est drôle, vraiment.* And now—*la p'tite maman*—she go *toute seule . . . comme un soldat. V'là.*" Her poor thin hand struck her breast. "*Moi— la p'tite maman.*" There was a pause. Then she sighed. "I dwelt, not far from Albert, *vous savez? C'est drôle, ca. Regardez.*" Again she turned her empty little bag upside down. "That is all that remains, m'sieu. But perhaps you have a little snuff?" She nodded, scarcely noticing the coin B—— gave her. "One would have thought that of five—ah, it is droll, this life. Ha! Ha!" She chuckled to herself, shuffling away in the darkness.

I suppose it's nice to be able to laugh, even if you have to be quite mad to do it.

Met M—— to-day, the fellow who was taken ashore at Halifax—to die, we thought. Perfectly well, but full of grievance. Seems he followed us over, got into one casual depot after another, and in six months here hasn't even attended a school. Just where he was when he left Ft. Sheridan—and no prospects.

Rather envy those who stayed in States. Got continuity of training, one job, and usually one regiment. Though P——— has stayed at Ft. Sill as canteen-keeper, and H—— as Adjutant.

Liaison service not turning out as planned. No dispute as to regional work, buying forage, renting warehouses etc.; but military end still in hands of divisional commanders. Most liaison officers at Front are French. Easier to get Frenchman speaking good English than *vice versa*.

Letter to-day from D—— R——. *Ventre à terre* at Nantes in I.O. Wanted to know what I had to say about my famous prophecy of June 26. Think's my month's right, but year about five too soon.

Learn from home that Barbousse' "Le Feu" considered enemy propaganda. Reaction here depends on reactor. If radical, likes it. If conservative—thumbs down.

Educated French, officers, business men, "nice" people generally, all conservative. Narrow, believe in caste, suspect new ideas—like "better classes" world over. Comfort seems to kill imagination. Well-dressed, well-fed people usually hostile to change. Even from war to peace.

Tues., 25th.—To deT——'s. Mlle. Christine and

her amazement that an American should know the story
of Noah's ark! No worse, though than "Y" worker
on boat coming over, who "hoped to teach French some
appreciation of home life." Explained to me that
French had no word for "home." True: but not so
important as that they have no word for "friend"—
feminine gender.

Poor strays—the "casuals." All longing for battery
—some sense of *belonging* to something.

Wed., 26th.—Der Tag! Nothing happened all day.
Kidded by everybody. Then K—— bounced in, with
evening paper and Von Kuhlmann's address to Reichstag. Admits frankly Germany's inability to reach a
military decision. So far as I know, first official recog-
nition of fact! Dumfounded! Begin to believe I *am*
a prophet!

Essentially childlike quality of French that makes
them really and deeply interested in other people's affairs. Found chambermaid this A.M. waiting with request she be allowed to show pictures of S—— and
babies below stairs. She rushed down three flights and
now everyone in hotel comes up to tell me how *charmante*
is my family.

Thur., 27th.—Busy all A.M. with "Y" sec'y arranging
for 4th celebration. On remount job for Col. R——,
G.H.Q. Usual discussion in *rapport* on *maisons de
tolérance*. Asked by Col. B—— to explain American attitude toward sex. Large order and no success. French
think us all wrong trying to regulate this matter. Prefer to let Nature take her course. Our attitude that it's
no moral problem but military one. Japs first to tackle
it in this light. Understand we're making better record

in percentage of ineffectives than they did. Remains to
be seen.

Saw Marcelle and sister. Latter put her child away,
and indicated her decks cleared for action. Not interested. B—— again fixed up with M——.

Such an enormous process of disintegration in things
that used to matter so much, now matter so little. More
than a sea between us and home. Things sacrosanct become theme for callous jest. Too much life in the raw
—too tolerant. Realists, perforce. No putting tawdry
tinsel in box, labeled "adventure." No making roses
out of cabbages. Significant that favorite word of
Germans seems to be "stinks."

Fri., 28th.—Usual routine. After dinner, out among
'em with K—— and T——. Saw Loulette—wistful
little flower on the primrose path. Poor kid become
something of a nuisance. Already spending that 300 fr.
Impossible to be rough with her, though. Too damned
gentle!

Sat., 29th.—To Major de Garnison. Terrific poten-
tate. Surrounded by *très gallonés*. Got so excited
shook hands earnestly with *planton*. Lots of work.
Saw Marcelle and sister. Latter queer. Drink, dope—
or worse. Probably the worse. Walked home with
them. Joined by Yvonne and kid brother. To Lion
d'Or for long philosophical bicker.

Sun., 30th.—Office A.M. Lunch with DeM—— and
out to country place. Made one of family. Grand-
daughter, Odette, so like my baby. Literary discussion,
with special reference to merits of Racine, with Charles,
age 14. Bully kid, not a trace of prig—they merely

work them hard in French schools. You've got to be educated to get by at all in France. Unlike U.S., where it's handicap.

Delightful picture of family life. Such content with simple things. Such absence of pretense, such an atmosphere of courtesy. Enchanted with DeM——'s little daughter, Gabrielle. She and other children talked same brand of inaccurate French I do.

July, 1918

Mon., *1st.*—Awakened by chambermaid, very severe. "A person" below to see me. Found Loulette! The first of month, and I all set, doubtless, to accept her little proposition? Hard to explain things. She went away very sad, not understanding, of course. Thought I didn't love her, poor child. Matter of fact, never met anybody more lovable.

Took Col. H—— and Capt. P—— to call on M. le Général. Hard enough to have big-wigs on hands without having to do their talking for them. But old boy helped a lot. He's a dear.

Bought some toys for DeM—— children. Gaby's birthday.

Busy with odd jobs. Hate this God damned puttering. Sick of this accursed town. Why don't I hook up with Loulette? It would help my French certainly.

Tues., *2nd.*—Excessively hot. Choke collar galling neck—to say nothing of soul. Some day, maybe, they'll realize you can fight a war without being so damned uncomfortable. British seem to manage it.

Took P—— E—— to show. Long walk to her abode. Nice girl. Makes me feel how much I miss American women.

Wed., *3rd.*—Learned that some letters home had been passed around. Felt like chap in Paris who picked up *fille* and went to *maison d'amour*. In midst of things heard a chuckle. Around wall some tiny holes, behind each some one who had paid small fee for privilege.

Christ! So they want "anecdotes, amusing or pathetic incidents, descriptions of daily life"—if I told them what daily life really *is*, they'd pass out!

Unofficial application for tanks receives no encouragement. Told I was "pretty old." Also, except for motors, lacked necessary training.

Col. H—— here to-day. Promised berth at Front, at first vacancy. Told him I was sick of this. Burden of reply, there were hell of a lot of other men sick, too; one unpleasant feature of war being large number of sickening jobs. Pulled old blah about "service," "doing one's bit," etc. Almost had me in tears, telling about beauties of life in S.O.S. *Quoi merde!*

Got great compliment on French. Asked shopkeeper for Manual of Conversation. Wanted to know "what for?" Trust it was not Gallic guile!

Social-Democrats in Reichstag refusing to vote war-budget—first time it's happened. From such seeds the end will sprout.

Thur., 4th.—*Défile* of school children on Champ de Foire. Impressive. R—— and I only spots of O.D. in flashing group of *bleu d'horizon* and gold braid, as we stepped out for ceremony of saluting flags. Huge crowd.

Afternoon—games at Velodrome. Yanks thought they'd go big in grenade throwing. Bet accordingly. But it's a cricket throw—not baseball—and French cleaned up. Day a great success. Lots of enthusiasm. Entirely spontaneous letter from French to American non-coms., expressing sentiments of fraternity. Also, roomful of flowers, gift of school children to Gen.

D——. Countless incidents indicating cordiality between two peoples. This alliance very real and profound. Mere tolerant politeness has given place to real regard and affection on both sides.

Formal dinner at Cercle—*beaucoup boissons*. Later, fell in with boys and large evening ensued. One old man, well pickled, made speech. Said this day will be celebrated henceforth, not as Independence Day of Americans, but of *World*. This particular Fourth certainly marks considerable change in organization of the old planet.

Fri., 5th.—Awakened with information that "lady from America" was below. Mme. M—— with letters and gifts. I, slightly foggy, talked all sorts of irrelevancies, like Limousin accent and difficulties in checking baggage. Fact that *two weeks ago* she was *talking* to S—— knocked me flat.

Spent morning with Geo. W. Hangover. Heard new toast: "May your identification tags never be separated." Going to drink my toasts in Vitel after this.

Sat., 6th.—Ferrero's conception of this war—a conflict between extensive and intensive living. Conflict between two conceptions of living, rather than government. In thought and habit, we've spread out too much. Got to learn to concentrate—to extract all the fragrance from a single blossom, instead of always yearning for a larger garden.

French know that better than we. DeM——s, with their little home, offer no "entertainment." No tennis courts, no swimming pool, etc. All they have is children, flowers, a lovely view, and friendly conversation —never dull, yet never frivolous.

A contrast to our own feverish hunt for "pleasure."
The vulgar noise of our restaurants, the hardly less vulgar ostentation of our week-ends. The French find happiness on a fraction of what we spend for privilege of
boring ourselves. Much more practical than we. When
they go after pleasure, they get it. The competitiveness
of our social life would be absurd to them, since it does
not bring what they seek.

They like above all things to talk. The *escrime* of
ideas a real sport. Like to sit for an hour over glass
of mineral water in a quiet café, and just bicker. Take
two hours for lunch, and don't talk business. No topic
considered "dull" if handled with wit. Much more serious than we, and rather more mature. Also more entertaining. The scurry of our "efficient" life, of which
we are so proud, strikes them as energy of three year
old making mud pies. Perfectly clear to them we
haven't grown up.

Germans having some difficulty disposing of us.
Their communiqué announced taking of Cantigny by
"the enemy." Did not mention Americans. Prisoners
asked what they think of the Yanks, say they aren't
Yanks, but Canadians, dressed up in a new British
trick!

The great chance of the Allies, now, is Austria. Hope
they won't miss it. Salonique, the front door. A grand
time to declare war on Bulgaria, and back up Greece.
The A.E.F. discovering it has a freshness of view and
freedom from precedent that justifies it in doing things
its own way: Our diplomacy should do no less.

So M—— C—— is chucking his desk job and seeking "action" via the Artillery. Lots of credit for spirit,
but can't hand him much on brains.

Can't understand the home-folks—they're so full of

hate. Mme. DeM——, who lost her first-born, doesn't especially hate the Boche. And the wretched refugees, who've lost everything, don't. But they're cockeyed, throughout, in the U.S. H—— W——, with varicose veins—*drafted*. Probably put him in the Infantry.

So Washington thinks we can finish this God damned war by 1920. Nice of them to set date. Used to think it was somehow going to wind up automatically. At least now we talk of ending it ourselves. Everybody here says next summer. Still think Boche can't stick it through winter. Significant, no news coming out of Austria. When tough old hide of German Empire finally punctured, we'll find nothing in it but rotting bones.

Burlesque of Official Communiqué: "Paris, 3 P.M. Stubborn fighting continues at the Gare de Lyon and other stations. Long lines of commuters, fighting shoulder to shoulder. Trouillard family has been able to take the train. Baggage registry window captured, lost and re-taken. At end of day remains in employees' hands, who have issued an important bulletin. Civilians continue to fall back strategically. Have abandoned La Muette, Passy, the Boulevards, as far as Blvd. St. Germain. Their morale excellent. Comédie Française continues to hold out with feeble detachment of spectators. Some raids behind the abattoirs of La Villette and the fortifications. No change in other sectors."

Sun., 7th.—P—— E—— invited me to go driving with her. Found our vehicle an unpainted two-wheeled cart, with moribund miniature of a pony to draw it. Crawled through main streets of town at 1 mi. p.h., pony pausing to rest at every tram crossing. Huge entertainment of populace. From audible comment, qualified certainly as event of season.

A hard life, this, with Venus pulling at one arm, Bacchus on the other, and Mercury waiting in the background. Still sound in hull and rigging, but God knows how long before I'll hit a reef. War is hell—such slaughter of innocent and defenseless time!

Mon., 8th.—Hot, sticky day. Put in most of it getting out statement of regional strength. After which R—— decided on different way, so did it all over again. Great boy, R——. Hate his guts!

Tues., 9th.—Dined with Lt. G——, —th Inf. Dour but singularly thoughtful youth, much interested in philology. Knows all about French, but can't speak it.

Wed., 10th.—K—— been here for months, studying radio. Graduated high on list. Now sent to regiment as gunnery officer. B—— also in radio course. Resented it, wouldn't study, and was canned. He goes to a battery as radio officer. It's a great little army.

What is going on behind veil in Germany? Possible to prove, with figures, that they can go on, defensively, for long time yet. But if Teuton is good fighter when things are going good, he's not an up-hill one. Think he'll crumble when he realizes cards are running against him.

Question is, how clearly does he realize that now? Think he's realizing it with startling rapidity. Seems childish to think of his suddenly throwing down arms, with plea for mercy, but not a bit more incredible than his recorded plans for domination of world. Every German believed in them. So if he could astonish the world when he thought he was winning, he can astonish it again when he knows he isn't. When the rush for the band wagon starts, every last one will claim somebody else was responsible, and he's the only good Indian.

On strictly military factors we may get decision sometime in 1919. But Von Kuhlmann's speech must have meant something. An internal ferment, of some sort, and he the voice of a powerful party—the great industrials, maybe, who see no sense in further struggle. For first time coming over Germans, conservative as well as radicals, that cause is doomed, and nearly time to toss up sponge. They can thank their good old German God for W. Wilson.

Asked to *"prendre une tasse de thé"* with Gen. and Mme. O——. Significant that "Mr." always precedes "Mrs." in French usage. B—— reproves me for not wearing wedding ring. Says I get invitations under false pretenses.

Great changes coming. DeM—— gave me book, written by Frenchman, burlesque of America and Americans. Said: "No Frenchman can ever again write such a book." Wonderful, the understanding and mutual admiration growing up. Sometimes hear an American—newcomer—say unpleasant things of French. Likely to get called by other Americans. As for French, even that crusty patriot, Col. B——, beginning to wonder if there may not be something in our attitude about *maisons de tolérance.*

Occasional instances of bad behavior of Americans. In general, simply marvelous. Drunken soldier a rarity —M. P's very much on job. In T——'s battery a soldier accused by French family of having stolen 200 fr. Before wheels of military justice could begin to turn, battery took up collection. Right or wrong, weren't going to give anybody excuse to say Yank soldiers were thieves. French so moved at that, refused to accept money. Thief so moved at refusal, collection, etc., he confessed, and told where money was.

People at home seem to think that to be court-martialed means to be shot. Anybody liable to trial, since any officer can prefer charges against another officer. Acquittal after trial leaves no disgrace.

Thur., 11th.—30 yrs. old to-day. Older, probably, than I'll ever be again.

Early this morning, drums and *clairons* coming up street, in half plaintive, half triumphant *Chant de Départ.* Two companies of *coquelicots*—name of little blue flower worn by Class of '19. Full equipment, brand new, swinging along, *très militaire.* On way to station —and *au feu.*

Not a cheer. Perfectly silent streets. Few kids, trudging silently beside steel-blue column, wordless, holding hand of brother, perhaps. On sidewalks, here and there, woman, old-looking, furtively dabbing at eyes.

Spoke to one—peasant, obviously. *"Oui, mon lieutenant*—I have heard the *Chant de Départ* before— twice. Two others went like this. They have not returned. And now, *le p'tit* Jeanot—*le bambin.* The last, m'sieu."

And at my "You are very sad?" Shrug of shoulders. *"Sans doubte, m'sieu. Oui.* I am sad. And yet—I am not sad." And then, with curiously classic speech so often found among illiterate: "I am not so unworthy of the soil I till!"

One hears France is *fini.* But throbbing of *clairons* gives lie to that. Sad—and very, very tired. Soundless tear or two. Catch in the throat. And then a sigh— unutterably weary . . . but always a sparkle in the

eye. *Quand même, m'sieu.......jusqu'au bout!"*
The fine steel of this people bent very, very far. But
not in power of heavy-handed German to break it.
Heavy-handed and heavy-hearted, too! Doubt if Teuton lives who could understand depth of cold contempt
with which old peasant woman spoke as squad of German prisoners halted, waiting for French column to
pass. "Fools!" all she said. Voice of embattled Mari-
anne before mad barbarian bull. No hate. No fear.
Sheer disdain.

Von Hertling's speech to Reichstag as indefinite as
usual. Have hunch he's whistling to keep his courage
up. Believe the Boche will take another crack at us
about the 17th.

To "vaudeville" by hospital unit. Memorable. In
courtyard of ancient stone caserne, about 500 Yanks,
around platform on which was piano—almost as ancient as barracks. Only light, flicker from lantern,
swinging above. Faces—clean, open, animated—made
one proud of one's own. Such names! And as many
tongues as ever chattered at Babel.

Show began with Grieg's "Spring," by master-mu-
sician in private's uniform. Marvelous ragging, some
songs, "Madelon" on violin, and a recitation of Service
poem. Encore after encore. Then on tower of Hôtel
de Ville, old clock slowly tolling 9:30. Singer stopped
abruptly in middle of song. Hush. And then, in stillness, far away, first notes of bugle. Instantly, such a
scurry and rush. Place deserted, save for officer or two,
sentries, and performers. Lights vanished. Caserne
walls great black shadows. In the distance the clatter of
hobnailed boots as some straggler hurried to get under
wire of "check." Then, very sweetly, the melancholy
notes of "taps." Died in a silence that was complete.

Only sound, clang of great gate closing behind me, and resounding echo of my footsteps on worn old cobbles.

Interesting, that where Yankee soldiers sang of Broadway, dragoons of Bonaparte had once been quartered.

When Sarrail was busted and sent to Salonique, they said he was "Limogé." Letters often come to Limoges, addressed to him.

At *rapport* to-day, order from G.H.Q. to locate English-speaking French for interpreters. Order transmitted to French unit-commanders.

Fri., 12th.—Got uniform repaired. Charge—50 centimes.

Saw Réjané in "Mme. Sans Gêne." Gassed and helpless in midst of garlic-eating natives. Got in conversation with Jean B——, *rapatrié*—27 months in Bocheland. So gentle and polite. Spoke exquisite English. Father professor Univ. of Angoulême. Asked what he's doing. Ans.: Sweeping out canteen at station! Thought of order from G.H.Q. Seized him for interpreter. He said he was beginning to believe in fairies.

Sat., 13th.—Good example *argot des tranchées: "Un gradé veut arroser un nouveau galon."* Means chap who's been promoted wants to throw a party in celebration.

Of the metropolis, by taste as well as birth. Provincials are provincials, the world over. Variety to life in a great city, in people and things—a saltiness. Not much here but scenery (some miles out) several cafés, a commonplace cathedral, and a couple of movies. Women, innumerable, of course—but there's a *sameness!*

People at home, like E——, talk of "settling" Russian problem in terms of 6% interest, compounded semi-annually. And, with approval, of sending Roosevelt there. T.R.'s medievalism would make no hit with Bolshevik. Significant, Trotzky's declaration in favor of Germans, not because he liked them better than Entente, but because they were nearer revolution.

Heard to-day that L—— B—— esteemed most valuable man in Red Cross. Smoother of troubled waters. Everybody's friend. Keeps things going. Great fellow. Wish he were here.

And that F—— was trying to make R—— jealous. What fools some women are! Doesn't feel she's had all emotions a woman's entitled to until she's had jealous husband. Thread which holds man to woman sometimes pretty slender. F—— has keen blade in her hand, but her curiosity to use it may prove dangerous.

Shined up belt and boots—got to be *bien astiqué* for grand review of troops to-morrow. All gilt and glitter of région to be there. "Best people" don't approve of 14th, it being republican holiday, and so, not so many flags as on 4th. But rabble regard it highly. We've got to put on brave show.

Great row at *rapport* to-day. Seems old woman, tired of life, jumped off bridge over river. Lt. M——, American, was on bank. Jumped in and saved her. French think it would be grand thing for International Relations to hang a medal on him. Col. B—— dead against it. Said in first place, American interfered with personal liberty of old woman—had a right to drown herself if she wanted to. In second place, if there was any decorating for courage to be done, medal ought to go to old woman. She jumped off high bridge, which took nerve. Finally compromised on *Médaille de Sauvetage*—O.K. for policeman, *pompiers*, etc., but *pas militaire.*   M—— will never know the difference.

Sun., 14th.—First time I ever reviewed an army. Conspicuous as hell. With R—— only O.D. in glitter of Gen. O——'s staff. When band played S.S.B., Gen. O—— saluted, and went on. But R—— stood at attention until anthem was finished—all alone in midst of army. Bawled me out for not "obeying regulations." My point that I followed lead of C.O., in this case, Gen. O——. Our "regulations" written before we ever had anybody on foreign staffs.

Had lunch at —th Hospital Unit. Met M—— B——. Extremely attractive girl, with a bean. Good to talk again of books and bookmen with one so simpatico.

Then *en campagne* with B——, with "all his sisters, cousins and his aunts." 16 sat down to tea—all talking French, and all in unison, according to custom of the country. One little old man, *drôle type*, gave *allocution* to "glorious" Americans, "glorious" Wilson, winding up with my "glorious" self—first American with whom "he had had privilege of conversing." Wore little gilt Statue of Liberty in buttonhole, and tiny flag.

One old lady wanted to know if we, *en Amérique*, also employed Arabic system of numerals!

Curious paradox of French. Renowned for artistic taste, but house furnishings generally atrocious. Cluttered with junk, which they insist on showing, in detail. Also, fiddler in every family, and worst slaughter of good music draws hearty applause.

Even the educated incredibly uninformed about rest of world. Dear old lady wanted to know if it was true that in Chicago, *"la ville des cochons,"* one had really learned how to manufacture eggs. Another said she understood that it was customary in *les Etats Unis* to have milk piped to houses.

This the place where enameling first flourished. Mme. F—— said that as little girl they played duck-on-rock with pieces now held priceless and kept in museum. *Autre temps, autre mœurs.*

All chance of conciliatory, Made-in-Germany peace now gone. Very apparent stiffening of Allied spine. Thanks to Wilson and the U.S., it is going to be a "victorious" peace, with the Hun on his knees, taking what is given him.

Struggling with French proves great training in English. So hard to say things *exactly*. Very richness of English clouds precision. Little appreciation of *mot juste*. French have nicety of speech—perforce. Their vocabulary not a tenth of ours. Such simplicity—certainly the highest ideal of expression.

Mon., 15th.—To-day a *jour de fête. En campagne* with DeM—— and countless daughters and grandchildren. Played Pied Piper to a dozen youngsters of all ages. Little Gaby gave me bunch of purple flowers to match my cigarette case, and "Nenette and Rintintin" to send to my little Americans. Nobody, of course, can be found to believe this famous pair really does protect against bombs, etc.: but *tout le monde* always has them somewhere about his person.

Encouraging incident. Called H—— on phone. Answered by interpreter who said H—— was there, but spoke no French. Assured him I spoke English fluently! Ooh, la! la!

Evening with B—— family. Delightful. French more intellectual, though less informed than we. Not so "wise." But rather closer to things that count. Boy of 16 better company, in some ways, than our average college graduate.

Frank affection of family life. Stranger not held aloof from rigidly polite circle. Slow to invite, but once committed, all bars down. Electric responsiveness of French gathering. Full of stimulus. Not surprising they are famed for wit. They make dullness difficult.

The French woman—marvelous! Not a family the hand of war hasn't scarred. But got to know them long and intimately before you know *how* scarred. No talk of life's hardness, not many words wasted on enemy. Don't *talk* of "carrying on": just do it.

Amused at Americans, with few weeks' experience of the land and a dozen words of the language, expressing opinions, favorable or otherwise, of French. And the second-hand literary eulogy one reads. Fact is, you can't appreciate the Gaul until you know him. And despite surface appearances, he's not easy to know. An extraordinarily sensitive bird.

Tues., 16th.—Hun offensive launched! One day ahead of schedule. Damn—I *must* be a prophet! J—— completely flabbergasted!

Extremely hot, and blinding white dust worse than tropical. Wonder if I'll shiver through another French winter? Nix. All over in October—maybe.

Telegram rec'd from G.H.Q., stating I was "desired" for G2. Information requested whether "this officer's services could be spared." Very excited. What to do? R—— away. Not much doubt he'll see his way clear to dispensing with my services. The "serving" I've done you could put in your eye.

Touched at way French at Etat received news. Full of felicitations, and professed to be downcast. Insisted

wives, children, all downcast, too. Great fellows. Certainly have genius for making one feel all hell on wheels.

Took M—— B—— to dinner and wasted bottle of
Beaune on her. Probably preferred mineral water, anyway. Much talk, and pleasant, concerning books and
people. Remarkable person.

Wed., 17th.—Very sad at thought of leaving. Did
work in daze. Never met a finer lot than these gallant
crocks of —th· Region. *Sans peur*, and all rest of it.
Consommation with R—— and DeM——. Nearly
wept.

Thur., 18th.—Great excitement at *rapport*. Mutiny
of remount detail (American) quartered on French *intendance*. Chief cause, apparently, the food. French
puzzled. Col. B—— insisted orders been given to treat
les Américains extra special. *Intendance* reported back
they *had*. "Delicacies of all sorts." Col. B—— astonished at "ungratefulness" of Americans.

Much running about and investigating. Found source
of difficulty in fact Americans did not consider horse-
entrails, especially *le pine*, and eyes of cows, as "delicacies." Another case of *autre pays—autres mœurs*.

DeM—— very droll handling French end of "up-
rising." "*Les punaises*"—"meatless days" suppressed.
Stomach certainly rules soul. Roast beef and *pommes
frits*—no more trouble.

Hun attack faltering. American successes reported.

Fri., 19th.—R—— returned this A.M. Debated
problem of his authority *re* wire from G.H.Q., and then
phoned Paris for instructions. Said work of office was
increasing, and I "of great value." Loath to let me go.

Paris urged me to stay, painting **G.H.Q.** in horrid light, but left it to my choice. I'm to "think about it."

Everything true, maybe, but feel need of traveling. Don't know where I'm going, nor why—but on my way. R—— can turn over *les petits embêtements* of this office to somebody else. Pershing needs me now.

Great counter-attack to-day. **W.K.** war ought to be over somewhere in October or November. Be home, if still whole, some time next Spring. The vines on the house ought to be pretty good by then.

Lunch with Capt. R—— of Etat. Splendid old chap. *"Soldat du métier,"* i.e., a *regular.* Curious tragedy. At Front a year. Then fell in ditch and crippled, badly. Can scarcely walk, but can't carry wound-stripe, and professional career ended. Told me that of 300 contemporaries who started war, only 42 survive.

Hoped his boy would not adopt military career. Curious reason. All the old regulars having been killed off, officers of future would be rankers, good fighters, but not gentlemen and devoid of culture. Said if lad insisted upon going into soldiering, he'd see to it he joined Artillery or Engineers, because their technical character demanded men of brains, education and superior intelligence.

Tried to make him understand why I laughed, but couldn't!

Antipathy in French army, as in ours, between professional and amateur. Each, though making exceptions, despises other as class. In French army, this antagonism is intensified, because remaining regulars are well on in years. To natural hostility is added that between youth and age.

Remember dear old Col B——'s remark that if Civil War had lasted another six months, history would have had different set of generals to revere. What an upstart the Royalists must have considered Cromwell.

Great mistake in our army to have different groups, like U.S., U.S.R., U.S.N.A., and U.S.N.G. Foreigners can't grasp distinctions—nor can we. Better if we had one army—one insignia.

Heard L—— H——'s brother, W——, gassed. Shocking. Remember him as only infant. Well, the infants are fighting this war—like every other. They make better soldiers than their elders.

S—— writes inquiring if we now wear the lapelled blouse like British. Thinks it would be both practical and comfortable. That answers her question, of course.

Sat., 20th.—Good news from Front—17,000 prisoners.

Told R—— of my "reflections." Couldn't bear to have Pershing worrying along at G.H.Q. without me. Thought I'd better go. No cheers from R——. He'd like to keep me to do his errands for him.

Telephone from Paris that G.H.Q.'s inquiry regarding me had been answered with "indispensable." Oh, my God! Thanks to that flat-footed, sniveling son-of-a-bitch, A——, I'm S.O.L. Limogé, and no mistake. Well, what the hell.

Read "Cyrano" for comfort. What a poem!" *"J'aurai tout manqué, même ma mort."* Poor Gascon, sublime and droll.

> Philosophe, physicien,
> Rimeur, bretteur, musicien
>   Et voyageur aérien,
> Grand riposteur du tac au tac
> Amant aussi—pas pour son bien!—
>   Cyrano de Bergerac
> Qui fut tout, et qui ne fut rien!

And those altogether splendid lines:

> Que dites-vous? . . . C'est pas inutile? . . . Je le sais!
> Mais on ne se bat pas dans l'espoir du succes!
> Non! Non! C'est bien plus beau lorsque c'est inutile!
> —Qu'est-ce qu' c'est que tous ceux-la? Vous etes mille?
> Ah! Je vous reconnais, tous mes vieux enemis!
> Le Mensonge?
>   Tiens, tiens!—Ha! ha! les Compromis,
> Les Préjudges, les Lachetes!
>   Que je pactise?
> Jamais! jamais!—Ah! te voila, toi, la Sottise!
> —Je sais bien qu'a la fin vous me mettrez a bas;
> N'importe: je me bats! je me bats! je me bats!

To Theater in evening—"Cyrano" the piece. But enormous disappointment. In place of Rostand's sublimely pathetic character, there was a cheap comedian, a burlesquer—much emphasis on the *nose* . . . couldn't stand it and quit.

Hell of a day, all round.

Sun., 21st.—B——'s picture under my eye, smiling up at me from under his little helmet. Never a sweeter smile on mortal lips. Hard to think of it smiling so far away.

Speaking of helmets, P—— tells story of British Tommy. Old soldiers never have taken kindly to them, considering them modern and depraved. This old chap, hit on head with shrapnel fragment. Came to, rubbing his eyes groggily. "Shook me up somefink orful," he growled. "Never did like them damned things, I didn't!"

Situation between Soissons and Marne looks bright. Impossible to say yet whether success tactical or strategical. Certain the Yanks played part in it. Morale of French at high pitch. That of Boche must be low. The check on the Piave, followed by decreasing strength of German *morde*, must have repercussions.

Plain that war not to be ended in compromise. *That* time has passed. No more thought of concessions. *We* to decide the terms—not Germans. When they ask for terms, they'll get Grant's reply to Lee.

Probably do just what Lee did. Conviction must be crystallizing in Germany that all chance of victory has passed. Must know they're fighting for lost cause. Contrary to human nature to fight for that. Once idea gets to people that it *is* lost cause, they'll just go to pieces. One hears talk of what we'll do next summer. No stock in that. If this year ends with Germany on defensive, knowing that next year our strength will be quintupled, their morale will never stand through winter.

Probabilities are—constant fighting, three or four months more. Then, if no decision, it will either be "unconditional surrender," or Junkers will try to hold on, and a popular protestation will do their surrendering for them. More certain every day that this fall will see Hun on knees, squealing for mercy.

This theory so pleasing that few dare accept it. After four years of dashed hopes, they have a sort of pagan, superstitious fear of optimism.

To B——'s in evening. Dear, kindly people, professing to derive great personal satisfaction from fact that I am not to leave them. But also so sympathetic over my misfortune.

Wonder if I hadn't better kill R——. But *cui bono?* Merely change jails.

Mon., 22nd.—Tried to get leave, but R—— passed buck. Nice fellow. Nothing at office—not even chair to sit in.

Tues., 23rd.—Tried R——again on leave. All he'd say: "Find me some authority. *I* haven't time." Went hunting through Army Reg. If I shot the bastard, any court would call it justifiable homicide. Finally got him to call Paris. Wouldn't say anything about results, except to hint of possible transfer to Besançon. That bird certainly works in the dark.

Wed., 24th.—Awakened by wire from Col. H——, relieving me further duty X——, and directing immediate presence Paris for further instructions. What now?

Busy winding up loose ends, most important being farewells, beginning with Gen. C——, whose kindly words almost made me weep. The French have genius for saying nice things and contriving to say them in such way you find yourself believing them.

All *désolé*, they insisted. Capt. C—— said I was *brave garçon*, and—highest compliment he could pay—"more French than American." Mme. L—— even phoned in from country to say adieu. Profoundly moved by it all.

In evening, a dinner at the Cercle, tendered by members of Etat Major. Champagne ad lib. To bed fuzzy, but very *content*.

Thur., 25th.—Final farewells at Etat Major—an ordeal! When crusty old Col. B——, at the rapport, made what he called *le prononcement officiel*, broke down and fled.

Found B—— and DeM—— at station . . . long way from Etat, too. Insisted on fixing up baggage. B—— already nailed place in train. A wonderful experience, and eyes were misty as train pulled out.

Arrived Paris, 7 P.M. and to old pension. Overwhelmed by welcome of *femme de chambre*. Delightful
old Col. de la R—— on train. Same who asked permission of Gen. D—— to deliver some little *causeries* to
American officers on How to Drink Champagne. Been
so shocked, he said—wild lads actually drank it by
bottle!

Some new and charming American girls there. Also
L—— B——. Bickered half the night with him.

Fri., 26th.—*Butter* for breakfast! Reported Capt.
L—— on Ave. Montaigne. Given orders to proceed
forthwith to Etat Major, 7th Région, at Besançon.
These orders, however, pending return of Maj. H——,
who was at G.H.Q., and would have further information
regarding call thereto.

Afternoon—Maj. H—— telephoned from Chaumont
he had learned nothing definite about me and G.H.Q. I
therefore directed to take night train for Besançon.
Capt. L——, however, very decent, and consented to
postponement of execution until to-morrow.

See the Great Cham himself to-morrow. Usual palaver
about Liaison Service short of men, splendid work I've
been doing, etc. And so—on to Besançon. After that—
over the Alps.

Sat., 27th.—Couldn't see Maj. H—— all morning.
Regular damned pope! "Could not be disturbed." Did
some errands. Saw J—— B——. After leaving Ft.
Sheridan, went to Camp Something-or-other in Iowa.
Sat on his tail there, doing nothing. Asked for 90 day
leave. Said army evidently didn't need him, so he
might as well go back and be useful in business till they
did. Nearly court-martialed for request eminently sen-

sible. Little later, transferred from Artillery at Col.' D——'s request, and sent over here. Doing purchasing work—which is what he ought to be doing.

Also saw P—— R——. Also out of Artillery and at desk—though for other reasons. Poor devil—he had a miserable time trying to prove the self-evident fact that he wasn't made for Artillery.

Time was when insignia man wore bore some relation to work man did. That was long ago. Run into crossed rifles, bursting bombs, etc. all over Elysée Palace. T—— W——, also T.B. from Artillery, says he petitioned G.H.Q. for crossed fountain pens, but never got answer.

Met G——, on way to join staff 1st Army. Lt. Col's job, and only question of time when he gets silver leaf. Able lad. Lunched at Crillon. G—— full of good advice, and presently full of assorted spirits.

Back to Ave. Montaigne. Capt. L—— said useless to wait longer. Better beat it for Besançon. Disagreed. Full of Dutch courage and intimated somebody was "stalling." L—— finally went into holy of holies . . . and came out with order directing me to proceed to G.H.Q.!

To dinner with D—— S—— and A—— H——, good fellows, both. And to see "The Mollusc," played in English. Audience more interesting than play—English, Australians, Canadians, Americans, soldiers, nurses, etc. So responsive to slightest joke on stage. Like a visit home. Atmosphere so unlike French theaters.

Endowed enterprise, enlisted men getting in for 5 fr. Great idea. Nothing soldier *en perm* needs more than clean amusement. What he really *wants*. But not much of it to be had.

On street, afterward, accosted by stranger, American, with slap on back and mealy stuff about "you soldier boys." Sweating well, coat thrown back, exposing suspenders not so very new, and shirt not so very clean. At intervals, geysers of tobacco juice. U.S. Representative —— from Kentucky. One of delegation "studying conditions." "Yessir, had dinner with King of Italy t'other day. An' as I was tellin' McAdoo 'fore I left," etc., etc.

Unpleasant to reflect that he represented what "we boys" were fighting to make the world safe for.

D—— had new one on War Aims. England fighting for Freedom of Sea; France for La Patrie; U.S. for Souvenirs.

Sun., 28th.—Stored some more baggage. With time and experience, be able, maybe, to travel like French officers—handkerchief, bottle of perfume and steel helmet. Also small locker, about half size of ours. Now and then an Anglophile, with collapsible bath tub.

Called on Mons. H——. Suspicious at first. When he found I didn't want to borrow money, became cordiality itself, and put purse at my disposal.

Lunched with J—— B—— at Cercle Interallié, residence of Baron Rothschild, now club for Allied officers. Gorgeous place, service *al fresco*. Loveliest gardens in Paris, and Lucullian fare. Hard to believe a war's on only forty-odd miles away.

Saw E—— J——. Now trying to get in army. Been offered 2nd Lieutenancy, but says he can't live on less than Captain's pay. Seems to see nothing comic in situation.

Long talk with L—— B——. Thoughtful, pleasant company. Excessively conscientious and rather too upright. Repressed, with fear of careless living that dulls his edge. The vestigial Scot in him, probably. He could learn much from French.

Letter from R—— K——, mostly about D——. Latter "leading very weary existence with one of these highly efficient N.G. outfits. Battalion Liaison Officer, said job consisting of Officer of the Day, duty every two or three days, and running the H.Q. mess."

Mon., 29th.—Delicious bit of *tartuferie.* Order issued by German commander at St. Quentin: "I have been disagreeably struck by the way the French inhabitants take home with them the fowl and game which they have bought alive in the markets, doing it in such manner as to cause these animals useless torture.

"The units of French police must be issued an order to take energetic repressive measures every time such an outrage is observed.

"The animals should be carried under the arm, or placed in a basket.

"COMTE BERNSTORFF
"capitaine et commandant."

Another yarn current among French: A *poilu*, on leave, was discussing military equipment, especially helmets. Civilian friend hazarded opinion that German helmet was better, since it protected the back of the neck. "True enough," replied the *poilu*. "But that would be of no advantage to *us*. The Germans have no opportunity to shoot us in the back."

Tues., 30th.—Left Paris, 8 A.M. Train jammed, S.R.O. Arrived Chaumont 2:30. Saw Billeting Officer and got room. 60 fr. Then to G.H.Q. reporting Capt. W——.

G.H.Q. a shock! Expected to see Gen. Pershing like Napoleon at Friedland, on white charger, spy glass under arm, surrounded by gold laced officers in swords and high boots. Found instead group huge stone barracks, around court, with million typewriters all clicking at once. Reminded me of Sears Roebuck.

More field clerks and stenogs than soldiers, though slight concession to fitness of things in sentries, band, and retreat with bugles.

Bon mot, attributed to Mlle. Géniat, just back from tour in Switzerland. At Berne, while out walking, a German accosted her, making many compliments in German. "I am French," says she. "Speak French." "Ah," sezze, *"Permettez-moi de vous accompagner."* To which she disdainfully replies: "Is it not enough for you to be knocked down—do you want to be stepped on?"

French morale very much on the make.

Wed., 31st.—Started to work under Capt. W——. To fill in for another man for few days. Tested as to French-speaking by W——. Passed *cum laude*, since W—— knew practically no French himself! Intimation that next move would be to Base Censor's office, where French-speaking officer was needed. Well—all right. *Je m'en fiche.*

Official designation this office—"Press Section, G2, General Staff." Chief is Col. M——, a Regular whom I knew years ago as Lt. 5th Cav. Later in Artillery. Now here, and somewhat sour on job. Scheming to get a regiment. Charming man. His greeting most cordial.

Met A——, Capt. in Intelligence—in civil life "F.P.A." of "Conning Tower."

Dined with W——, also old newspaper man. Talked mostly of books and music. Little "shop." Pleasant fellow. The town incredibly dull. Have to walk miles even to eat, and no diversions.

No clear idea of what next for me—and reached point of not caring much. W—— says ability to speak French makes for complications—so many branches after men of that sort. Intimates part of G2 dealing with counter-espionage been making improper proposals for my person. Or may go to field press station to "learn ropes." Perhaps be Conducting Officer—tote distinguished guests and undistinguished correspondents to war. Completely resigned—come what may.

The Hun having rude and rather comic awakening as to Yanks. Finding them fighters more savage than his own ideal. Has tried "Kamarad" stuff several times —hasn't proved profitable. American, aroused by what he considers unfair play, a murderous fighter. Refuses to *hate* Hun. Considers him merely a peculiarly objectionable pig—to be quickly stuck.

German still strong. Can hang on for while. But longer he hangs, worse it will be for him. So obvious, exasperating to have to wait for him to realize it. According to best military opinion here, we shall whip him into peace some time next summer. Back in long pants some time after Xmas, 1919.

Shocked by tilted mirror in front of me. Reveals top of head and march of years. Old hair going like snow in sunshine. No longer merely "thin." Have to wear cap, pretty soon, so as not to *catch cold!* Awful. No wonder tanks wouldn't take me.

August, 1918

Thur., 1st.—Handed orders to proceed to Paris, reporting to Capt. W——, Visitors' Bureau. Same old stuff—short of personnel, temporary assignment, etc. But ours not to reason why.

Dinner with G—— S—— and three T.B.'s—so grateful for kindness. Couldn't help thinking: "There, but for the grace of God,' 'etc.

Fri., 2nd.—To office. *Rien à faire.* Saw Burton Holmes, Paul Scott Mowrer, Floyd Gibbons. Wound like latter's almost worse than death—though *he* doesn't think so.

Left Chaumont 2:15. Met Capt. M—— of French Mission at G.H.Q. on train. Most interesting. So full of ideas, and aptness in expression. Told several instances, from own experience, that fill in colorless statistics of German's plight. Passing through town which had been occupied by Hun, people kept marveling at how well French *looked.* Said there was such contrast, physically, with Germans. Also, in German hospital, containing both German and French wounded, there were ten German deaths to one French, following operations. German soldiers getting 2 oz. fat per *week.*

No feeling that war can end this year. I still think though that October-November will be crisis. If no peace then—won't come for another year. Those stupid Germans—always obey their leaders. Usual thing,
161

for officers to skip in face of certain defeat. Men think
nothing of it. And men who will fire machine guns
when chained to them, incapable of reasoning out simplest problem.

Arrived Paris at 7. Spent hour capturing last taxi
in town. Cheering welcome at pension.

Sat., 3rd.—Reported to 10 Rue St. Anne—Visitors'
Bureau. Has charge of people who come to see war.
Hoover, this week. Issue passes, route party, make all
arrangements, and provide conductor. Capt. W——
C.O., too much detail. Needs understudy. I'm it.

A year, now, since I put on O.D.—and look at me!
Well, *c'est la guerre.*

Sun., 4th.—Only event, courier cleaning automatic in
office—went off, and bullet just missed field clerk on
floor below.

Mon., 5th.—Big Bertha began spitting at 10. Silly
waste of powder.

Office all day. Ran into W—— H——, very low.
After leaving Saumur, went to Front. Got ordered home
as instructor, but C.O. wouldn't let him go—too valuable. Disgusted. Lots of cases like that. H—— sent
home as instructor. Never been to Front, not even
Saumur. Exasperating to better men who have to stick
it.

W—— had pocket full of francs and keen desire for
Maxim's. Great argument about it, with two pals.
One, C—— very quiet chap, all against it. Over-ruled
by G——, famous drunkard. Out for large evening.
Had lot of wine. C—— got tight and went off with
girl named Suzanne. G—— drank little, and home

quietly to bed! Everything upside down these days.
Saw L—— C—— with girl, evidently well ac-
quainted. She called me over. Explained I mustn't
draw wrong conclusions. Their relations purely platonic.

To Olympia. Slight flicker and usual lure of women.
Survived. Métro closed. Walked "home."

Tues., 6th.—Up early and got Cong. S—— of N.Y.,
D—— of N. Dak. and L—— of Minn. Took 8:15 to
war. Met F—— on train, famous hero who insisted on
showing everybody **D.S.C.** citation, and telling all details. Most awful ass.

Changed to motor car at Meaux. To La Ferté,
Veaux, Château Thierry, Fere-en-Tardenoise, outskirts
of Fismes.

War just as pictured. Mud. Wrecked buildings.
Loot accumulated in dugouts, but not carried off.
Dead horses at roadside. First sign of Front, unutterable
smell thereof. Troops, guns, dispatch riders, bursting
shells, balloons, planes—everything just as movies show
it.

Most impressive thing—the *cleaning up*. Dead
quickly buried. Small army goes through fields salvag-
ing equipment. Hard to find souvenirs three days after
battle. Roads, right up to Front, better than our boulevards. Big army keeps them so. Saw almost as many
steam-rollers as guns. Still another army maintains
traffic. Easier to find way than at home. Signs everywhere, with traffic cops, very much on job. Mixed
police—French and American. Signs—German, French,
English. And tell more than directions. Every now
and then one with dry information: "This road under

observation; divide convoys." Inference obvious, and no complaints when chauffeur steps on it.

Incredible quantities of ammunition left by Hun— not all destroyed. Must have moved fast. Americans did not have all, or even large part in job; what they did was important. Saw secret report from G.Q.G. (French) on operations just preceding counter-offensive. Stated work of Americans beggared all praise, and in all probability, one American division stood between Paris and capture.

Passed through Belleau Wood. Also saw Big Bertha emplacement. All there but tube. Clever camouflage. Hard to believe in range of gun, even after seeing it.

Visiting dignitaries full of questions. "Look, is that a high-explosive cannon?" Viewing a neatly ploughed field: "Gosh, the firin' there must 'a been something awful!" And "Say, how many men will a shell kill?" Incredible, number of things those nimble brains thought up.

S—— insisted on finding 165th. Had to turn off road and find camp. Immediately a political meeting. Pathetic—boys clustered around him like flies on a cake. Eager inquiries about the Subway! Pressing scribbled addresses into hands, with plea to write folks they were O.K. His pockets and mine stuffed with these commissions. At leaving, lots of handshaking, and: "Well, boys, take good care of yourselves." One "boy" muttered: "Christ—it's a wonder he didn't tell us to take umbrellas!" (This outfit just out of line, lost most of officers, and been bombed all night.)

Other Congressmen disapproved of half hour thus "wasted." All for hurrying on. Reason presently apparent. Furtive inquiries for troops from *their* states.

Halting progress. Much stopping and handshaking, and "well boys, where do you hail from?"

Had to have souvenirs. Countless Boche helmets collected. Would have taken tank if there had been room in car. Suggested at Big Bertha emplacement that few bolts, etc., would be much prized at home. They took enough rusty old iron to sink a ship. Mr. D—— wanted to buy my gas-mask, until I explained its possession would land him in jail.

Skeptical, at first, about gas. But after while, all I could do to keep them from wearing masks constantly, and tin hats, too.

Their notion of "Front"—a line, like a string. Rather shocked to discover, after riding an hour, they'd been at the Front all the time. Stopped at crossroads, explaining that Vesle was just over hill, couple of hundred yards, and the c.r. had been shelled vigorously day before. They decided it was time to turn around.

No shells. But they had plenty of thrills. Thought firing of our own artillery was big shells dropping on both sides of road. Had great comfort being jaunty about it, and probably go through life telling about time they were "under fire."

Back in Paris at 6. More war talk. Hun sure to make strong effort for negotiation. France and England favorably disposed. U.S. position questionable. Sure to be trouble if idea is "on to Berlin." Wouldn't be surprised to see abdication of Hohenzollerns—grand gesture of self-sacrifice, etc.—no consequence, but would save Allies' face. Next few months crucial.

Wed., 7th.—Got title of "Adjutant." Hell!

Item in newspaper: "Ace of the trenches, was René-Louis Lambin. Minus right arm and left leg, he swanked it in the cafés, his uniform covered with crosses and medals. There was clamor for his portrait and his autographs, and the *Marseillaise* saluted his entry into theaters. The skepticism of a police inspector put an end to this apotheosis. The ace of the trenches was only a pastry-cook. The loss of his two members was in consequence of a railway accident. His only citations were seven convictions for theft, burglary and *abus de confiance*. Two years imprisonment."

Interesting workings of G2, and the *why* of censorship. G.H.Q. extremely anxious to locate two divisions of German guards, prior to big counter offensive. One lost for two weeks. Finally found through item in obscure German provincial newspaper, about band of Guards Division, etc. Lots of howl about stupidity of censorship. Don't understand how important seemingly trivial facts can be, properly interpreted, and put together with other facts. Most complaints unjustified.

Rumor that present quiet on Italian front presages separate peace. Constant remark of German prisoners, being taken back after Marne battle, and seeing enormous masses of Americans: "We have been fooled." Significant of what must soon reach their civilians. Americans no longer a promise—delivering. Have heartened French tremendously.

German morale certainly crumbling. "Disgusting," say French, of fawning and whining of German papers. Ignoble people. No pride. Can therefore break with suddenness and completeness of which finer-grained people would be incapable.

Big Bertha's shells continue to drop. No effect. One fell near Embassy other day, killing two people. Less excitement than a street car accident at home. Only effect of shelling is to add to already considerable contempt French feel for enemy—a contempt even thick-skinned Boche himself feels.

Worst feature of Paris life the boys from the line, in on 48 hr. leave. No 6 fr. *brasserie*, beer included, for them. Pockets full of francs. My purse may hold out, but my stomach won't.

Thur., 8th.—In office all day, arranging details for Rabbi S——'s trip. Never met "Mr. Foster," but know how he feels. Dined at Ciro's (32 fr.!) with N——M——and gang from Front.

Letter from B——. "I will not expect longer for writte to you (in my negro's english) that i have not forgotten you and that i hope you will soon send to me your news. Where are you? What are you doing? . . . I hope you will not us completely forgotten and we have soon a long letter of you. I remain your good and truly friend."

Fri., 9th.—Letter from A—— D——, at the Front with 155 G.P.F. outfit. Pattern of burst so long, using them for enfilade fire. Well in front of 75's. Must be shock to some of the boys.

Sat., 10th.—Met T——. Graduate of C.P.A.L.T. Then to Limoges, duty—mess officer. Flunked artillery exams there, and sent away. Had busy time since. Instead of job in rear somewhere, as he and everybody else expected, was assigned to Infantry—saw action almost immediately, and now recuperating from shell-shock!

Significance of D'Annunzio's flight over Vienna. The first crack will appear in Austria. Kaiser Bill will descend in flourish of democracy, etc., intending merely to change his coat. But descent will be permanent. The Germans themselves will see to that.

Germany, hitherto, shown nothing but military intelligence. The m.i. is going to take her back, in a few weeks, to the Hindenburg Line. What will social intelligence think of that?

Another thing: German commercial interests not overlooking fact that another year of war will close only remaining door they have to civilized world—the U.S. Three months more should tell the story.

Saw P—— R—— in Crillon bar. Cursing his fate. A "ferry pilot." Flies planes to Front. Says if he does good work, and delivers planes undamaged, he'll be kept at it indefinitely. If he crashes them, he'll be sent to rear. Doesn't know what to do. Says he's had enough danger. Wants some glory now.

Saw little lad in Tuileries, so like my own. Filled with strange sadness. Half the soul-sickness of these days is out of fear of what he will think of me, when he grows up and learns how I fought the war from behind a typewriter. And yet, it is the thought of children that damps audacity. Odd paradox! When he is old enough to understand some measure of it, it will be too late to matter.

When God finished making the first man, He left him for a moment. And while His back was turned, the devil slipped up and slyly inserted *imagination* into the head of the unhappy creature. How much happier we would be if God had never turned His back!

The purple cigarette case S—— sent, cause of much trouble. All right in darkness. To-day, on boulevard, had to withdraw to privacy of comfort station to get cigarette. Bad enough being on boulevards at all, without pulling out thing as conspicuous as a peacock's tail.

Sun., 11th.—Chat with *femme de chambre*, frail little woman. Asked many questions about S—— and the babies. Told me she had a little boy, five years old —her husband had disappeared in Sept., 1914. No word since. Did I, perhaps, think he was prisoner? What words of sympathy are there worth the uttering? Wonder if people really know what they say when they talk of "bringing the war to German soil," and "punishing" the Hun. His women have been punished already.

Les vieux pepères. Among the most pathetic figures of war. The dreary, drab lives these wretched old men lead, without even the blessed chance of being killed. One look in their faces tells how long these weary years have been—no trumpets, no flash of bayonets, no decorations. Just long hours of toil, and weary monotony and discomfort. The incredible imbecility of war!

A long, lonesome day.

Mon., 12th.—Stopped at kiosk for *Cri de Paris*. Proprietor, under counter, popped up at my request. "Oh—I thought you were a Frenchman!" he exclaimed. So flattered, I bought half his stock. Business geniuses —these French!

To office. Combination "adjutant"-errand-boy. Busy delivering messages around Paris. High degree of efficiency. 2 officers, 2 men, 1 limousine. Like delivering needles in a 5-ton truck.

At dinner, French officer, fine looking lad, sat down at same table. Conversation. Spoke English well. Two years at Cornell, and had visited extensively. Did I, perchance, know a girl in Chicago, T—— A——. So

told him I'd met T——'s husband only few nights before, and that he had letters to French family, the
W——s. Did he, *par hazard*, know them? Did he
know them? "Ma foi—I am Jean W—— myself!"

To Abri with him—"Boules à Gauche." All French
audience, but three Americans came in later. Made a
lot of racket, kidding actors—all the usual prankery of
undergraduates in liquor. Shared disgust of rest of
audience, and pained to find one of them was B——
H—— of Cleveland.

Tues. 13th.—Rien à signaler. Spent most of day
hunting Sen. J. Ham. Lewis.

Wed., 14th.—Got Rep. C—— of Michigan, and
took him to war. Very much higher caliber than other
specimens. At Meaux picked up two French journalists.
M. Ginisty of *Petit Parisien*, and M. Maurice Soulié,
of *Le Matin*, and also author of many musical comedies,
including "Girl from Rector's"—a quiet, scholarly,
curiously youthful gentleman of 61. Strange story of
his life. Development arrested until about 20, and re-
membered little or nothing prior to that age.

Frenchmen not interested in pictorial side—smashed
buildings, shell-pitted hillsides, endless columns of supply wagons etc. Bent on "local color" in daily life
of *les soldats Américains*.

Took them to —th Infantry, just *en repos*. Got some
of officers together and begged them to spin some yarns.
Frenchman particularly interested in Germanism in U.S.
Knocked over by first tale. A company lost contact with
supports, and left with flanks exposed. Several hundred
yards away a body of troops, but friend or foe, nobody
knew. So officer in charge called for volunteer to

cross intervening space, under heavy machine gun fire, to find out. First to step up a sergeant of pure German blood. "Hell," he said. "The Boche won't kill one of their own." Miraculously, he returned whole, with desired information—and received citation for D.S.C.

Frenchmen dumfounded to learn what large proportion of Germans in this regiment. When they learned that this regiment had earned some fame for taking prisoners "for identification purposes only" they were aghast. And when they were told that one entire company, without exception, was made up of university graduates, they threw up their hands.

They had heard of Yank mascot habit, and were much interested. So, for them, asked if this outfit had mascot. No—but they had Johnny. Temporarily out with the boys, watering the mules. A lad of twelve, it appeared, father dead, mother disappeared, sister on the town, etc., who had adopted the regiment. Came in presently, diminutive lad, dressed in O.D. correct to smallest detail of insignia. Looked frightened when he saw the two civilians. Ginisty spoke to him in French. Boy looked up, half defiantly. "No spik French!" Evidently afraid he might be taken away. But officers said whole regiment idolized him, and would need a division, at least, with heavy artillery, to get him away. Had a fund for him, and intended to take him to U.S. for education.

Visited grave of Quentin Roosevelt, on spot where he crashed. Curious twist in German nature: bodies of fliers always interred, usually with some ornamentation; but ordinary soldiery left to rot where they fall. Roosevelt's grave surrounded by curious mélange of things, partly work of Hun, partly our own. An old rifle, a broken trench knife, a row of white stones, rude wooden cross, several bunches of wild flowers, some fragments of the wrecked plane, and a bottle, containing his name. Spot been surveyed by engineers, for post-war monument, probably.

Lunched at a spot with brand new cross, bearing name P——, —th Inf., U.S.A. Two feet away, a battered old board, name half obliterated—and date—August, 1914. Underneath, no doubt, bodies of Gaul and Teuton. Been fighting over this field for thousand years. Wonder if they'll ever find better way?

Tempted by first "souvenir." A skull I stumbled over, nearly breaking own neck. Perfect for small jardiniere, with top already neatly removed. But an appropriate poppy grew in it, so let it lie. "On Hohenlinden when the sun was red, and Yser rolling rapidly." "I do not know, my son—but it was a glorious victory."

Speeding through La Ferté, held up by convoy, and group of horsemen clattered by—B—— J—— leading. Jumped off horse, as usual, equal to situation. Said he wished he was French, so he could kiss me. Just out of Marne show. Time only for few hurried words, to note the British decoration, to see his old smile, to have him say how much he liked being with his "boys." And then —a quick clasp of the hand, a frankly tearful wave. Wonder if we'll ever meet again?

Missed train. Dined in Meaux. To Paris by motor. Pitch black night, and no lights on car. A nerve-wracking ride.

Thur., 15th.—Life here ought to give most apathetic patriot a wild and lyric enthusiasm for the American soldier. Not only as fighting man, but as *man*. Gentleman, in truest sense of word, splendidly disciplined, and yet, as L—— (Dutch journalist) says, with *freeman*

written on every act, sounding in every word. No soldier
could be more completely respectful to his officers, more
docile under rigid discipline, and yet be so completely
and candidly His Majesty, the American Citizen.
Has dignity, charm, and a helpful friendliness enormously appealing. The Yank has proved himself as his
best friend never thought he could. Proud to be of
same breed.

Met B——. Many vicissitudes in way of schools,
and just graduating from anti-aircraft school. Urged
possibilities of that line. Took me to Brentano's and
consulted work on solid geometry. Finished, ere begun!

Fri., 16th.—Ordered to take Sen. J. Ham. Lewis to
British Front. Made hasty preparations. Ordered not
to. Senator's explanations to French of his function in
U.S. *"Le fouet"* of the Senate. French failure to
understand.

Letter from J—— S——: "You're right about war
being over in Sept. or Oct.—but in *1923*. Don't kid
yourself, son, it won't be over for a hell of a while.
You've got the wrong dope."

Letter from R—— D—— wondering why *gardes
barrières* are always pregnant, and *chefs de gare*, always
cocus.

Abortive air raid, shared with Rev. H——.

Sat., 17th.—Met E—— deL——. War for another
year, his opinion. Curious fellow. Roman Catholic,
looks like Jew, born in Spain, lives in France, job in
N.Y., speaks every language, and *intime* with big-wigs
everywhere, especially Germany. Comes straight from
an E. Phillips Oppenheim novel.

Office all day, making arrangements for visiting
Spaniards.

To dance at Passy apartment. Doubtful, de-national-ized—probably de-natured—women, and soft, effeminate Red Crossers, S.O.S. fellows in *tenu de fantaisie,* etc. Poisonous atmosphere.

Sun., 18th.—Debate with Rev. H—— Subject: as-sininities of religion. No decision. Beyond that—*rien.*

Mon., 19th.—Met P——R——, en route to line. Perfectly certain he's going to be shot. Unshakably fatalist, and resigned. No amount of argument could shake him.*

Saw R—— L——, private, M.C. Extremely dirty. Said sadly he was looking for some one to make world safe for *aristocracy.*

Funny how drop of alcohol acts as lens to bring out subvisible femininity of boulevards. Bacchus, Venus, et Cie. Strong corporation.

Tues., 20th.—Routed out of bed with orders to take Rep. B—— of Minnesota, and *wife,* to Meaux. Mr. B., totally *blind.* Progress slow because he had to stop and *feel* every shell-hole, scarred tree and pitted wall. 4:30 before we reached Fère-en-Tardenois. Suggested turning round. Bawled out handsomely. Explained going further meant all night, and sleeping arrangements at Front for visitors, especially ladies, not of best. Pleasant remarks about "tin soldiers afraid to stay out all night." Kept temper and explained further that advance C.O.'s not too cordial to visitors, and because of ration-shortage, orders out to feed none. "Take me to your commander! *I'll* show 'em what orders to take."

*Never touched, but died by his own hand in 1925.

Demurred at that, and he made comment to wife about "God damned kid officers, etc." Nice fellow.

About enough, I thought. Ordered chauffeur to return. But before leaving, dropped into "Y." The Sec'y much amused at tale. "Don't take them back," he said, "We'll fix 'em up for night, somehow—and give him taste of war he won't forget."

My charges puzzled at being told that Front was miles away, and by "Y" fellow that we were *in* it. Couldn't understand that you can be very much at "Front" many miles before you can see a Hun. Shells and planes travel far.

Went to Roosevelt grave. In ten minutes, throbbing high over head, Boche plane. Dropped like stone to 300 meters, circling. Had seen our staff car, and come to investigate. Expected machine gun activity—open prairie and no cover. Suggested we move on—without delay. To which incredible B—— made ironic comment, anent some people's courage, etc. The chauffeur saved situation. Took B——, dumped him in car without ceremony, and stepped on gas. Highly practical youth, that driver!

On to Chery. Stayed just long enough for C.O.'s tearful entreaties to get our God damned car out of way, as Fritz had been dropping heavy stuff all day.

Then to crossroads, shelled vigorously all day, but comparatively quiet at dinner hour. Only *comparatively*, though. No place for prolonged visit, and chauffeur went through like beam of light. Guest's only articulate comment: "That one was pretty close, wasn't it?" Suggested going back for measurement, but he declined.

Next visitor I get who insists on *seeing* war, will crawl half a mile on his belly through a *boyau*, well floored with mud and human excrement. It'll be at night, and he'll creep over decomposing Germans, sleep in a mud-puddle, and eat his breakfast on the flank of a horse nine days dead, scraping the corpse flies from his bread, when his hands aren't occupied with lice on his own person. He'll see "the Front," all right!

Fairly lively night. Plenty of shelling, planes buzzing overhead, and a number of bombs in vicinity. Visitors properly thrilled: but chauffeur groused bitterly. Said "camping out" was no fun for him, and he got no thrills out of sleeping on bare boards.

Wed., 21st.—All over sector hunting some regiment that wasn't there. Finally stopped beside —th Engineers, building roads. Had to call in men, and Mr. B—— for 56 minutes in the sun, gave address.!

Politicians—like them not. Insincere, wishful of effect, and so crafty. Ugh!

Of Y.M.C.A., *au contraire*. These fellows here—personally charming, working so hard, at menial jobs, and at considerable risk. One under fire, without relief for 5 wks. All of them working harder, longer and with less conveniences, than most army officers. All over 30, real fellows, in no sense professional uplifters. Smoke, drink, swear as befits, etc. One told following story on colleague:

He was delivering lecture on beauties of a pure life. "I," said he, "take a long walk every night, followed by a cold shower and a brisk rub. Then I jump into bed and feel rosy all over." Paused at this point, and plaintive voice from back of hall pipes up: "Go on, mister. Tell us some more about Rosie."

Another one: Negro stevedore came to regimental doctor, asking to have head examined. Doctor complied but could find nothing wrong. "What makes you think there's something the matter with your head?" he queried. "Dere mus' be, boss," was the reply. "If dey wasn't somethin' de matuh wif ma head, I'd nevuh be in dis here wah."

Back to Paris by night, Sgt. M—— (chauffeur) says to cheer up: Liberty Loan campaign starting soon, and Congressmen will return to States.

Thur., 22nd.—*Rien à signaler* but extreme heat and touch of dysentery.

Fri., 23rd.—Ordered to take Sec'y Roosevelt and party to Chaumont. Ordered not to.

Met Julius Rosenwald. Vigorous, wholesome type, not at all *avisé*. As proud of his catalogue as any author of his novel. Don't know what he's here for. Neither does he. Who *does* know why he's here?

Universal talk of what we'll do "next year." My own notions look silly.

Newspaper comment on overseas cap—"brimless, peakless, permits all the sun to strike where it will cause the maximum of discomfort, and in the rain is so designed as to collect all the water in ingenious little pool, the edges of which melt at frequent intervals, depositing water down neck."

Full moon. Stood on Pont de l'Alma at midnight, pondering the fact of human existence. A singularly over-rated institution—Life. Emotions probably consequent upon sluggish bowels.

Sat., 24th.—To Base Hospital No. 9 to see D——. Tragic case. Unblemished record. Then tight, one night, picked a hooker and fell—first time. "*N'y á pas que le premier pas.*" Got everything there was.

Dined with C—— M——, J—— B—— and S——
H——. All pessimistic about war. My own hopes of
early settlement vanished, but prophesied everything
over by Nov. 15. Laughed at.

Sun., 25th.—With Congressmen R—— (Cal.),
B—— (Ky.) and W—— (Utah) visited Base Hospital
at Neuilly. Facial wards—horrible and yet marvelous.
"Before and after" photographs. And the faces—*obliterated* . . . no possible "after." Has the Lord ordained that from this hideous mangling of flesh beautiful things should come? The decaying, fetid flower
by the roadside, sweetening the fields of to-morrow
. . . hard to find meaning in torn bodies and torn
hearts, forget the shining grains of life ground between
stones of circumstance to make bread that will nourish
souls as yet in the making.

Old surgeon, still sensitive to pain, but with thoughts
ahead. The individual—a stone in wall—chipped,
broken, fitted. Sees more than *Schrecklichkeit.* Not
fighting Germans, nor they us. Both against ever-vital
powers of darkness, both groping toward light—victory, in the end, to both.

Beyond the Rhine, the same agony. The justness of
the cause, of no moment. Men suffer gloriously in un-
just causes, too. The big thing the immolation
on the altar of a cause—fitting and chipping the million
stones that new bit of wall may rise along the eternal
road.

Grotesque analogy—the German, as carrier of a
bacillus. Slaughter the plague-bearing rat—in blood
wash the plague away. So the slaughter of men, that
a new order may bless his children. Fruits of victory to
German, as to us. Though we *seem* to fight each other,
to the thoughtful gods who watch on Valhalla, it is

but man struggling upward another step on the long road which he is ordained to travel, and whose end, lost in the mist, he knows not.

Homage to the nurses. Few motives, and simple, lead men to war. Compulsion, pride, thirst of adventure. But these girls—a thousand adjectives, and subject not touched. For lives so splendid, one needs an incense of respect more fragrant that any that comes of ink. Eloquent enough, words that came through clenched teeth of one poor devil, writhing in pain: "By Christ, you gotta hand it to 'em!"

Can't evade it—there *is* sublimity in war. Man made in mold of divinity, and more than a flavor of his origin still clinging to his soul. The cheer of these lads, their quiet grave resignation, too beautiful for marring touch of praise. Life has buffeted .them sorely: for some it has not yet given its hardest blows. But no quarreling with terms of the game: they carry on.

One comes away from this eddy of human wreckage, a little sick at heart. But one presently forgets the bodies shattered, the faces marred, the freshness of lives become stale and useless, and remembers only that "God fulfills himself in many ways." The singular evangelism of blood. Coming out of this shadow-place into the sunlight, with some new measure of religion. Not freshened respect for dusty words, moldy thoughts, stupid priestcraft, fantastic divinities—*no!* But the soul is revived in this tabernacle of agony, and one comes out from the temple as from a revelation, more religious, essentially, more ready to bend the knees in simple worship—of *man!*

This all sounds like a "Y" Sec'y, 4 days over! Blah, perhaps. Not expressing what I feel. Words can't, damn it!

Lunch with Julius Rosenwald. Crude, unpolished,
naïve, but genuine and likable and worthy of respect.
Very friendly and democratic, stopping soldiers on
street to introduce himself and get their names, so
that he could write home about them. Not subtle, but refreshingly direct and honest. Disdainful
of money, per se, but proud that world knows his
business.

Had to smile at Carl Sandburg's conception of J.R.,
when he wrote his bitter articles. Carl right, perhaps,
but only half. Sees only injustice, and tries to per-
sonalize it. Damning millionaires, forgets that they are
humans. Forgets, also, his own weaknesses. Rosenwald
seems so very wrong on so many things. But not smug.
His soul not dead. Only those who are neither big nor
right, shelled in their own contentment, worthy of being
hated.

My poor parents! How perplexed they have been
through the years, their first-born, apparently intelligent
enough, so full in promise of a sort, dreaming along,
heedless and irresponsible, yet so strangely willful. They
haven't understood. Nor have I myself. It comes over
me that my life, so far, has been a pensive drift toward
understanding, a tasting of life here and there, in some
ways, as of love, drinking surpassing deep, and all as
a preparation for something only dimly grasped. At
times a curiously vivid feeling that it was all to a purpose, that though to all outward view, stagnant, that
none the less I was moving toward a something which
would be in some measure fruition of it all, a gathering
together of loose threads. It has been a conviction
almost mystical, a placid faith in my own star, that one
day, when I had sat on my stone by the slow moving
waters long enough, I would rise up, and that then they

would see that my pensive waiting had not altogether been in vain.

Here by my window, watching the clouds rolling slowly by, I see symbolry in them. I have seen clouds of many sorts, and some I have taken apart to assay their quality. It comes over me, elusively, vanishing when I try to pin it, but ever returning, that the long years of sitting by the window, and going down occasionally into the street, are drawing to an end. That now is coming the time appointed, when what I have seen there shall be brought together, and set down. That perhaps, now, those who have waited and wondered, and wept a little, may have some reward for the patience that has been theirs.

A dreaming thought, a reverie I would not voice to aught but S——. The dear dream of my life that she may one day find justice for her faith in me. Above the clouds, as it grows dark, is a soft, unwinking star. It has always been there, never wavering, brightest in the blackness of the night. It is the one thing I pray to—that its pure light may not have burned in vain.

The unutterably stupid Germans! Not yet to have learned, what all her spies know, that the will to victory on our side is now practically universal, and stronger than ever before. What was once hyperbole—"peace in Berlin"—is now a conviction.

The Yanks thoroughly aroused, thinking they have Jerry on the run. And with a savage but understandable desire to shell German towns—which, sure as next summer comes, they'll do.

Against the Hun is a new, competent, and increasingly powerful army, which has tasted victory and found it sweet. The more it has, the more it will want. He ought to recognize that the game is up.

The day when his army definitely cracks may be a
year off, or nearer. But when that day comes, the crack
at home will be simultaneous, and the whole fabric
which has frightened us for so long will crumple up.

No long, tedious fighting progress toward Berlin.
The fire will be out long before that.

Mon., 26th.—Party of Congressmen to Front. B——
(Ky.), W—— (Utah), J—— (Texas), R—— (Cal.),
A—— (La.). Route No. 1. Through Belleau, etc., to
Fère and return.

Chief interest of party—souvenirs. Half the time
spent collecting iron. Only thing they had more of was
misinformation. Got so tired of their digging through
rusty scrap iron, asking "And what's this, Lieutenant?"
I'd answer: "Oh, part of fuse on German 4000 milli-
meter shell." Probably piece of jam-tin.

Lord, what questions! "How deep are the dead buried?" Etc. Tried to answer honestly, at first—which
meant "I don't know" 99% of time. But was human.
By end of day had Munchausen looking like a piker.

On lovely hillside near Vesle, observed two men and
horse pass suddenly to a happier life. A second bang on
other side of road indicated advisability of going hence,
without tarrying in process. Some glory, perhaps, in
impending progress of shell while leading a charge; none
whatever while merely showing Congressmen the scenery. Nothing more ignominious than appearing in
casualty lists under "Accidental Deaths."

Great stuff for visitors, though. Thrilled at being
able to go home and tell everybody what it feels like to
be "under fire." My thrills all gone. Most satisfactory
visitor, Swiss from Zurich—extreme interest in Meaux
Cathedral, and very little in distant rumble of guns.

To-morrow, 3 Congressmen—section of Naval Affairs Committee of House—for 3 days in sector. Talk with enthusiasm of "camping out." Not so keen myself. Prefer a bed. Hope to scare them into early return. Only, knowing so little, it takes a lot to scare these birds— and got to get pretty damned well scared myself!

Average of intelligence among Congressmen seen so far, makes for wonder at what Binet of Congress would reveal. But it's their God damned *frivolity* that infuriates. Treat the war as circus, put on for their especial benefit. Most of them here as nothing but curiosity seekers, getting material for re-election campaigns, and be able to talk familiarly of "the brave boys Over There." Keen for getting pictures snapped "on the battlefields." Etc.

Sen. Lodge's speech, with its *jusquauboutismes* ought to bolster the Junker contention that they're fighting in self-defense. Americans—those well removed from Front—bitterest of bitter-enders. Curious how a little personal experience of H.E. tempers passion for triumphal march down Unter den Linden. If a storm-brigade of editorial writers, officered by politicians, were put on the line, the old war would be over in 45 minutes.

Next best thing, the raising of the draft age. The oldsters won't see any war, of course, but they're having a beautiful scare. There's a ludicrous rushing around here, in search of commissions. Hard put to it achieving safety commensurate with honor.

An election in England about Nov. 17. Simultaneously, Hun going to make most serious effort for peace, yet. Even to surrender. A military defeat to the Junker interest. If he gives up, not licked, there's always room for the contention that he quit too soon.

Unconditional surrender rapidly becoming Allied

slogan. I see no peace until Germany accepts it. So no return to fireside for another year. Horrible thought, but facts must be faced. Nothing on other side but purely superstitious "hunch."

How I thought, when I first got here, that the pangs of *mal du pays* would ease with time. Vain hope!

Tues., 27th.—Visited sanitary train, with M. Ginisty. All Pullmans and spotless. G. tremendously impressed. Took me, then, to see corresponding train of French— box cars, of the "Hommes 48, Chevaux, 8" type, dirty straw on floor, and iron racks for stretchers. In early days, he said, no straw or iron racks. Just piled the wounded in—some survived.

Wed. 28th.—Took Mons. S——, Municipal Councilor of Zurich, to war. Copious notes. Much struck with Belleau Wood, and fought that battle all over again. Getting very good at it. Talk now so they think I fought it.

Old woman at Lucy-le-Bocage. Living in a tar paper shelter—God knows on *what*. Furniture, cow, chickens —everything gone. One son killed, other a prisoner. Twice a refugee, 1914, 1918. "*Embêtant—oui, que c'est embêtant, ca*" all she'd say. Goes every day to put flowers on graves of *les Américains—ces beaux garçons* —"in place of their mothers."

Thur., 29th.—W—— L—— in office. Genial *bavardeur*. Certainly learned the army game, that boy! Could talk himself into anything.*

Sore throat, grippy, and low in spirits. 250th day out of Hoboken. Wish to hell I'd stayed there.

---

*Now a brilliant banker-promoter, with large achievements behind him, and probably larger ahead.

Fri., 30th.—Left in navy car at 8, with bos'n, admiral or something, driving, and Rep's W—— (Tex.), O—— (Ala.), and H—— (N.Y.), House Naval Affairs Committee. Found they had provided themselves with bedding rolls, and enough food for a battalion. All set for long campaign.

From Meaux, Oulchy-le-Chateau, etc., picnic lunch, en route, to Hdqtrs, —th Div. at Fère. Difficult traveling at Front without knowing changing battle maps. So Lt. W——, aide to C.O., came aboard ship.

Misty weather, and able to reach points ordinarily impossible. One spot on hill, directly over Bazoches, not 200 yards from Boche machine guns. *Beaucoup* shells, one near enough to spatter visitors with earth—tremendously thrilled.

Stumbled into gas pocket in ravine, but safely out. One fellow been caught. Still alive when fished out, but future problematical.

At one spot, under observation, warned charges against exposing selves. No sooner said than three heads popped up. No casualties, however.

Back to Div. Hdqtrs. Reported to Gen. A—— that I had 3 Congressmen in tow. He cursed vividly, seeming to blame me for it. But all sweetness when they came in. Generals know who pays their wages. Had them in to his mess, I left outside with the help. What the hell's a lieutenant? Felt like a step-child.

Visitors wanted to sleep out—"just like the boys do." Found nice smooth board for myself in ruined château, wrapped myself in handkerchief, and pretended for some hours I wasn't frozen.

Sat., 31st.—Went forward, overlooking Thibaut and Bazoches. Boches did their stuff for occasion. Scared —though not scared so much as by efforts of statesmen to accumulate souvenirs in shape of unexploded shells. Despite watchfulness, one succeeded in hanging panier of three 77's on back of car.

Gen. A——, good type. Not so keen about aides. Next step in animal kingdom to *amœbæ*. Lunch with Gen. J—— at Brigade H.Q. Charming *gentleman*, and thorough soldier. When a brigadier's polite to a Lt. he's a 14 karat. Curious riffraff of troops—N.Y.'s East Side. No wonder division's known as "The Traveling Circus."

Mr. H—— provided excitement. Saw empty shell case hanging from tree. Cracked it with bayonet he'd picked up. Sudden energy in vicinity. He'd given gas alarm! Certainly have to watch these birds every minute!

Knights of Columbus—frying doughnuts. Great lads. Most popular with troops—probably because they're further ahead than anybody—and no charge for anything. Too damned much *business* to "Y."

To Corps Hdqtrs. Gen. Bullard asleep—told he couldn't be waked. Did it myself. Looked bad for moment, but beat him to it by announcing rank of visitors. Hell of a thing to wake a man to! Student type, and charming, once awake.

Route No. 1 again. Roosevelt grave, etc. Tawdry sentimentality of visitors. Only variation, gang of niggers disinterring bodies. Sweet job.

Back to Div. Hdqtrs. at 5. Same bed, but more comfort, thanks to straw provided by French orderly. Fritz put on grand bombing party, and H—— D——, exquisite musician, offset it with battered old piano. Charming fellow. Memorable night in dugout, talking art and such matters, with him—in French! *Un copain!*

September, 1918

Sun., 1st.—Breakfast with "Spare Parts" mess. Good lads. Stole Congressmen's food and contributed to mess. On road again. Visitors satiated. All the war their natures craved. Especially when made to see more of Graves Registration Service—digging up isolated cadavers and placing them in one grave. A body, after three or four weeks of Nature's work, no lovely spectacle. Tried to make charges see that war something more than glorified hippodrome.

Not entirely successful. Fully convinced they've seen war at close range—actually lived daily life of soldier. Been shot at, all right, but not enough to have professional attitude. Their thought, when they hear sizzling whistle of an "arrival," is, "How exciting." Haven't yet learned how exciting it is to duck for nearest funkhole.

The navy driver learned that quickly. Least curious of party. No desire whatever to see Front, admitted it frankly, and went under car at least provocation. Said he didn't like war, and saw no sense pretending to.

More souvenir-collecting on road back. Constant vigilance price of safety! "Oh, lieutenant—what's this?" Found Congressman kicking unexploded *potato masher*. Found Mr. W——'s coat pockets suspiciously stuffed—proved to be several grenades—also unexploded.

Lunch with Div. Supply Train—nice crowd—and on

187

to Paris.   Arrived with car looking like Salvage Corps truck, but visitors all happy.   Enough lying-material for the rest of their lives.

Mon., 2nd.—Rec'd orders transferring me to Field Censor's Hdqtrs. at Meaux.   "Moving up to the Front." No details.

"Listened in" at examination of prisoners.   All of opinion that war must end before Christmas—in some form of negotiated peace.   Failing that, next Spring, in Germany's complete exhaustion.   Fifty-fifty.   In back of my head mystic number "17"—applied to November. Rot!

Tues., 3rd.—Out to Meaux.   Wondering what my job is.

Wed., 4th.—Reported Press Section Hdqtrs.   Took couple French journalists to Soissons, etc., and back via Fère.   Found —th Div. on move.   Back at 7.   Dined with Gen. Gouraud—i.e., in same dining room.

Thur., 5th.—Nothing much all day, except listening to correspondents fabricate their dispatches.   First question of H—— B—— on appearing: "Well, how many towns has —th lost *this* morning?"   Pressmen been crustily treated by —th: result—pan it at every chance.

Dined with M. Soulié.   Said I "thought like Frenchman"—highest compliment Frenchman can give.

Fri., 6th.—To Soissons, St. Thibault, Bazoches, etc., with Miss D—— and Mr. F——.   Imbecilic but docile pair.   Did everything told not to do.   Insisted on going into Soissons.   Town full of gas, and didn't know how to use masks, so wouldn't let them. Much put out. One thrill not on program. Watching battery near Vesle. Gun burst. Narrow escape. 8″ fragment finished No. 2. Another piece slit coat sleeve. Fell down on nose. *Blessures* severe—but no wound stripe. Not even walking casualty. Sore face but no glory.

C.O. quick witted. Ordered remaining gunners to another piece. Saved their nerve. Gun-bursts not so common as formerly. High rate of firing then. But steel, same as men, got to rest between jobs. Rate reduced— bursts also. Though French calculate that loss from bursts less than advantage gained in rapid fire. 75 once shot 20 a minute. Rarely more than 6 now. But fuses exceedingly sensitive, and factors of dirt and carelessness always present.

Detachment plodding along in blistering sun. Lt. commanding carrying as heavy pack as any. Asked what for. Said: "When I have the damned thing on I know when the boys need a rest." Competence and conscientiousness of our junior officers something to be proud of.

Dined Château Thierry. Complaint from visitors of "service."

Acute dyspepsia. Nothing else to report.

Sun., 8th.—Solemn high mass in Cathedral, commemorating first victory of Marne. If Gallieni had had planes as well as taxis, war would be over now. Very moving sight. Drums and *clairons*. Poorly dressed old men, carrying flags of communal and labor societies. Stirring sermon by Archbishop of Arras.

France forever gay—except at occasions like this, when mask is lifted. The Frenchman, temperamentally, a rotten Protestant. And too rational to be Catholic. Ancient struggle of head and heart.

Clever, the Germans. But in no important virtues have they even approximated French. Swine in victory. Ignoble in defeat. Boor among nations, cowardly as cruel. Watching faces in Cathedral, sad yet proud, notion of bloody Hun that he could ever impose will on them becomes absurd.

Pomp and circumstance of churches, flowers over graves of those gone, symbolry and mysticism, prayers, incense—all dead leaves of tree long since crumbled in dust. Mummery of children. But of no importance what we believe, what ideals we die for. Our gods may be of clay. But if we *think* them gods, perhaps they *are*. Nothing, bad or good, save as thinking makes it so.

Lunch with H——. Disgusted with life. "Two years in army and haven't done an honest day's work." So many anxious to get back to *work*—not destruction. But perhaps this is not all destruction. Maybe not building a new world, but strengthening foundations a little. Trouble is, we're down with pick and shovel. Want to go back upstairs and finish mural decorations. And without uniform, without bosses, without being *hurried!*

So B—— H—— is drafted! Lots worse fates. One, wondering what you ought to be doing. Enlisted man has less comfort. But less worry. And only one person to look after!

Advantage in being drafted—no use stewing. Can't move. Volunteer cursed with *choice*—semblance if not reality. L—— one honest man. Here from bombing school at Langres. Curses self for *embusqué*. Helpless. But isn't sure he'd go back to Infantry if he could. Rather lost taste for trying.

Most of real *embusqués* of Paris seem content enough. But covering up, probably. Secretly, all little Hamlets

—to do or not to do. Some, though, blessed with no imagination. Content to fill niche fate put them in. Others not so lucky. No peace of soul. B—— L——, writhing constantly between glory and Red Cross. Kind of suffering not much talked about—perhaps the worst.

Saw T——. Graduated from Saumur, been to Front, now assigned Base Censor's office, Paris. T.B. probably.

Mon., 9th.—Example of keeping mind off work—sitting on hill above Soissons, watching bombardment of heights beyond, paper in hand, figuring number of bricks required for 7 ft. wall around *lopin** at home. Joy to forget guns and dream of Sears Roebuck catalogue!

Comfort in official report on information gathered from 12,000 prisoners. "Morale lowering rapidly. Only hope—'holding on'." Striking recurrence of "we have been deceived." Food difficulties acute, even in army. Physique deteriorating. Crisis in effectives. Criticism of indecision and vacillation of High Command. Also growing friction between German states. In prison camps, actual fighting between Bavarians, Prussians, etc.

Fritz plainly slipping. Only question, how long it will take to hit bottom. Even with taste for "fresh and glorious war" must look at another winter of it with small enthusiasm. So far, though, no resentment at leaders. Blind, passive resignation to whatever fate dishes up. The perfect soldier. Witless animals, led by the nose—all the way to extinction.

Warnings from home against Demon Rum. Unnecessary. *Défendu.* Beer out, also. Colored liquid of indifferent taste and no potency. Wine a blessing. Mellows, warms and stimulates sense of humor. Case of

*Little patch of ground all one's own: the Frenchman's idea of heaven on earth.

Paris firemen, after air raid, driving wagon up and down Rue de Rivoli, half sounding *alerte*, other half, *berloque*. But no getting drunk on wine. Haven't tried that since night in Bordeaux with D——. Still shudder at recollection. Probably most decorous drunk ever staged, and days of agony following entirely unmerited.

Earnest old ladies in pants over here "investigating" must be disappointed. Less drunkenness in all France than N.Y. can show on one Saturday night. We're strong on bath tubs, Pullmans, express elevators, etc. But for temperance in food and drink, French have us scratched at post.

The *blague* of "leave." Been here 9 mos. and haven't had one yet. Same yarn from everyone I meet. Probably our newness at game. All in rush, etc. Allies get leaves, regardless. A *coup d'état* certain if Frenchman's *perm* held up thirty seconds.

Saw G.H.Q. report on conditions in Italy. French tried to teach them something about war, but Italians too busy to listen. High praise for enlisted man, but nix on officer. Cocky as hell—think they've got Cæsar's blood in them, etc. Bad case of swelled head. Roads on this sector, in back areas, full of Cæsar's descendants, each with hammer and pile of stones. Rifles turned over to barbarians. Censored newspaper spoke of "glorious Franco-Britannic-American victory of the Piave." Every time Italians get too cocky, Allies threaten to shut off coal. Military power of future evidently going to reside where coal and iron do. Nothing else matters much.

Hate this God damned army life—but some don't. Some like it. Most, maybe. Seems as if thing most people hate most in this life, is responsibility—and *choice*. Idea of democracy more and more silly.

Sent home Boche helmet. Make novel and com-
modious gobboon.

Talked with de la C—— about drinking. Told of
M——'s being carted off N.Y., dance floor. "Social
suicide" in France. No prejudice against booze, *per se*,
except few cranks like "Ligue contre Alcool." But supposed to use it with sense. Matter of education. Getting too tight, like bad table manners. Simply "not
done." No *laws*—except public opinion, infinitely
more powerful.

Drollery of having *two* meat courses. Explanation:
Smallness of grain crop, due to man-shortage, and necessity of killing cattle that can't be fed.

Tues., 10th.—Beginning of melancholy days—cold
and damp. Orders to *filer* for Nancy. Rumor big
American push to start soon.

Wed., 11th.—All packed, ready to go—ordered to
stay behind. Felt like step-child. Whole section, and
correspondents, piled off. Nothing to do but sit beside
probably disconnected phone, in deserted office, overlooking malodorous alley, and reflect on vanity of
life.

No one left but little boob of censor—happy at
chance to sneak up to line and see for first time stuff he's
been censoring.

Smoke innumerable Luckies, read all newspapers,
dance solitary clogs in effort to keep warm, and watch
unending rain. Occasionally stroll down to court to
chat with hotel's one and only waiter, ancient gentleman, apparently born in clothes—never since removed,
and whose otherwise perfect French is marred by excess
of mustache and total absence of teeth. Back to silent

phone, play tit-tat-toe, and even *sing* to relieve awful stillness.

> And gentlemen in England now abed
> Shall think themselves accursed they were not here,
> And hold their manhoods cheap whiles any speaks
> That fought with us upon Saint Crispin's Day.

Read *"Ceux qui s'en f . . ."* by Gyp. Interesting picture of French life.

Thur., 12th.—Home folks hoping I'll be returned as "instructor." Fat chance! Only things I know—funk holes between Soissons and Rheims, and more healthful of *abris* along Marne and Aisne. Can also distinguish between departures and arrivals, even to caliber. But that knowledge can't be imparted.

Rumor that big Yank push has started. Moral effect tremendous, regardless of success. According to French G.Q.G., "German of to-day not German of three months ago, or even of July 18, either physically or in morale."

Germans great fighters, en masse. Individually, not so good. Briton, Gaul or Yank could fight to last man against defeat. Not the "invincible" Hun. Remove his conviction of ultimate victory—nothing's left. Nothing to talk of campaign to Rhine and beyond. Hun will be squealing like stuck pig long before that.

Times have changed. No peace by negotiation now. The German a pragmatist. Thinks he's gotten where he is, through force. When thoroughly licked, he'll cease to believe in force. Q.E.D.

Much talk in press about "wanton" destruction of French towns. Nothing of sort. Diabolically system-

atic. Part of plot to ruin France industrially. Looking to an economic war in future.

Mistake to endow Germany with same intellectual
processes as ourselves. Never grown up. Still has
medieval mentality. Charlemagne with machine guns.

Puerile gabble about "punishment." No sincerity
to it. Like wrath of baseball crowd at umpire. How
many prepared personally to blow up German towns,
hang Germans, strangle German babies, etc.?

Even if possible to lay country waste and sell people
into bondage, no positive benefit thereby. Modernize
mens Germanicus—our only assurance of ultimate
safety. How to do it? Ford and Bryan thought German hyena could be tamed with gentle ululations on
ten-stringed humanitarian lute. Used to think, myself,
German *people* amenable to same sort of reasoning as
ourselves. That faith not altogether gone. But got
to realize that our sort of thinking is in Germany in-
hibited and clouded by notions we discarded centuries
ago.

Saw M.P's lugging in drunk. Fought like wildcat,
until a couple of cedar sticks began playing arpeggios
on his stubborn skull.

As Boche mind works now, it responds only to clubbing. Therefore, he must get a clubbing. Got to go
on till he admits he's had enough. Essential he *admit* he's
licked. Got to knock pride out of him. Freed of that,
he'll feel his sore head, and then go for the men, institutions and ideas that have kept him in intellectual short
pants, while the rest of the world is allowed to stay out
nights and carry latch key to doors of truth.

Then, only, can we say war is won. Meantime, talk
of boundaries, treaties, rights of nations, economic agree-
ments, punishments, etc., merely obscure main issue—

which is to make Fritz realize what a nuisance he's been, and, of his own volition, lead a life more in harmony with the date.

How to do? No "negotiations" whatever. To every suggestion of terms, etc., Grant's answer. But no vengeance afterward. And no silly attempts at "guarantees." Can't determine future. Can only make groove for ball of fate and hope it won't jump out.

K——, dispatch rider, has perfect program: "Lick hell out of 'em and then treat 'em decent."

Large part of our "advance" so far, merely German withdrawal. True offensive not yet begun. Success of Foch, to this point, in getting self out of bad hole. Real knockout not in this round.

Le Temps very earnest about pronunciation of "Foch." Says that he's a Basque, and sound a soft *"ch."* Fortunate, since "normal pronunciation would be confused with word not uncommon in England and *les Etats-Unis!"*

Fri., 13th.—Definite news of Amex success. 8000 prisoners.

In to Paris to see if telephone worked. Saw lot of people. All Red Cross going into "gas." The latest thing, evidently.

Feverish—probably got flu. Letter from M——. "Done nothing worse than knock foundation out of fine macadam road, paying homage to passing 105's."

Sat., 14th.—To Meaux, got baggage, and back to Paris on *soi-disant* 5 o'clock. No taxis.

Sun., 15.—Office A.M. *Rien à faire.* Saw W——. Philosopher, takes life as it comes, finding it humorous.

Put in afternoon getting and moving trunk. Lone taxi refused all financial inducement, yielding only on ground of "L'Union Sacrée." Sick. To pension and to bed. Two violent air raids. Stayed abed, not at all happy. Thrills gone from air raids.

Mon., 16th.—Austrian peace offensive. launched. No news from Argonne.

Wire from G.H.Q., ordering me to report Rue St. Anne, *Stars and Stripes.* No idea what for. Reported. Nobody there had idea, either. Comical Pvte. H——. A fiend for saluting. Always snapped to attention when spoken to, etc. *Très militaire,* but a nuisance in a newspaper office!

Back to office to sit on tail till lunch. Fell in with M—— J——, up from Rome. Like everybody, sick of his job. To Crillon for cocktails. Met S—— J—— back from leave and golf at Trouville. More drinks. Ciro's for dinner. 48 fr. Ouch! Saw P—— H——, recovering from wounds and shock incidental to ash-can dropping on him, and quite drunk.

Off to some low dive. Quickly ejected. S——, noisy, quarrelsome, but virtue unassailable. M—— in bad shape. Took him to hotel. Waited outside, while S—— put him away. No signs of S——, so followed. Started upstairs, but stopped by *maître d'hôtel.* Offered to put me out. Full of vim, vigor and *vin rouge,* I said it was public place, and dared him to try.* He called out all the help. Things looking serious. Threatened to call cop. Answered with suggestion he call Paris garrison. In comes gendarme, pulling whiskers—"*Que se passe-t-il donc, hein?*" *Maître d'hôtel* started expla-

---

*The chap was right. Unlike the U.S., a hotel in France is in the eyes of the law, private domain, and I was a "trespasser."

nations. Interrupted with my own. Didn't Monsieur le Gendarme, being man of the world, *comme moi-même,* agree that most of these God damned *hôteliers* were grafters—Portuguese pigs? Clapped his hands. *"Mais que c'est vrai!"* All for pinching maître d'hôtel and waiters. Curtain—cop and I marching out, arm in arm!

Long walk home. Violent rain storm. Blew cap away. Pitch black. On hands and knees, hunting cap all around Etoile. Stalked by cop, very suspicious. Finally overcome by curiosity. Revealed himself. Eplanations. Persuaded me it was hopeless task. home at 2, drenched to skin, and evidently, *un peu sou.*

Tues., 17th.—Orders to report to Col. W——, C.O. Counter Espionage Section, G2, S.O.S.—the more-or-less "secret service." Feeling too rocky to be excited.

Saw H—— B——. Enlisted in navy. Now navigating Paris in command of fleet of typewriters.

Wed., 18th.—Reported to Maj. C—— and R——. Good fellows and competent. Brief exam in ability to manage French. Passed. To go to some base section for few weeks training with British Intelligence. After that, more training with our own. Then job of my own, somewhere. A flat in Baker Street, maybe!

Saw D—— again. Business of sighs. Every man has string of beads, souvenirs of dalliance, one or two, perhaps, with luster of genuine, the rest of glass. But best to keep it, save for fleeting moments of revery, in pocket, along with more practical keys, more necessary purse, and more comfortable pipe.

Thur. 19th.—Left Paris 7:30. International

mélange in compartment.   Jap, silent, and reading. East Indian, silent—doing nothing.   Englishman who kept opening window.   Frenchman, who kept closing it. Serb and Swiss.   Significant of what's coming over world.   Common language—English.

Havre at noon.   Back to spot where first trod soil of France, etc.   Met W—— W——, just arriving in "Y." Made me feel like old vet.

Checked baggage and reported to I.O. Lt. C——, capable and charming, C.O.   Two other officers in training. Studied all afternoon, and Southampton boat control, P.M.   Like Rembrandt picture.   Long tables, with Allied army representatives and French civilian secret police behind, and "fiches"— card in- dex of undesirables underneath.   Passports checked against it.   Met Capt. B—— and Lt. H——, English Green Tabs.   Nice fellows.   Also Sgt. C—— some time Scotland Yard.   Aboard ship for "scotch & soda."

Monsieur C——, Commissaire Speciale de la Surete. *Drole type.*   Incident of Greek—fur collar, etc., "a trifle too Italian tenor."   Standing behind C—— as Greek presented passport.   Whole story in *fiches*—bad egg, German agent working out of Barcelona.   Dum- founded to see C—— hand passport back—*"Tout en règle, monsieur. Passez."*   Smirk on Greek's face.   Evi- dently thought he was putting something over.   Tried to warn C——, but waved aside.   Actually took Greek to boat, introduced him to skipper and expressed hope for pleasant voyage.   Demanded of C—— if he'd gone crazy or blind.   Shrewd smile.   "The French, *mon petit,* are the thriftiest people in Europe. *Bien entendu.* If we jug this *costaud* here, we are put to expense of try- ing and shooting him.   I shall now signal the U.K. to arrange accommodations for him in the Tower—and let our Britannic ally foot the *addition.*"

First lesson in spy-catching!

Fri., 20th.—Awakened at 5 by clatter of field shoes—arriving Yanks, headed for rest camps. Coming by thousands, now.

Busy at office, all day, getting hang of job. Interesting, but difficult and complicated. Moved into billet. Feel like E. Phillips Oppenheim.

Sat., 21st. Studied cipher code and files. To Fox's Bar for cocktails. Dined Francois I. Champagne. Discussion of Jewish influence in French govt. Surprising how many in the Ministries and close to Le Tigre. Suppressed speech of Sen. D——. Probably nonsense, but interesting. Analogous to mistrust of Catholic "influence."

To dive at 8 Rue de Galleon. Singular district. Blacks, chinks, lascars and what not. *Défendu* to Americans and M.P.'s posted. But carry authorization to "Pass anywhere by day or night, either in plain clothes or uniform." Also French pass: *"En raison de son service spéciale . . . est autorisé à passer en tout endroit et à toute heure de jour et de nuit aussi bien en civile qu'en uniforme (au même titre que les agents français de la Sureté).*

Great hit with inmates by singing D——'s: *"Je fais parti d'une société,* etc." Insisted I came from Pas du Calais. Very elaborate house. Mirrors over beds, etc. Wound up in row about champagne. Usual thing. Took us for *poires.* Horns in and handsome apologies for mistake.

Sun., 22nd.—Worked all morning on reports. Bleak weather. Lunch and billiards at Cercle, with C——. Remarkable lad. Extraordinarily mature for years. Commissioned Infantry, transferred G2 in Washington, and trying for nearly year to get back to regiment. No chance. Spent youth in France and knows language and people. Perfect for this job. Very popular with both French and English—no mean achievement.

Tea at Legation with Brand Whitlock and wife. Simple, unaffected people. B.W. "radical," perhaps, by some standards. Seems not to understand French. Obsessed with surface objections, antiquated sewage methods, etc. Likes Belgians very much. No Frenchman does. This place now Belgian capital. Some 70,-000 here—mostly resting. Never heard Belgian referred to as such, in France. Always *salle belge.*

Met Gen. N——, British O.C. Trianon Bar and dinner at Grosse Tonne. Quaint place. In heart of Rue de Galleon district, but run most decorously by Frenchman and daughters. Perfect illustration of French conservatism. Bad Lands developed subsequent to G.T. Never occurred to proprietor to move. Wooden benches, whitewashed walls, sawdust on floor, etc., but superb cuisine and excellent cellar. Very handy to boat control.

Mon., 23rd.—Morning in B.I.O. News of successes in Palestine and Salonique. Rest of war quiet. Not much sign of end. Exasperating.

Story of Mlle. S—— - M—— — C—— party at Deauville. Prominent people—Cabinet Minister, newspaper owner, *grands industriels*, etc. M——'s villa haunt of prominent folk. Great influence wielded by such as she. Her *ami*, C——, captured. Pulled some wires. Liberated in two weeks. Wires evidently reach Berlin. Nothing in U.S. to compare with such women.

Tues., 24th.—Talk with Capt. P——, British I.O. Extraordinary man. Botanist of note, *en civile*, (grandfather invented soda-water!), musician of ability, and very charming. Much interested in growing estrangement between Yanks and English. Voluminous reports on subject. Also G2 reports on Belgium and Germany. The *real* truth.

Pavements resounding day and night, with shuffle of incoming Americans. No effort at concealment. Regimental numbers painted on bass drums. But must give German agents no comfort to make reports.

Wed., 25th.—Advance party —th Div. arrived. Out to see them. Riffraff confined to camp, but J—— M——, being Major, allowed to dine *en ville*. Felt old and case-hardened. Commonplaces so wonderful to them. So full of enthusiasm. Little differences, too subtle for expression. Envious of them, coming over with own troops and going through business just as planned.

Picked up postals with pictures of *Ceinture de Chasteté XVI ème siècle*. From stories of U.S. must be field for these ingenious devices there. Poor little creature, man, and his pitiful efforts through ages to harness vagaries of sex. His principles and habits totally divorced. Difficult to see slightest progress since ejection from Eden. Must be discouraging to moralists —except they never know anything anyway, and so, nothing to be discouraged about.

Interesting—daily *manchette* in *Le Matin.* Shows importance study of English has attained in popular esteem. Probably be world-language when Esperanto, etc., forgotten.

To St. Jouin. Hotel perfect museum, full of paintings and MSS. Run by "La Belle Ernestine," mistress of Albert Besnard, lately deceased, ætat 77. Once haunt of De Maupassant, Flaubert, etc. High above blue waters of La Manche, with rolling Norman hills behind, still remains sanctuary for painters and writers, and ancient fireplace still hears good talk.

Visited Etretat, lovely little bite into Norman coast, where Archbishop still comes every year in all his vestments to bless the fruitful sea. British hospital, where rich used to play golf and sun on the *plage.*

Dinner at Tortoni, with J—— M——, and two other Majors. Very stiff in neck. Constantly "majoring" each other. J—— highly regarded. Character won respect and affection of everybody.

Place full of newcomers, trying to dry up France in one evening. Also full of tarts, with Yanks falling *en masse.* Two of them, E—— and C——, caught my eye. Came over and begged not to spoil game. Agreed, provided they did their part, and reported all information gathered.*

Le cafard! Desire to see S—— and infants assails sometimes with poignancy almost unendurable. Comes suddenly—reminiscent flash of face in crowd, sound of child's voice, etc. Sailed 9 mos. ago to-day. More than that before I return. Hard to be patient.

---

*The amount, variety and value of information gathered this way, was amazing. With *les officiers Américains,* wine, women and a wagging tongue formed an unfailing combination.

Letter from H—— D——. His division moving. *"La musique ne marche plus. Il nous manque, tout simplement, un piano!"**

Thur., 26th.—C——, rare combination of culture, imagination and virility. By pre-war standards, young. But phenomenon of these times that age no index to friendships. One pals with sixteen and sixty. *"Je fais parti d'une société, où sont admis tous les jeunes gens,"* etc.

Found one man sharing optimism about war—N——, British I.O. Bases theories on experience in business with German character. Anticipates no long drawn out retreat, but sudden crumbling, with every damned Boche trying to prove *he* was good Indian. Looks for end before Xmas. The Hun in the ropes and groggy. Bulgaria gone under and Turkey soon with her. Austria hurrying to get warm seat on mourner's bench, and then —*kaput!*

Interesting life, this, but sordid. Behind scenes and see wheels work. Close to French and British, military and civilian, latter Scotland Yard and "flics" of Prefecture. Not as romantic as tired business man gets them in fiction. No secrets, and one long process of disillusionment. As D—— says: "Only through daily contemplation of one's own impeccable virtue one escapes abyss of cynicism."

British mind works more slowly than French. Apt to take things seriously, with consequences sometimes disastrous. Usually a jump or two behind French—

*D——, it was, who one memorable night at Fere-en- Tardenois, pitted one battered piano against a number of Gothas in a raid—and outplayed them!

*blagueurs** always, with love of subtlety. Logical where British are incurably romantic. Case of irresistible force and immovable body. Small wonder they've fought for centuries.

Lunch with G——, Chef de la Sûreté. Unsmiling man with twinkling eye and mind like lightning. Flared in wrath at suggestion that France would become Morocco of U.S. Agreed, however, that idea was good, if we first got ourselves a king. French love to screen serious thoughts in *blague*.

Australians making trouble for English. "Digger" private passed on street by English "brass hat." Former saw nothing. English wrath: "Don't you salute your superior officers?" "Yes" (with unpleasant emphasis on pronoun), "*my* superior officers." Then, spotting English soldier across street: "Hi, Tommy, 'ere's one o' yer fuckin' English hofficers wants t' be saluted. Kindly oblige!"

Clothes beginning to wear out, and forgotten how to tie a necktie. But enough *soap* left for another thirty years.

Days getting wet and cold. Winter en route. No enthusiasm for prospect. Hun probably even less keen. 200,000 prisoners since July 18. *Ça marche.* One explanation, perhaps, in card distributed by planes over German lines, containing facsimile of letter sent home by prisoner, with description of menu. Germans sur-

---

*"Blague," says Prof. Feuillerat, "is the satirical, jesting pretense of not taking seriously what one actually respects—hiding the most sincere convictions under an appearance of cynicism, ridiculing what in one's heart one considers sacred, steeling oneself against emotion and tenderness. *Blague* is certainly the most characteristic of French traits, and the most difficult for a foreigner to comprehend."

rendering ever since, each one with card—all keen to join club!

Fri., 27th.—Bulgar peace offer. Turkey and *les Autriches* next. Hopes for end before Jan. revived.

Marvelous British! Dined with B—— last night, breaking up about 1. Said this morning he'd ordered bath for 10 P.M., and found "batman" waiting for him when he got home, still prepared to offer bath. Picture Yank soldier doing that! B—— saw nothing strange about it. Puzzled at our amusement. Great fellow, J. Bull—who doesn't understand us at all. Nor we, him.

Met way-up British chaplain. Sized us up as having no thoughts above drink and childish gabble, and promptly came down to our supposed level. Thoroughly bored and disgusted. Sincerity the greatest of virtues in a cleric. Nothing worse than one who tries to be "one of the boys." The "boys" wants clerics to be clerics.

To Belgian Ministère de la Guerre. Pathos of situation. Housed in a shack. Complicated Belgian politics—two races, two languages, two habits of thought. Sad—patient confidence that immediately after peace they'll return home and take up life where they left it. Small chance. Post-war problems terrific, and ill prepared to cope with them. They'll need us more than they or we realize.

The more I learn of European politics and what lies behind the countless veils, the more am struck by fact that of all nations in war, U.S. by far the most thoroughly homogeneous and united. All others torn constantly with internal dissension. We alone present perfect front. We the one guaranty of Germany's thorough defeat.

Belgians' nationalistic problem hard to solve, and has led them into foolish and unhappy paths. But can't forget it was her heroic decision to stand against the might of the Hun for a few bloody weeks that saved the Western world. The U.S. may give the *coup de grâce*, but Belgium made it possible.

Wondering how life will be *chez moi*, without wine. Contemplate the possibility of having cellar. Pleasant to go below and come up with dust-covered bottle of Château Yquem, or luscious, velvety Beaune. Curious that where best wines come from, drinking to excess frowned upon. Not much strength to total abstinence societies among French, but nowhere is damnation of drunkard more rapid or complete. Simply isn't done.

Women, too. Western observer, here for week-end, thinks France land of libertine. Fact is, Frenchman's knowledge of life much more profound than ours. Makes us look like children. Frenchmen lament our innocence, and its disastrous consequences. On surface, French morals inferior to ours. But as practical solution of problem, his results vastly better. Pays smaller price for fall of man than we. Less sepsis in his wounds. May lack reticence in speech—not in conduct. "I Cure Men" ads plastered everywhere, but probably no more to cure than we have. His sophistication, in long run, seems more valuable than our head-in-sand policy.

Droll scribble on *pissoir* wall: "Three seconds of Venus . . . three years of Mercury." *Réflections astronomiques!*

And on the wall of a *cabinet d'aisance:* "*C'est ici la ruine du talent—de la cuisine. Hélas!*"

Frenchman not yet perfect—nor near it. Hasn't

discovered woman as much more than female. English language has synonyms beyond number for sin which made Adam's landlord cancel lease. But only one in French—*l'amour*. Hasn't conception of possibilities in word. Saxon way ahead of Gaul in that respect.

C—— and I lunched with two newly arrived men. Scandalized them. Points of view so different. Frivolous, calloused and bored with things that interested them most. Shocked at our disillusionment. The surgeon's attitude. Got to have it or go nuts. Double bridle and stiff hand on emotion.

Letter from T——. Still at C.P.A.L.T. as Administration Officer.

C—— busy pulling strings to get back to regiment. No chance. Nobody gets out of this service. Col. C—— mysteriously influential, with argument we've been too well trained, and know too many secrets to be at large.

Astonishing English! B——, born in France, speaks language, as far as vocabulary, better than most natives. But *accent atrocious!* Asked why he didn't talk so Frenchman could understand. Replied: "Didn't believe in encouraging the beggars." Surprising how few English, out for four years, even begin to speak French. Seem to consider it beneath them.

Contrast—U.S. reception of news of Bulgar defection, bells, whistles, cheering crowds, etc. Here—absolutely nothing. Grave nodding of heads. *Pas mal,* and an occasional *ça gaz, hein*—that was all. Less enthusiasm than at home over news 18th ward had gone Democratic. But great news, despite surface calm, and morale up. German notions of conciliation out of the window. Allies have tasted blood. What had come to seem impossible, so no longer. If one invincible foe could go under, so can another. *Demain—les Autriches.* The end is certain.

Sat., 28th. Spent A.M with Capt. C——, secret ink fellow. Told of latest dodge for carrying ink in bottle labeled venereal disease medicine. Another trick—shoestrings saturated with soluble ink, and dried. Amazing story of ingenuity and counter-ingenuity. Increasingly involved chemistry of it. Up to four reactions.

More Australian trouble. Being sent home "on leave." Laugh at that. No intention of ever coming back. "Let the God damned English finish their own war."

Letter from J—— S——. "While at Havre, keep away from the British navy. They do other things beside sail boats!"

And from R—— D——. "We S.O.S.'ers may not be glorious and heroic, but we're plucky little endeavorers at our daily tasks."

Sun., 29th.—Put in morning on study of Belgian conditions—economic and political. The high-road for German *defaitism.* To G.T. for dinner. First acquaintance of Calvados—colorless liquid, pure alcohol, with faint taste of apples. Felt like calling out fire department. Interesting discussion of real cause of war— Teutonic logic *vs.* Anglo-Saxon game-spirit. N——'s illustration. German attack at Ypres. British busy all day, plugging Boches. Rifles hot. German soldier in canal—can't swim—British Tommy jumps in and rescues him. German incapable of understanding. Why do damndest all day to kill me, and when I obligingly offer to drown myself, prevent it? Those two points of view basis of whole war. Cavell incident another illustration. Undoubtedly everything Germans said she was. But British would have turned her loose, with some grand remark about British lion never touching lady, etc. —loud cheers from gallery. Poor Germans too damned logical. Committed capital military crime. Even admitted it. Had to be shot.

Everybody with pleasant shiner. N——, as usual, pretending to be Yank, by endless repetition of "Wal, I guess," and *spitting!*

Mon., 30th.—Rocky rising. Full of biliousness and noble resolutions. Bulgaria takes the count. Very cold and dreary. Low in stomach and spirit.

One job here ascertaining morale, etc., of new troops coming through. I.P.'s mingle with newcomers and get slant on things. Make individual reports, checking against each other. Strikingly anti-British feeling among Yanks. Much more hostile than toward Germans. Common remark: "When we get through with Jerry, we'll clean up them God damned limeys!"

Incredulity of B.I.O.'s. Provided P—— with detailed report for transmission to War Office. Serious thing.

October, 1918

Tues., 1st.—Tour of shipping with French and British I.P.'s. Captured frightened Spanish tailor from Bordeaux with copy of Karl Marx. Felt like elephant, stepping on gnat.

Got bread tickets by *Système D.** Afternoon in rest-camp areas.

Wed. 2nd.—Nothing much all day. In evening, joined in raid on *bordel.* Navy lads being hunted. Puzzled *sous-maîtresse.* Couldn't understand why *les flics Américains* insisted on bothering lads in their simple, natural pleasures. Complained she was treated as enemy to society, when it was plain to see she was in fact public benefactor.

Thur., 3rd.—Visited C——, Commissaire Spéciale. Droll little man. Think he speaks English, but can't get him to. Calls himself *Monsieur Sait Tout.* Characteristic treatment of spy. Latter came in tears, said he'd been spying for some time, but French people of neighborhood been so kind to him, couldn't bear to keep it

---

*Many words beginning with "d," such as *débarasser,* *débrouiler,* etc., in general signifying to get around. Hence *le système D* signifies all extra-legal procedure. French army, French government, etc., all operate on it. No country has more rules and regulations, less observed. The English had an analogous word in "wangle." We, perhaps, in "graft."

up. C—— told him not to be troubled. Had known all along he was spying. Was, in fact, rather grateful than otherwise, since he'd been rather dumb spy, and furnished excellent channels for news of things that weren't so. '

Counter-espionage developed along those lines. Difficult and costly to catch spy, try him, etc. Much more satisfactory to isolate him, and either feed false information for transmission, or intercept dope he sends. Like talking into telephone with wires cut. Keeps spy busy and no harm done.

To François I. for dinner in honor of R——'s departure. Champagne and much pleasant bicker. But this nightly lushing has got to stop! Wind up in home for dipsomaniacs!

Fri., 4th.—To Rouen with C—— and Lt. L——, M.T.C., as passenger. Visited police H.Q. Interesting personnel. M. le Chef—little man with sallow skin, protruding lead-gray eyes, baleful in expression, but twinkling now and then with humor that few Frenchmen lack. Dark gray beard, almost concealing bloodless lip—perfect picture of M. Lecoq and all his tribe. Tremendous pride in profession and insistence it be recognized. Also, le Chef de la Sûreté, with passion for his *Service de Mœurs*. Showed dossiers of prostitutes. Enthusiastic, full of ideas for control of sex-problem. Also, *Chef du Service Anthropométrique*, equally fanatic. Finding listener familiar with Ellis, Kraft-Ebbing, etc, opened up heart and files.

Saw *"chameau"* in operation—wooden device on which girls examined for disease. Line waiting for inspection—half defiant, half in humiliation. Their records—shocking! Long stretches of disease with intervals of "health." Mathematical chance of not picking up something from average ticketed female on streets, about 1 to 1,000,000.

Lunch with P—— and *adjoint*, Italian, who introduced us to *Vin du Pape Clément*. Called on M. le Comte d'A—— and Capt. L——, British I.O.

Dined at Duclair. Proprietor of little inn, M. Denise, renowned among gourmets. *Caneton pressé* ordered in advance, so ceremonies began immediately on arrival. The *mise en scène*—ancient kitchen, lined with gleaming copper and planished iron. Duck, impaled on huge skewer, placed before specially prepared hickory fire on hearth, with chain device, actuated by hot air in chimney, turning bird slowly around. 22 minutes—exact. Carving, a ceremony in itself. Surrounded by daughters and grandchildren, holding special knives, old man went about work, like poet writing sonnet, with monologue on history of *caneton à la Denise*. Carcass, marvelously dissected, placed in press, and blood extracted. Essential process—gave "quality" to creation. Entrails, cut up, mixed with recondite assortment of spices, blood, *fine* champagne, wine, etc., supplied sauce. Long job, but results a justification. To wash it down, a velvety old Burgundy, selected by Master himself. Had we ordered champagne, probably been thrown out of place!

Ordinary *restaurateur* to M. Denise, what Belasco is to life. His *caneton* not an excuse to extract francs from gullible wayfarer, but expression of himself. His response to our fulsome praise, congratulating him on creation, that of perfect artist: "Everyone says that. It is very good."

No picture complete without frame. As old man spitted duck, L——, the perfect American, said: "I've often had chickens done that way in N'Yawk." And

at the end, as capstone to arch, inquired if it was necessary to "tip the cook."

On way from Rouen, C—— fell asleep, head on
shoulder. Roused such vivid picture—taking family
into town for Sunday dinner. How bravely B——
would begin, sitting beside me, his little legs sticking
straight out. And how, about half way, his head would
nod and he would tumble over against my arm. Sweet,
gentle little lad . . . so many pictures come back to
dim the eyes.*

C—— showed me letter from mother, with "you
brave boy," "splendid courage," etc., in it. Helpless
oath and query as to what I did in like case. We loom
large through haze of distance—an optical illusion.

Back to Havre. Wondering where path leads now.
New I.O. at Nice. May go there. Also to Nantes.
But what's use of dreaming? Whatever you expect in
this God damned army, some order comes along and
knocks it out.

Many people now believe in peace this year. But as
peace now dependent on unconditional surrender, no
telling how long it will take to achieve it. Evacuation
of Belgium, from all signs, imminent. How long can
they hold shorter lines? The end so certain, the delay
exasperates.

Sat., 5th.—Popular notion that spy-catching's maze
of romantic intrigue, about as right as most popular notions. Spying, most of it, pretty sordid business of
selling out to highest bidder. Counter-espionage—
raising the ante. Silly ideas of "underworld." Crime
as unnatural as indigestion, and about as romantic.

---

*Just finished administration of corporeal punishment to same
gentle lad for bumming from school. Times change.

Cold, dreary weather, with spirits to match. Nothing to report save end of daylight-saving. About time to be transferred somewhere. *Où? Je m'en fou!*

Sun., 6th.—Central powers ask armistice! Anticipate no immediate results. U.S. papers probably flaunt headlines: "Hun Asks Peace." They haven't. Won't be armistice, and Hun knew it when he asked for it. Not clear what his motives were. Probably for home consumption. Rejection will support contention he's fighting for fireside. But also confession that victorious or Deutscher peace now beyond hope.

Only thing left for Hun is fight with back to wall. Beginning of disintegration. Convinced that Austria and Turkey ready to give up ghost.

As cold, wet and generally dreary evening as Norman coast can produce. Tired of talk and dined *solus* on *plage*—tender juicy *tournedos*, with *pettis pois*, very sweet and delicate, and Beaujolais, 1903, with sunshine of Burgundy in every drop. One of numerous friendly cats shared chair, and waiter, *réformé*, with more ribbons than Turk, supplied talk. Needed cheering and got it. Madame's *au revoir* seemed more than professional.

High regard for Jimmie Hopper's articles. Also Mc-Nutt's. Seen stuff they write about, and still approve. Contrast with lot of so-called war-correspondents.

A great job, this—learning dark and devious ways of fellow man. Makes for cynicism, the police point of view, belief that all men, certainly all women, have price. All illusions gone about character so dear to magazine editors—the spy. Rarely romantic. Sometimes not even clever. Often with less courage than cornered rat.

Curious that experiences have come in such undra-

matic sequence that I have no sense of what is worth
recording. Significant that I should write in detail of
dinner. Later, perhaps, in retrospect of time and distance, may regain sense of proportion as to *here*—lose
it as to *there*. Long before I'll get over simple wonder
of *water*—hot and running!

Letter from B—— H——. Attitude toward Hun.
The more one suffers personally, less violent hate for
enemy. Being shelled, impossible not to feel sympathy
for chap on other side, getting same thing.

Many Boche prisoners coming through here, many of
them freshly wounded. Such pitiful cattle. Is Teuton
of to-day different and dirtier clay than rest of us?
Sometimes think so. Treacherous, cruel, cowardly,
without honor. But any river dirty near sewer. When
source of his iniquities blown up and swift flowing time
done its work, with sunshine of truth and oxygen of
common sense to help, German waters will run sweet
again.

Can't feel friendly toward 1918 model Fritz. Had
a touch of Kultur in lungs, and hardly enjoyed Kriegs-
herr's holiday. But can't hate unborn children. Even
in funk-hole, compressing carcass into size and shape of
cabbage, pretending to be grateful for gas-mask, chief
thought one of pity for fools who've brought it about.
Fritz just as unhappy as we are. Bleeds and dies, just
as gloriously, according to lights, and over graves:
"Here rests . . . for God and Fatherland."

Sitting in muddy shell-hole, listening to that dam-
nable *whee-e-e* overhead, no comfort to reflect that four
thousand miles away some slob, his fat belly cushioned
in arm-chair, is telling neighbors Hun should be punished for crimes.

Germans, and *a* German—so different. Fishing

through poor torn pockets of shabby German body, drooped over wreck of machine gun, to find well-thumbed photograph of woman and little boy and little girl—so like one's own . . . impossible to hate what had been that body.

Nothing so revolting as bitter, pitiless cruelty of those who know nothing of reality of it all. Those damned Germano-baiters at home, so much more cruel than those who have the right—and are not!

The churches, and the sort of men that fill them. Unending compromise. Sickening, now, to hear quibbles of anointed, to see them taking another hitch in doctrines not big enough to fill. "Forgive them that do hurt to you"—a big order. Too God damned big for pygmies in the pulpits. Honor to Nietzsche, who believed Christianity puling, two-faced sentimentality—and said so. No hell deep enough for smooth-skinned harlots in vestments who prate Sundays of their Lord—and sneak like rats from splendid words the Man uttered. Deeper than one reserved for Huns they want to "punish." Hun may have crucified Christ, slaughtered, raped and burned. But faithful to own gods, at least.

Indelicate item, culled by censor, from soldier's letter: "Take a long look at the floor, Martha, because when I get home, you aren't going to see anything but the ceiling for a long, long time!"

Every letter censored to-day carried request for chocolate. Seems to be thing most missed. Possible to get a little here, but *ersatz*—made out of sand. Shipment of Maillard's in recently. Put away whole pound at one sitting.

Amused at account from home of bombing of Federal Bldg. Troops brought in, etc. Probably think they know what air raid in Paris is like.

Mother overdoing Red Cross stuff. Probably.thinks any let-up would ruin Foch's plans. Wrote her to take it easy—Haig plays golf in middle of battle.

Mon., 7th.—Talk with Maj. F——, San. C., *re* food conditions in England and bearing on Yank morale. Unquestionably big cause for dislike of English. Come over on English transports, boiled fish, boiled *everything*, no salt, dough pudding, with bill-poster paste for sauce. And ham sandwiches and hot dogs sold at high prices by concessionnaires! No wonder they arrive sore. Stomach the seat of all emotions. No American can ever kiss hand that feeds him "bubble and squeak." *

Dined with B.I.O.'s. Couldn't convince them of seriousness of problem. So talked about art, instead. Home early, rather glowing.

Tues., 8th.—Black-bordered card from B—— in Limoges:

"*Mon cher ami: J'ai le douleur de vous annoncer la mort de mon jeune frère, M——, tué à l'enemi à l'âge de 19 ans. Il était engagé volontaire et avait dévancé l'appel de sa classe. C'est le second de mes frères que la querre nous prend. Les victoires se paient avec ces terribles sacrifices. Heureusement qu'ils ne seront pas inutiles.*" †

---

*An English pudding, peculiarly without taste.

†Letter received from B—— under date of July 12, 1926: "Mon cher ami: Je ne sais si vous suivez la question des dettes interalliés. Elle n'a certes pas pour vous la même importance que pour nous.

J'ignore quelle est votre opinion a ce sujet. Mais j'ai tenu à vous faire connaître celle qui est enracinée au fond de la conscience de tous les Français. Vous la trouverez dans un article que je joins à ma lettre où elle a été formulée avec plus

Not so certain. Much hangs on Wilson's response
to Germans, and consequences thereof.

News of transfer to St. Nazaire. Oh, Gawd!

Interrogation, with C——, ex-Scotland Yard, of
N—— R——. Deserter-spy(?). Claimed former,
wore O.D., had story, but no papers. Gave him 3rd
degree in French cell. No go. Left him with assurance
French would shoot him Thursday A.M. Won't—but
he doesn't know that. Pale green and nearly ready to
spill story.

Wed., 9th.—Left early with C—— and Capt. A——,
wounded and returning to outfit. Dieppe—recollection
of last visit, so many years ago, and so different. Abbeville, British G.H.Q.—dreary, depressing place. On
to Amiens. Never before realized meaning of word
"destruction." Signs: "This *was* so-and-so." Literal

de moderation que les paysans ou les ouvriers n'apportent à
l'exprimer habituellement.

Il est possible que les combinaisons politiques du personnel
en place aboutissent à la ratification des accords au subet de
la dette. Ce n'est pas certain.

Ce qui l'est incontestablement, c'est l'existence autre fond
de l'âme populaire de ces deux idées fondamentales:

(1) Nous ne devons pas le prix d'une guerre faite dans un
interet commun et dans laquelle nous avons fait les plus grands
sacrifices;

(2) alors qu'on nous a empêchés d'obtenir du coupable la
réparation du dommage, on ne peut nous demander plus que
nous ne recevrons de lui.

Vous me direz que ce sont deux idées morales, et non
financières. Mais nous vivons par des idées morales et ce sont
celles qui survivent aux incidents passagers de la vie des
peuples.

Pardonnez-moi cette lettre ennuyeuse, qui a l'allure d'un
document diplomatique!

description. Felt it more keenly than on Rheims-Soissons sector, because not so new. Ground in north, fought over four years, and grass done best to heal old wounds—only intensifies them.

Brass plate at Etains; put up by —th Inf. (French): "On this spot the Tiger of France emptied his bladder. The grass will forever grow greener in consequence."

Only one hotel in Amiens—and filled. Found woman to lodge us for night. Nothing in rooms but beds. No window-glass, no furniture, no carpets. Usual story. Husband prisoner for four years, no news for two, and little boy of five. So cheerful, withal. Full of refugees, waiting to go back to homes at Arras, Douai, Cambrai, etc.—so pitifully confident they'd find their homes waiting for them. No heart to tell them honestly of piles of broken stone and charred timber they'll find.

Thur., 10th.—Visited cathedral—exquisite, and not noticeably damaged. Streets practically deserted. Civilians only lately allowed to return.

On to Peronne, Villers Bretonneux, etc. What desolation! Unlike anything seen before. Country very flat. Desolate at best, but with all trees on landscape either cut down or shot away, and once ripe fields gray and muddy waste of overlapping shell-holes, impossible to convey impression of forlornness. Nothing for miles and miles but *mud*. Absolutely colorless.

One incident accentuated gloomy feelings to pitch of nausea. Chauffeur drove too fast. Passed party of German prisoners—lorry got in way—hit one poor devil. Fortunately not badly hurt. But what must comrades have thought—brutal, cowardly Americans, doing very thing we're told German officers do and laugh about! Sentiments of English guards probably little different.

Lunched near Bohain at Brigade H.Q. —th Div.
Left A—— there with outfit. German soil night before.
Unburied bodies everywhere, and quantities of materiel.
Never get used to sight of dead. Those gray faces,
turned up, with outstretched fingers still clutching at
soil they tried to hold—for what?

Decided time had come to acquire souvenir. Relieved
deceased German of bayonet he had no further use for.
Removed dried blood, and now have excellent imple-
ment for chopping kindling at home fireside.

C—— found this, in English paper. Pretty bum
poetry, in spots—but it seemed to fit:

> German boy with cold blue eyes,
> In the cold and blue moonrise,
> I who live and still shall know
> Flowers that smell and winds that blow,
> I who live to walk again,
> Fired the shot that broke your brain.
>
> By your hair, all stiff with blood,
> By your lips befouled with mud,
> By your dreams that shall no more
> Leave the nest and sing and soar,
> By the children never born
> From your body smashed and torn,
> When I too shall stand at last,
>   In the deadland vast,
> Shall you heap upon my soul
>   Agonies of coal?
> Shall you bind my throat with cords,
>   Stab me through with swords?
>
> Or shall you be gentler far,
> Than a bird or than a star?
> Shall you say—"The way was hid,
> Lord, he knew not what he did?"
> Shall you know that I was bound,

In the noose that choked you round?
Shall your eyes that day be mild,
Like the Sacrifice, the Child?
. . . German boy with cold blue eyes,
In the cold and blue moonrise.

Amusing spectacle of entire British army, sitting in
sunshine beside Cambrai road, engaged in picking ani-
malculæ from shirts!

Overwhelmed at thought of being many miles beyond
once famous Hindenburg line. And Boche indeterminate number of miles beyond us. Moving so fast, impossible to tell, from hour to hour, just how many. His
goose is certainly cooked.

Strange thoughts roaming through houses of shattered
towns, few hours after enemy had left them, and with
his dead lying about amidst débris of last meal. Boche
have done rotten, unbelievably savage things. But sum
of emotions—sheer bewilderment. These boys, whose
bodies lie strewn about, or alive, toiling like dumb cattle
on the roads, have been worse than any savages. Be-
fouled every nest they occupied. Disgusting in nastiness.
And so wanton. Tear up pictures, smash mirrors—God
knows why. And Boche dugouts almost untenable for
stench. How can fellow humans be so dead to what we
believe essentials of even animal? Simply no answer.

Visited Canal of Escaut at Bellincourt. Supposed to
have housed two entire divisions, on canal boats brought
into tunnel. Americans nearly caught in trap, but saved
by Australians. Place pitch dark and stinking. Encountered Australian, with candle. Great lad. Down
into one of · canal boats, poking around in débris.
"Wot's this naow?" seizing tangled bunch of wires.
Nearly had heart failure, place being full of mines.
Nothing happened. "Not a bloody fuckin' thing!"—

very disappointed! Ventured to remonstrate against wisdom of performance. His philosophy complete and disarming. "If it's a mine, it does you in, if it ain't why, then it don't. An' that's all there is to it." Hastened to free myself of overstimulating company. Opportunities to be "done in" unsolicited numerous enough.

Saw big copper kettle—supposed to be trying-oven where Germans cooked cadavers for fat. No idea what it is, but certain not *that*. Probably nothing but *field lazaret*.

To French sector—St. Quentin, etc. Marked differences. Country not quite so desolate. Not so many signs—French seem to need fewer directions than British. To Ham, Chaulnes, Nesles, Montdidier—little more than heap of stones and splintered trees, looking as if giant had chewed them.

Nightfall about Beauvais. Ran on in dark, getting thoroughly lost. C—— saw light and made inquiries. Found ourselves in brightly lighted room with strange company—three French officers and wives, with honored guest—very black Jamaica negro, surgeon, British Medic. C. Champagne and everybody mellow. Urged to join party and did. Song, dance and talk. *Soirée* such as only Gaul, who knows not self-consciousness, could stage. Cordial hopes that adieus might prove *au revoirs*.

Arrived Rouen 3:30. Pried open hotel and achieved bed of sorts.

Fri., 11th.—Reached Havre at 11, well fagged.

Lunch with new man, Capt. F——, ex-A.D.C., C.O. —rd Div. His blunders. (1) Smelled bottle of Cointreau and pronounced it "not bad." (2) Professed knowing all about I.O. job. (3) Fell into C——'s disingenuous invitation to tell adventures at Front. C——'s perverted sense of humor. Decided such chance to give wise guy education too good to be missed. Guaranteed thorough course. Casually inquired if F—— had noticed one Capt. N——, B.I.O. With urging let out horrid truth—this N—— very *suspect!* Extreme caution necessary. *"Méfiez-vous, taisez-vous, les oreilles enemis vous écoutent,"* etc. F—— sealed own fate. Allowed he'd observed very thing—that he "knew the type," etc. Said N—— had tried to worm information from him, but had cleverly frustrated plot!

C—— carried on. Began F——'s course of training in "shadowing." To practice on N——. Dark hints about latter being German-born, etc. F—— took it all, hook, line and sinker.

Great amusement reading home papers. Article in *New Republic*—prophetic sheet—with grave assurance that nothing can happen in Balkans . . . some weeks after Bulgaria has gone under!

Rumor abroad that Kaiser has abdicated. Not true, yet; but convinced it will come.

Sat., 12th.—Significant picture: Huns, prisoners in cage, faces against wire, in earnest confab with Wisconsin Yanks—all talking German. Shadow of coming events. When enough Yanks have talked with enough Germans, war will be over, all objectives attained, regardless of what is done to map.

Squib picked up at Chaulnes:

PRECEPTES DU PARFAIT MILITAIRE

1. Il y a toujours une circulaire, mais il y a toujours une autre circulaire de façon qu'on est toujours le bouc.
2. Il ne faut jamais chercher à comprendre.

3. Il ne faut jamais s'en faire, car il n'y a pas d'exemple que les bidons ne se soient arrangés.
4. Avant d'exécuter un ordre, il faut toujours attendre le contre-ordre et encore.
5. Toute initiative non commandée est coupable.
6. Rien n'est plus désagréable à celui qui n'a rien à faire que de voir quelqu'un travailler.
7. Rien ne sert de partir à coups il faut tout de même courir.
8. Ne faites jamais le jour même ce que vous pouvez faire par un autre le lendemain.
9. Avant d'assumer une responsiblité assurez-vous toujours d'une victime de rang inférieur mais suffisant.
10. Soit.

FONCTIONS DE L'OFFICIER SUIVANT SON GRADE
Le sous-lieutenant n'existe pas.
Le lieutenant fait tout et ne sait rien.
Le capitaine ne sait rien et ne fait rien.
Le major sait tout et ne fait rien.
Le lieutenant-colonel s'en f . . .
Le colonel rappelle les paragraphs des O.J.
Le général s'étonne.

Lunched at le Petit Vatel. Quaint name. Original Vatel, Condé's chef. Killed self because fish were frozen. Now patron saint of French kitchens. Met Lt. M——, I.O., London, over as convoy to somebody's dog.

Dined G.T. with N——. Story of days with Manchester Yeomanry. Ordered sergeant to serve out grog. Latter drank it all and passed out. Just then brigadier arrived with staff on inspection. Serious offense—being drunk at Front. Sergeant too good a man to lose. N—— ordered tarpaulin thrown over him, and carried off on stretcher. As cortege passed, brigadier brass hat came to stiff salute: "Gentlemen,—our glorious dead." At which supposed corpse comes to, and wants to know

"what th' fuckin' 'ell th' bloody old bloke's starin' at?"
Tableau!

N—— greatly upset when promoted to majority.
Hated horses and majors mounted. Tried demotion to
captaincy and feet. Failing, made batman ride, while
he walked.

Sun., 13th.—Further progress in F——'s "education." Tipped off N——. Scandalized, but acquiescent.

Introduced F—— to Mons. "Sait Tout." Told
F—— latter was remarkable detective, able to tell man's
occupation by merely feeling fingers. "Sait Tout,"
previously tipped off, played up, and promptly told
F—— he was wire mfr. in civil life. Latter dumfounded! M. Fil de Fer, his title henceforth.

F—— busy sleuthing, and a scream! Caught N——
nosing through supposedly "secret" documents at office. All suspicions confirmed! Rest of us almost in
hysterics!

A monstrous *blague*, and twinges of conscience at
times. Possibilities of international complication! But
C—— obdurate. F—— too wise by half. His latest:
"In France they frequently put cognac in coffee." And
so chummy with Lloyd-George. Found him "rather
capable chap."

Hopes rise and fall these days—vast range and great
speed. Last night—our conditions accepted without
reservation—nothing more to war. To-day—reserva-
tions, and trap apparent. Emotions damp and soggy.
And to-night, news of Boche counter-attack on grand
scale and some success.

Still, *average* points to end by Xmas. Bet C——
best dinner to be bought in Paris on *Réveillon*, end of
fighting by Nov. 15. He thinks me crazy.

More convinced than ever of Kaiser's ultimate abdication. An essential predicate to discussion. Evident that own people have no further use for him.

Not so keen for being I.O. after peace. Speaking French, too damned useful getting things wound up. Dreadful prospect of being here till last of A.E.F. on high seas.

Curious that rank counts for so much more among Yanks, than with any of Allies. Newer at game, look more closely at insignia. Promotion very slow in French army. Chap may have functions of general, with one stripe on sleeve. In consequence, pay small attention to tunic. We pay a lot, and rather droll in deference to outward symbols of importance. Plenty of morons carrying silver hardware.

Havre, being in *zone des armées*, has less than share of wild women. Can't get here easily. Those here mostly local product. But enough at that. Common lament for security of old home town, with constant surveillance and virtue less a matter of personal choice.

News from home that place is rented for another year. Depressing, but perhaps just as well, when I'm trying to regain bearings in normal world, to have something coming in. Pleasant enough, just to wear soft shirt and pad around without explanations to some sentry.

So damned hard writing letters home! Dull as ditch-water. What's use, when magazines do it for you? Mostly bunk, of course, but better than letters. Stuff a chap writes his first month over, likely to be his best. So tired of talking about it.

W—— in at last. Never see service, of course, but good experience, training camp, etc. And always able to say he was "in it."

Mon., 14th.—More work on Anglo-American relations. Fundamental English misunderstanding of U.S. In law, literature and education, take color from England. Political and social leaders mostly of British stock. But small amount of Anglo-Saxon blood in American population. English immigration long since ceased. Bulk of new blood, until '50's, Teutonic and Celtic, followed by Scandinavian and Italian. Last ten years, predominance of Slavic and Levantine.

English like to think of U.S. as mere enlargement of Thirteen Colonies. English imprint far from obliterated, but U.S. to-day entirely new nation. Not due entirely to influx of other races. Climate and environment producing new ethnic group. Autocthonous American of to-day probably physically nearer North American Indian than any race of origin.

As long as English regard Yank as racial kin, sure to be puzzled and hurt. Got to learn American is "foreigner." No more nonsense like "blood thicker than water," etc.

To English, Revolution was incident, unfortunate blunder in colonial managment. To American, it marked dawn of history. Taught vast nonsense about it in school, and never allowed to forget it. Juvenile fiction always has "red coat" for villain. War of 1812 unknown to most Europeans, gave U.S. some of its best heroes. Memory of English position in Civil War still rankles.

American, regardless of ancestry, apt to begin life with prejudice against Britain. Deepens into dogma, with politicians, professional Irish, helping all they can. German propaganda found fruitful soil. Legitimate sympathy of many Americans for Germany, land of origin. Most of wealthy and educated in sympathy with Allies. Bourgeoisie divided. Farmers and labor, indifferent.

English necessities, "blacklist," etc., exploited by Hearst newspapers. Old scandals, like opium wars, dragged out. Cries of alarm at gold shipments. English character distorted, and weaknesses magnified.

English criticism of American delay in entering war, as tactless as unjustified. Failure to grasp enormity of Wilson's task in bringing huge territorial agglomeration, of doubtful homogeneity, into struggle spiritually and geographically so remote.

Peculiarities of temperament. Aggressive egotism characteristic of Americans, as of all *young* peoples. Appearance of excessive sophistication, to conceal lack of it. First contact with older and more stabilized civilization apt to cause irritation on both sides.

Problem of vast importance. Relations between U.S. and British, after war, likely to determine orientation of world politically, economically and socially.

Put F—— to work on "Harbor Control." Posted out on breakwater, with sheet on which to mark description of passing ships, especially color of smoke—important information to be deduced from this! Swallowed it all. Very funny—till French sentry nearly shot him!

Tues., 15th.—St. Nazaire order canceled. Probably to take over I.O. job at La Rochelle.

Wilson's splendid and very clever answer. No reaction yet. Probabilities that Hun weaker than we have dared hope. Gossip that Gen. Staff asked for armistice. That—or military disaster.

Abdication of Kaiser certain now. Many changes in government, all tending definitely toward democratization. Undoubtedly *ersatz*, at first. But maybe Germans never democratic because never tasted charms of self-government. One taste—even at hands of autocrat, with motives of self-interest—and they will not revert.

Possibility of last-ditch fight. But spirit of defeat seems in their blood. On brink of crumbling altogether. No surprise to hear, any day, of capitulation. No hope of compromise, and they know it. For first time, find many people agreeing with me.

State of my pants gives direct and personal interest in progress towards peace. Question—how long can we hold out? Wearing thin in many spots. Can hold out, maybe, till new year. After that, tremble for consequences.

Letter culled by censor. Yank soldier mentions casually that "division received *fouragère* six times from both Pershing and Foch." Only flaws, no division received *fouragère* six times—or even once—and writer didn't belong to division anyway, being carpenter, working in base hospital. Otherwise, hot stuff!

Letter from Red Cross girl. Referred to destroyers as "darling" and "adorable." Ought to get ten years hard labor!

Strange things out of censorship. Anything interesting or peculiar turned over to us, for investigation. Sometimes considerable consequences. But nothing ever said. Case, "closed," goes to files. Hope those files burnt when war's over. With them anybody could get rich on blackmail.*

Sent home saw-tooth bayonet picked up near Cambrai. Supposed evidence of German ferocity. Really used for woodcutting, only one issued to squad. Saw very few

---

*These files were burned, in the presence of a number of officers. But what remains in the files of memory can never be burned.

of them. Ironic that French "Josephine" doesn't get
share of attention as atrocity producer. Makes neat
hole, that closes up, with sepsis inevitable. French not
keen for bayonet-work. Silly to fight close-in, when
more damage possible with gun at half a mile. Disap-
prove of even odds in war. Not a *game*.

Letter from W——, "Convoy Officer, Destroyer of
Congressmen No. 1." Wants to get into this branch of
G2. C——, I.O. here, doing his damndest to get out
of it. And M——, at Front since March, with Artillery, wondering how he can get job as Conducting Officer and "see something of the God damned war!"

Pet peeve—the swine in the rear, afraid war will end
before we can "punish" Germany. Fellows in line all
for a knockout and out of the ring as quickly as possible.
Not much patience with blood-and-iron spirit of folk
who've never seen war outside a cinema.

Turkey asks peace! *Ça marche!*

Wed., 16th.—News I go to La Rochelle.

To boat-control. Interrogation of 17 year old—
minus papers. Tears and the truth. Wrath at F——,
dirty Corsican bully. Dinner with B.I.O's at G.T.
Bang on door and incoherent Yank voices demanding
admission. Proprietor in stew, knowing neither regulations nor English. Drunken soldiers. Profuse apologies on discovering American officer. Salutes and handshaking. One reason why Germans have no chance
against us. Couldn't picture German officer shaking
hands with drunken privates and giving advice on how
to elude M.P's.

Thur., 17th.—Fate sealed—on to La Rochelle. British I.O.'s threw party in celebration. Everybody pleas-

antly maudlin. Much kidding about Anglo-American relations. Played game of "consequences" with following extraordinary result:

"Anglo-Saxonism will rule world. Down with Latins. Exhaustive and painful researches incontestably proved truth of Darwinian hypothesis—particularly as regards England; and inasmuch as propinquity of two kindred relationships of necessity breeds certain amount of inter-communication, the honor and purity of womanhood, therefore, can only be upheld by animosity of British and American arms."

That, of course, true. But, on other hand, whatever may be said of leathern breeches of typical British buccaneer, beyond all dispute that he has shaggy ears—in short, demonstration of hardiness; for in all questions of economical prosperity, basis of stability must be matter of degree, looked at from standpoint of efficiency.

Only by marriage of Queen Mary's eldest daughter with Judge Hylan can future of two great monarchies be assured. Summarizing above, as Capt. F—— has so wisely said, a little jesting now and then is relished even by the worst of men; thus proving efficacy of famous but oft misquoted line: *Fortiter in re, suaviter in spe.*

Copies to:

C. in C. Spanish Army   La Ferté Massé
C. in C. Swiss Navy   W. J. Bryan, *Service de*
Chief Surgeon, Liberia   *Mœurs*
C. of S., G2, S.O.S., A.E.F.   C. in C., L. of C., B.E.F.
Associated Press   Manchester Guardian
The Vatican, *aux soins "un*   Die Deutsche Tageszeitung
  moutardier"   Tortoni's
Max of Bade

and general *affichage** voted.

*Promulgation of decrees by posting.

Fri., 18th.—300th day from Hoboken! Damned
cold. Shivering, fingers numb as lead, and not even
November yet.

Bought Liberty Bond, leaving me strapped. One of
those "doing his bit," etc. Thrilling! Rough and simple soldier, risking life on blood-soaked fields of France,
also helping pay own salary!

Race between Kaiser and pants still on. Vital interest in early termination of conflict! Each day another seam opens or another button drops from fatigue
—and can't keep pants up by merely gritting teeth.
Each morning, scan communiqués first—then breeches.
Strain beginning to tell.

Many people saying "long pull yet." Don't believe
it. Hun never would have made supine offer unless suffering vital weakness. May be able to withdraw Ant-
werp line and hold on month or two. But by own confession, bound to be licked in end. Likely to cut losses
now, and salvage what he can. Probably succession of
notes, with increasing military reverses, until final
cave-in. When Kaiser goes, whole dynastic idea with
him. Probably a Socialist government, before we—or
even Germans—realize it. Deutschland democratized,
and our essential war purposes realized. A mask, at
first, maybe, but soon a reality.

Problems of readjustment hitherto kept in background, going to make all sorts of trouble. League of
Nations, not mere imaginative, sentimental Utopia, but
only practicable solution of world in chaos. Reorgani-
zation of society going to require pooling of brains and
resources. Real job begins when peace treaty is signed.
Lord Buckmaster has the right dope: "The real victors
in this war will be determined 10 or 20 years afterwards,
and they will be the nation who will be the best able

to face the growing discontent of a disillusioned people, to ward off impending famine, and to save their people from the appalling consequences of the universal bankruptcy to which Europe is speeding every day with increasing pace."

Vast amount of nonsense about Germany. Silly idea of demanding huge indemnities, and in same breath refusing to allow access to raw material, i.e., ask tree to give fruit, but shut off sun and air.

No disposal of Germany after war by merely gnashing teeth. Got to take hold and make something out of mess, or war will have been waste of time. Won't do to slaughter dragon. Got to bury carcass, or turn it into fertilizer, or soap—or it will be worse offense dead than alive.

Policy of forgive and forget not merely laudable on moral grounds. Only way out. Does current squeak about "punishment" mean poisoning remaining Germans—or even child-bearing females? If so, it's childish hypocrisy. When professing Christians talk this way, they damn themselves for eternity, if recording angel isn't stone deaf.

Either slaughter entire Teutonic race, or take them back and try to make something of them. No middle ground. No sense hating *Germans*. Only proper object for hate, to anyone with brains God gave little snails, is an *idea*. And can't destroy ideas, or crush them, or punish them. Can only substitute good ideas for bad ones.

This life hard on illusions. Not many left. A hell of a way from best of all possible worlds, and man certainly a son-of-a-bitch when he puts his mind to it. But hope not to travel too far along road on which so many "realists" stub their silly toes, of believing there is no angel worth mentioning in poor, complex human heart. Heaven and hell both there.

Pride and wonderment for Yank soldier. Doing all and more than expected—and so blithely, so humorously. Manners superb, on duty and off. Held down by no traditions of servility, not only respectful to officers, but respects them. Very punctilious in military deportment. Not so attractive when first arrived. Noisy, crude, rather ill-mannered. But learns lot from native. Grows up fast.

Though this Belgian capital, probably more excitement in one city block in U.S. at fall of Ostende and Lille than in whole of Havre. A few flags, here and there—nothing more. After four years, feeling rather too deep for cheers. Whistles, parades, etc., at home. Here, a shrug of the shoulders, *ça marche*, and business as usual. Not even an extra.

Sat., 19th.—Still waiting La Rochelle order. Jump at every ring of phone. Don't dare send out laundry. Hell of a way to treat a fellow. Certainly tired of living out of *musette*.

Great pleasure in Sat. Ev. Post. Ads give link with past. Pore over announcements of new soaps, bacons, tires. Learn what home life is like now. And for humor —articles of war correspondents. Frequently know either writer or subject. Occasionally both. Full of lies, of course. But whoever would stop lies would stop writing.

Letter from G—— C——, Camp McClellan, Ala. Home as instructor. "With all the peace talk going on, haven't known till now whether I would get back to France. But with Wilson's last reply, no doubts now, and will be back in 6 wks., subs permitting."

Like hell he will!

Sun., 20th.—Watching usual batch of weary, straggling Boche prisoners, many wounded, passing office window. Struck by attitude of French populace. Not once heard prisoner addressed unkindly. Contrast, probably, with what our fellows get in Germany—with what prisoners would get in U.S.

French stop and look, curiously. A man smiles, perhaps: *"Ils ont eu assez, hein."* Children nudge each other, whispering. The mothers, like one to-day, raise eyebrows in wonderment: "But there are lads of only fifteen! *Pauvres gosses!"* Hate the Boche, *bien entendu*, and privately, use bad words about him. But *admit* it, come to level of that brutish foe? *Jamais!* Explains German "frightfulness." Much of it due to fear—the Hun a coward at heart. The rest of it, sheer jealousy. Never for an instant does Frenchman let German forget his inherent and permanent inferiority.

Depressing to study faces of prisoners. Feeling that one looks at herd of animals. Can't be *men*. Men never so filthy, nasty, pettily cruel. Possible to condone impalement of babes on spears, etc.—the conventional atrocities—after all, they are in tradition of good old savage warfare. But stomach as well as heart revolts at way these creatures befoul own nests, and destroy beauty in sheer madness. Can be nastier—only word—than any dog. Disgusting. One reacts, absolutely numb.

Hate things I can't understand. Can't take even first wee toddling step in understanding German. Not fair to call him brute, because no animal ever sank to depths he glories in. Can't even hate him—hate implies some common meeting-ground. The supreme puzzle.

German nation of to-day an abcess, discharging pus into sick world. We cut and cut. Drain, bandage and disinfect—"treaties," "guarantees," etc. But until germ is isolated and destroyed, real work not even begun. Merely trying to exorcise devil with charms and incantations. What world needs these days is more scientific spirit and less emotion.

Bubbling optimism of first few days following request for armistice, gone now. People again talking of "trickery" and "next spring." Boche so often *under*estimated, now have tendency to *over*estimate him. May be as weak as claimed—and weaker.

Retreating in good order. Some look for halt on Escaut. Don't think he'll stop before line of Meuse. Short line—but industrial centers in big gun range. Tired, half-mutinous troops fighting great enthusiastic American armies. Another note or two—then loud, ungrateful snarls, and turning on leaders who brought him where he is. Russia showed way. Pupil less bloody, but no less thorough.

Thoughts of going home! Thing in France I'll miss most is institution, found on every street corner, where demands of Nature conveniently if publicly answered.

Tea at Whitlock's. Seemed like man mentally tired. Expressed conviction Germans ought to be passed under yoke, just as Cæsar would have done it. Puritanical attitude toward French. Plumbing inadequacies and *la vie Parisienne.* Accurate but partial picture. Very interesting man, sympathetic and liberal, and both extremely kindly and cordial.

Saw R——. Disappointment in him. Not receptive to new ideas. Spiritually crystallized. Everything set and crystallized. Averse to any sort of inquiry. Bound with blank walls. Hope I never become mentally quite settled. Nothing so dreadful as arteriosclerosis of soul.

Possible explanation of sour reaction—nice case of grippe. Mixed some aspirin with thoughts, and so—to bed.

Mon., *21st.*—Discussing promotions with C——. No chance. G2 as full of 2nd Lieuts. as dugout is of rats. No further news of La Rochelle. Got to move somewhere, or have cirrhosis of liver!

Map shows how war stands. When Boche gets squeezed back to Forêt des Ardennes, he's through. With Foch as sledge, and mountains as hardie, he'll be split in two.

Marvelous, the way rumor spreads! Wonder why book-publishers don't use it to sell books. Plant dozen people around country, with orders to spring story to *one* person—absolutely *confidential*. Everywhere in twelve hours.

Have idea this war will be history by Nov. 17. Where did that date come from? Make it up, or what? For some reason, very strong in mind.

Tues, *22nd.*—Left on 8 A.M. boat for Trouville, to investigate American mutiny in English rest-camp. Tarried in Deauville. Few feet of water between two, but difference between Coney Island and Newport. Called on Gen. H——, British O.C. To camp 15. Mess with Col. · B——, O.C. Charming, cultivated Australian. Explanation of colonial attitude toward English—contemptuous of latter's inferior physique, and servile habit of mind.

Interview troublesome Yanks. Quite a bust-up, in which Diggers had helped. Yanks sore. Hadn't been paid. Short of uniforms. Worst of all, required to drill with British. Difference in regulations, etc. "Made a guy feel awkward." Ironed out difficulties, got Red Cross to bank boys until Uncle Samuel came through, visited hospitals, and left on 5 o'clock boat.

Hun note to Wilson. Of dubious value, but significant.

Wed., 23rd.—News from G.H.Q. I am to move "presently."

Long, dreary day, struggling to untangle details of LaS—— case, which decline to untangle. But wonderful evening. Dined with L—— M——, French officer—painter, *avant la guerre*. French and British medals. *Blessé* several times. First remark—had read *New Republic* all through war, and found it salvation of soul. Second—not since Christ had man risen with such vision, such calm superiority to passions of hour, and with promise of such succor to maddened humanity as W. Wilson. Recalled first experience of phrase, "Peace without victory"—early in '16, on lips of French *poilu*. Conversation to shock fireside bitter-enders!

Arm bandaged and in sling. Spoke of friend's children asking about arm. Mother laid it to "those wretched Germans." His answer: "How dare you poison child's heart? Is it not enough that yours and mine are rotting with hate, that you must carry it on to next generation?"

Talked of forgiveness and forgetfulness and future of world; why men died and what life was all about. Such talk as gives one new faith in greatness of human nature. And talk, such as on lips of East Side Jew, would mean Leavenworth!

All through it, with eyes on his wound stripes, my thoughts on distant drawing-rooms, full of soft comfortable creatures of both sexes—or none—as harsh and bitter as shallow and dull, who have done nothing and thought less, who mouth empty phrases and unselfishly shed other men's blood, who talk of "victory" as if it were end of world . . . who do lip-service to a noble creed o' Sundays, and dare to pretend Lord's Prayer not written for them. If there's a hell and a just God, there will be sterner punishment for such as they than for bloodiest German murderer. At least, he *dares*.

What a life! New people constantly—all ranks, creeds, nationalities, shades of thought. And meeting with a freedom and sincerity unknown to life en civile.

Thur. 24th.—Lt. M—— arrives. Belgian extraction, with wife somewhere in vicinity. My departure now certain.

All peace talk subsided. Convinced of German trickery—nothing more. My own optimism wavering. Probability of many months yet. Oh, the idiot Boche! Very low. Off with C——, F——, and N——. To François I, and Yvonne's. F—— quite tight.

Fri., 25th.—Wilson's response to Boche—splendid. So easy to have rendered merely curt dismissal—*fin de non recevoir*. Or as Parigot* would put it: "*Ferme ça gueule et fiche le camp!*"

Probable results—disruption of Austria, and Germany saving face by conceding eight millions in Alsace and Poland in exchange for fifteen million Austro-Germans. On basis of self-determination, etc., can't see where we can object. If they democratize at same time, what's left to fight for?

Waver up and down, day by day. But never lose

*A Parisian.

conviction that while *peace* may be far distant, end of
war is near. Few agree, but surprised if no cessation of
hostilities by Xmas. Dreadful if they ceased on or before Nov. 17! Be slave to superstition rest of life!

Lunch with B—— and Hon. H—— B——, niece of
Lord B——, and daughter Duke of A——. Also Col.
B——, O.C., British convalescent camp. Talk on everything from shell-shock, football and education, to world
politics and capital punishment. Unconcealed dislike
of English for Anglicised American, who affects London
fashions, says "right-o," and apologizes for own country.

Chaperoning party of Japanese officers. Inscrutable
chaps. Know more than they seem to. British mistrust
equal to ours. A trifle too *curious* for comfort.

Dinner with N——, British I.O. Australian Lieut.,
very drunk. Slapped N—— on back: "We're fightin'
troops, we are!" Emphasis deliberate and insulting.
English helpless. Nothing to do but get them out of
country as fast as possible.

Saw Mr. Whitlock, on request from British War Office, *re* Enver Pasha. Something in the wind!

Sat., 26th.—No news. What will Boche do now?
Turkish question. F——'s banquet. Château Yquem
by gallon. French disappointment. "But it is a *desert*
wine!" American notion that what's expensive must be
good. *Chez moi* at 1:30. About 82% sober.

Sun., 27th.—In bed all A.M. having pants repaired.
News that Ludendorf's got the hook. Dreadful sus-
picion of another "trick." So ofter underestimated
Hun that now going other way. Devil himself couldn't
be as full of wicked cleverness as Boche supposed to be.
About time to wonder if he isn't really in bad way.

Kaiser next for skids, with more or less of revolution to follow, and probability of German Republic in full working order before it dawns on us war actually *finie*.

Silly U.S. editorials: "Talk war, not peace." Ought to talk peace and think peace, because making of peace soon to be chief occupation of world. Beside peace problem, war-making relatively simple. Danger that we'll be plunged, unprepared, into huge task of setting world's house in order again. Got to do lot of talking about peace, or ghastly mess of making it.

Disgusted with cheap damnation of all things German at home. Hope children aren't already poisoned with it. Not possible to protect them against atmosphere of hate. But hope for counteracting reasonableness. Going to grow up in world tremendously different from one we have known. Have to grapple with new problems. Dreadful to think of them handicapped with useless rancors held over from past best forgotten.

Conviction that it's perfectly clear duty to bury hatchet. Hard enough, God knows—so much burned into memory: but got to do it. People who sign pledges to have nothing to do with Germans for seven years, etc., going to cut sorry figure before whatever God they are called to judgment. Feel sorry for them, but have first-class hate for those who, even by default, pass such cankers on to sweet souls of little people.

M—— entirely right. Germany not responsible for war. Just human nature, muddling and messing and bungling at things, as per usual. Doesn't matter, anyway, whether we're right or wrong, so long as we think we're right, and act accordingly. One thing certain—not going to get stumbling feet of human nature back on track of sanity if we waste effort trying to keep good-sized block of it in chains—physical or spiritual.

Home folks seem to think more of trumpets, banners
and fit of uniforms than of *why* of it all. We're behind other Allies in more ways than time. Their thinking, after four years of war, reaches wider horizon than
ours. Have learned wisdom in hard school. Look on
our fresh enthusiasm with kind of sadness, wondering if
they could ever have been like that.

Seems to get more clear—what war is all about. Germans put logic on pedestal and worshiped it. Studied
life scientifically and concluded force was right. Their
syllogism watertight. Invasion of Belgium, *Lusitania*,
rape of women, bombing of hospitals—everything fitted.
Nothing mattered but victory. That their religion—
have lived and died for it. But something in life higher
and better, more lasting, than logic. Kultur weighed
and measured brain of man, calculated range sharply—
but stopped there. World had to show him there was
soul, too—an unbroken word more to be treasured than
rich fields and thriving cities.

Life one long interrogation. Never an answer.
People not curious about why's and wherefore's probably more content, but miss something. Don't really
envy them.

Next step—terms of armistice. Hun may wriggle,
but bound to accept. Map shows precarious military
position. Disaster, any day. Political situation worse,
and crumbling process moving apace. Rumors of feverish fortification of Rhine. Nonsense. Fire's almost out.

Can't help thinking of Nov. 17. Ridiculous!

Mon., 28th.—Austrian capitulation. No excitement.
Feeling Germany must follow soon. No emotion in
crowd at bulletin board. *"Ca va bien."* Nothing more.

Letter from R——. Still at Saumur. "If you have

any use for about 20 lbs. of pure, concentrated, unadulterated ennui, just apply this office, using proper requisition form. Have certainly had belly-ful of S.O.S. Just my luck to have war end just as I was mounting my *cheval* to go galloping up to Front lines. Or do they do that at the war?"*

Certainly begins to look as if Germany would cave in by date appointed—Nov. 17. Remark of Gen. N—— (British): "Didn't see how we could keep them fighting." Always thought we were trying to make them *stop* fighting. Evidently mistaken.

To bed feeling miserable. Evidently have touch of flu. Hope not. Doctors busier than barbers on Saturday afternoon.

Tues., 29.—Still awaiting orders. Many changes in organization, due to evacuation of Belgium, etc. May get something hitherto not considered. British opening up new offices, nearer Front. Reported by them *persona grata*, and wanted in some forward post. But army way is by contraries, so probably to Spain—or Russia. *Quién sabe?*

Delighted to hear of W——, grooming, standing retreat, etc., suffering awful hardships I suffered in dear, dead days of youth in R.O.T.C.

Lunch with S——, ex-Foreign Legion. Strengthened in already strong contentment fate never called me to membership. A choice collection of unhung rascals. Good fighters—with friends or enemies.

Dined with W——, British I.P. Sergeant. *En*

---

*R——was flunked out of first R.O.T.C. and got 2nd Lieutenancy in 2nd Camp only by skin of teeth. But made brilliant record at Saumur, and was kept there all through war as instructor.

civile, Scotland Yard Inspector. Never carries gun.
Satisfied with piece of automobile tire. Calls it his
"persuader." Object of dinner to prove his contention
that Bordeaux wines intoxicate. Wagered I couldn't
drink bottle of his choosing and remain intact. He won.

Wed., 30th.—Wondering what I'll do when war is
over. Probably be made port or transport officer and in-
terpret till last Yank is fled. Thank God I don't speak
German! Those with troops will go *en bloc* and fast.
But us on detached service—gloomy prospect.

To boat control. Gen. K——, Q.M., very drunk.
Great fun for M.P.'s.

Thur., 31st.—In charge of office. C—— and B——
both away. Nothing much stirring. Tea and toast with
N—— at billet. The Britisher and his batman. Wher-
ever he goes, whatever he does—always the same. Marvelous!

No news in *communiqués*. End certain, though date
not.

November, 1918

Fri., 1st.—Events follow each other rapidly these days. Tension in air, though outwardly, no great change in life. Turkey officially under to-day. And Austria agrees to everything. To-morrow, probably, Allied terms for Armistice. Sure to be stiff dose for patient on Rhine. Opinions differ as to reception, but certain he'll swallow. Curious conviction that end is very, very near.

Still awaiting orders. Report that F—— had 6 seats on train, with several women, and all quite tight. Somewhat damaged as result of scrap night before.

Reading advertisement, occurs to me haven't had glass of *milk* in nearly a year! Calls to mind crisp, golden waffles, drowned in melted butter, with plenty of maple syrup . . . HALT!—that way madness lies!

To-day memorable for balmy loveliness. All Souls Day, and whole population, in finery, parading along *plage*. Except for planes and dirigibles in air, destroyers on water, uniforms everywhere, and prisoners drifting by, little to suggest war. To-morrow, *sans doubte*, cold and rainy again, with war only thought. Second only to stomach, in influence on soul, is w.k. weather.

Lunch, British Officers' Club. Question of British colonies, freedom of seas, etc., looming up. Rush for *les journaux*. Excitement in air. Hopes running high.

Sat., 2nd.—Letter from home expressing notion that

Wilson was popular with "intellectuals" here, but not *bas peuple*. 100% wrong. Funny ideas in thick skulls that presume to run politics in U.S. Solemn pronouncement by Mr. Hayes of Republican party, that W.W. is a "Socialist." Word evidently still has power to terrify in land of free. To average European, Wilson has Messiah quality: not too much to say, he's *revered*. T.R. simply *n'existe plus*. Never hear him mentioned. As for Republicans, one Frenchman expressed general feeling, declaring if he were German, he'd prefer Ludendorf to Lodge. T.R., with his obsolete bourgeois feudalism at world helm to-day, would be calamity beyond measure. Did his work, and did it well. But his day passed. Bigger things going on than he seems to dream of. Mustn't be allowed to interfere.

Resent idea we must go forth to battle, checking brains behind, and leaving to politicians decision as to what battle is for. See no contradiction in fighting and thinking—two can go on simultaneously. All wrong to fight blindly and leave *reasons* till afterward. Can lick Germany—and lose war.

Pitiful, sight of black-frocked politicos and woodenheaded generals around table at Versailles, determining what "peace" is to be. Man in street been thinking a lot. If ever man spoke for inarticulate world, it's Wilson.

Amusing phenomenon—terror of Bolsheviks. Solemn suggestions for occupation of territory, to preserve it from "infection," etc. Men who wouldn't try to evaporate ocean with penny fan, think they can regulate humanity into safety and sanity. Incantations to make ideas lie down and sleep. Things that made Bolshevism latent throughout whole world. Can be controlled. But sympathy and tact needed by those who try. Folly to think end of war means peace. World not going back to 1914.

Bolshevik, for better or worse, roaming in uncharted fields. Maybe quite mad, or maybe exceeding wise. Don't know yet. Fatal blunder in all plans for "helping" Russia, our going with advice, when we ought to go for information. Might help both of us.

Wilson's appeal less to intellectual than to emotional and religious. No conception at home of aura surrounding him in mind of common man here. Stands alone, calm, uttering first message of hope and good will among men heard these many years. Tommy and *poilu* hungry for such word—sick of politicians' empty jargon. If Germany doesn't know it yet, she will presently, that W.W.'s her best friend.

Sun., 3rd.—C—— back with news I go to Brussels or Nice—or both. But no date.

D——'s division en route to Archangel. Probably be there, quieting Bolshevik, when rest of us are telling lies to grandchildren. When he gets back and people ask where he's been lately, he'll say: "Fighting the great war." And they'll look blank: "War? *What* war?"

Republican attitude toward Wilson. Will not have sympathy of European peoples, who look on him as kind of god, his ideals and utterances, taken at face value, as absolutely inspired.

Politicians and "soldiers' point of view." Silly. As many different ways of looking at things among soldiers as among any other sort of men.

Had first frogs' legs to-night. Prefer chicken.

Story from home about W—— and B—— putting on new uniforms at night, and "looking stunning." Only

thing in way of uniform that would give me thrill—
derby hat and long pants.

Saw D—— and F————, champion grouser of
A.E.F.

Beginning to think of *après la guerre*—dreadful problem of *living*. Down to earth and job, after voyage on
coat-tails of fate.

Mon., 4th.—Austrian armistice signed. *"Next!"*

Col. C——, head of U.S. spy service, arrived with
wife. To British salvage shops. Passion for souvenirs.
Mrs. C—— acquired bayonet. To Southampton boat.
N——'s *blague*. Warning of severe penalties for taking
souvenirs out of France. Inquired if she had any. De-
nials. C—— insisted woman in her position wouldn't
think of such a thing, etc., etc. Just then, dropped bayonet! Great to-do. Extreme embarrassment of C——
family, and extreme delight of everybody else.

Dined with Maj. P—— at Guidon. Indian Army,
26 years. Knew China and East intimately. Said East
was place for poor man. Got to look into that for *après
la guerre!*

Tues., 5th.—British only take 10,000—"No news!"
Waiting for final smash. General impression—about
two weeks. Nov. 17th? "Shopping" with N——.
Hunting gifts for wives. Sans result. Dreary day. No
energy. Bored. Dinner, Tortoni's, with N——, B——,
and C——. Hilarious battle of siphons. One burst,
but no casualties. Extraordinary performance on Blvd.
Francois I. C—— holding up all vehicles, demanding
"passes." Also breaking into strange house—under
slight misapprehension. Stupefaction of landlady. Retreat in good order to Rue St. Quentin. Singular Antoi-

nette D———. Bureau full of dolls and clothes. Amazing evening. Home at 1—fairly tight.

Wed., 6th.—Poor old liver *hors du combat*. No news, except I.O. diaries suppressed! Lunch with P——— at billet. Capt. H———, London Rifle Brigade. Two types of Britisher—scholar and gentleman. Both charming.

Dreary, rainy day. Funeral of concierge's daughter —flu case. Feeling that war is over, universal. Dined, La Corniche, with N———. Hasty exit at 10—Police! *Contravention!* Shocking discovery of proprietress' past.

Thur., 7th.—Military advances continue. Eyes on Mézières. News that Boche *parlementaries* have started. From all signs mean to accept terms. Next steps—peace negotiations, occupation, and repatriation. Pleasant to think casualty lists and *communiqués* soon thing of past.

To Belgium to-morrow and Dutch frontier. Idea that Germans may try to slip over *défaitiste* agents. G.H.Q. wants information on condition of border.

Uppermost thought in all minds—location of wires whose pulling may lead to early release from this God damned army. Awful thought of being lost over here for years and years, while young, unattached persons, who'd really like to stay, get sent home.

According to papers, fiction-writing classed as essential occupation. Ought to let out 99% of A.E.F.

What to do with troops? Have army of thirty men, and battery of typewriters. Picked men, carefully trained, and linguists. Every tongue of Europe represented. Great fellows. More liberty than ordinary soldiers. Frequently in plain clothes. Never cease marveling at discipline—largely self-imposed. On their honor, and behavior beyond criticism. Yet to encounter American soldier failing to show respect for uniform of officer—or with any foolish notions about superior quality of individual under it!

Melting-pot process going on under high pressure. In making this heterogeneous mass into army, also making Americans. Separatist politicians going to have rude shocks when they try old tricks on these lads.

British very unlike French. Take a deal more knowing. Australians like Americans, with much mutual admiration. Hard to get intimate with Britisher. All sorts of inhibitions, things that "aren't done," veils of shyness to be pierced. But splendid pal, once bars are down.

At 5:26, report from A——, pop-eyed and reverting to native Anatolian, that armistice signed, at Sedan. To prefecture and on wire to G.H.Q. No armistice, but Americans have taken Sedan.

Downtown. Crowds and some excitement, but not much. To Cercle. Old man placidly reading *La Rire*. "Such excitement—*c'est idiot!*" *Vieux pepère* at bank: "*Vive l'Amérique!*"

Bulletin—"*officieux*"—put up, and more excitement. But not as much, nearly, as in American football crowd. 7:06: *Les parlimentaries sont arrivés chez M. Foch.* Things moving.

New bulletins every three minutes. Phone ringing, people in and out—impossible to tell what is what.

To Tortoni's. Wild night. Incipient party. Fight between V.C. fellow and A.S.C. chap. "Who won the war?" Who the hell *cares?* To Yvonne's. Champagne—*à la victoire.* Home intact.

Fri., 8th.—Note from F—— W——: "A sprig of mistletoe hung just under tails of my old dress suit for anyone who mentions war or the beauties of France."

Left at 7 in Cadillac, with "Sait Tout," N——, and C——. First *pannes* at Dieppes. Abbeville. Saw G——, B.I.O., there. Very cold. Montreuil by 4. British G.H.Q. Morgue, full of red-caps oppressed with own importance. Silent place, where no one speaks. Increasingly democratic friendliness of chauffeur. Happy thought of putting "Sait Tout," speaking no English, on front seat.

Nightfall in Boulogne, and one of Hotel Folkstone's famous champagne cocktails. Searchlights still playing over sky. Constant query along road: *"La guerre finie?"* Repeated injunctions of M.P's to keep lights dim didn't seem much like peace.

Calais at 7. Pitch black and cold. Dinner at Continental. To B.I.O. Turned in early, except chauffeur, who found friends and went for joy-ride.

Sat., 9th.—Early start. Dunkerque by 10. Hunted up I.O. No news. On to Furnes. Stark bones of what once were homes, tumbled about, and fields looking as if giant had stamped on them, and spit afterward. Country of marshes and shattered foot-bridges and rusty barbed wire, marking furthest advance of German civilization. Miles without sign of life, human, animal or vegetable. Silence that weighed like heavy pack. Marveled that man could ever have lived there, let alone fight for four years. Permanence of last line of Belgian trenches—brick, with chimneys and stray cats at thresholds, calmly domestic.

Nieuport—mere battered mass of brick. Especially interesting to N——. Been there six months. Purvis,

Dixmude, Ramscappelle—towns of a thousand communiqués—"towns" *en façon de parler*. In failing light of cold November afternoon, with dim redness of rising moon reflected in chill flashes of ubiquitous pools of muddy water, what was left of them stood like limbs of dead trees. Chilled with something more than chill of air.

Then, suddenly, into smiling land where cows grazed peacefully, people rode bicycles, and save for Boche signs everywhere and occasional shell-holes, no evidence of war. Hailed by Belgian soldier, laden with packages, and took him aboard. Had already made 40 kilos afoot. Failing us, would have taken at least two more days on journey. Attractive power of "home" counteracts obstacles that would chill heart of locomotive.

Many stories of German occupation. Holes in shoes mark of distinction for female Belges. Not honorable to be well dressed. Too many—*caractère légère*—whose first dislike of Hun had somewhat abated . . . such had not wanted for shoes. Boche trickery. Sent his own planes to bomb Ostende and blamed it on British. Fake exposed by discovery of unexploded Boche bomb.

Ostende at 7, dining surprisingly well at Hôtel de la Couronne. Little chambermaid, extremely pretty, acted scared as rabbit. Landlady explained—no reason to feel comfortable in presence of officers, and we first Americans town had seen. Difficulty getting rooms. Found one, with two beds, but wouldn't let us have it for long time—not even *see* it. Finally came out that it wasn't quite clean. Been made clear to them too often that when officers not satisfied, usually made trouble. Pathetic how cowed everybody is, particularly women. Frankly astonished at our mild demeanor.

Waiter, youth of 18, also had stories. So soon after

evacuation, everybody bursting to tell all he knows. Shattered mirror in dining room, where German soldier had used rifle, preliminary to shooting up place. Stopped by German officer, not for shooting, but because it was hotel reserved for *officers*.

Frequency with which we are saluted by civilians, doffing caps, etc., as required by Boche. Brass fittings on walls, door knobs, etc., all gone. All mattresses taken. Hun so short of linen, using paper for bandages in hospitals. Stories of pillage—very scientific—furniture, rugs, pictures, etc., neatly boxed and shipped to Germany. Probably never be recovered. Don't think I'll ever go into well-furnished German house without wondering where contents came from. German army commander—prince of blood, too—sent home trainloads of crockery and pictures. Hardly covered by *matériel de guerre* excuse.

Dominant note in all stories—irritating pettiness of Hun. Belgians hate him more for what he is, than for things he did. Might forgive him for murdering wife, burning home, and taking sons into slavery. But when put in jail for two weeks and fined because employee reputed to have talked back to officer, become implacable. Germans had no sense of humor. Many things he did would be laughable if not so tragic. Basis of harshness, his never-absent fear. Made himself a jest for centuries to come.

Sun., 10th.—Our hotel one of most expensive on *plage*. But bill for bed and breakfast—3 fr. 50. We first of liberators. Had neither smashed furniture nor raped chambermaid and everybody appreciative.

Chartered waiter to show us town. Constant flow of anecdote, mostly in Flemish. Saw mole and fortifica-

tions, whose very strength betrayed panic Fritz was in.
Also Tirpitz battery, which fired on Dunkerque and was
trial flight for Big Bertha. Gentle Hun left delayed
action mine in it, which went off, killing some fifty
women and children, and further endearing over-Rhine
Kultur to Belgians. Mass of twisted machinery and
shattered concrete.

Visited Kursaal, used by Boches as barracks—its
superb *Salle de Lecture*, a stable. The Hun would rather
keep his pigs in the parlor than anywhere else.

Wonderful *Gare Maritime*, begun before war, and one
of finest stations in world, completely dismantled for steel
in it. Docks, already being made ready for reception of
supplies, unhealthy place, well planted with mines, going
off at intervals still.

Pushed on along marvelous shore road, lined, every
inch, with fortifications, barbed wire and guns—all
testimony to nervous fear of landing, which guide told
us, never left heart of invader.

At Zeebrugge, saw famous blocked channel. Marveled long, despite intense cold, at nerve of British sail-
ors. Feelings peculiar, knowing that Americans would
have tried it if British hadn't. Never stated officially,
but reason to believe it fact.

Resumed journey northward, through changing country, incredibly neat, like old pictures of Spotless Town,
white houses with red roofs and green blinds, and rosy-
cheeked, plump little children playing on cobbled roads.
Not a sign of war. Reached Ecluse—Dutch frontier.
Unforgettable picture. White painted fence, with
barbed wire, formerly electrified by Germans—now full
of breaks. A narrow strip of land, with another gate,
and a long aisle, between tall trees, leading into Holland. Street-car tracks. Evidently no trick getting in

or out. Conversation with Belgian commanding guard, and invitation to cross border. Probably first American officers to be in neutral country without internment. Heard news of Kaiser's abdication from Dutch sentinel —told in gesture, mostly.

Lunch at Bruges, at table with Gen. Mangin, to music of *carillons*. Conversation with Belgian gendarme, speaking nothing but Flemish. By using style of Katzenjammer Kids, able to extract information desired. Pushed on. Roads choked with transport. Going slow. Picked up Belgian soldier, bound on bike for prodigious journey to attend funeral of father, civilian, killed by German shell—probably last of war.

Picked up quaint, black-bordered document:

"We have the honor to announce the death of His Majesty, William II, called '*Patte-Folle*,' or '*Le Saigneur de Naguère*.' Deceased following indigestion of French, English, Belgian, Italian, Portuguese and American soldiers, complicated by severe inflammations in Upper and Lower Rhine, coming on as result of surgical operation performed by Dr. Clemenceau.

"Funeral will take place in Berlin in temple of Good Old German God. The choir and Guards' Band will play the Te Deum *allegretto*, under direction of Marshal Foch, followed by grand *farandole* around the casket, with Gen Petain leading.

"After the ceremony, the body, reposing *sur la poudrette sèche*, furnished by Krupps, and in a coffin of English make, will be taken to the station, where, *au bout du quai*, a car will be reserved in a train *ultra rapide*.

"Burial will take place in a Holland cheese, of

the sort known as *Tête de Mort*, and the mourning will be conducted by the Crown Prince and the Association of Dethroned German Princelets. Charles I of Austria, Ferdinand of Bulgaria, and the Grand Turk will say a few words. All the bells of the civilized world will ring deliverance, and after the ceremonies a grand gorge will take place, of Frankfort sausage, ham from Mayence, Munich sauerkraut and other delicacies, washed down with Eau de Cologne. American bacon, being too indigestible, will be left off the menu. *Ni pleurs, ni couronnes. De profundis. Priez pour lui.*"

The Will of Wilhelm de Hohenzollern

At the moment when my Empire, formed from territories stolen from all my neighbors, is crumbling; and I foresee that a simple *casque à mêche* will soon replace the spiked helmet, I declare as follows: I bequeath—

(1) To my people, the shame of my past, and the weight of my crimes: I am sufficiently rich in them so that all can have a share.

(2) To my old friend, Hindenburg, all the nails which he has had driven into his head, and with which, in vain, he has tried to hold my tottering throne together.

(3) To Ludendorf, my faithful henchman, my big war sword, with which he will be able to frighten the sparrows.

(4) To the Fire Department, my numerous uniforms, which they may wear again at Mardi Gras.

(5) To all students of natural history, the right

to class me among the ferocious animals now ex-
tinct.

(6) Finally, to all my former subjects, the advice to keep cool, and to recall all the points of
President Wilson's peace, if they don't want to get
another crack on the jaw.

Done at Potsdam, regretting nothing but my
throne and the adoration of the imbecile crowd.
Signed G.H. EMPEROR AND KING—*en fuite*.

At Audenarde found —st American division coming
in, having advanced over four kilos without seeing Hun.
Terrific speed of war in last weeks. Roads jammed
with traffic and smashed with shell-holes. Couldn't
make much speed. Flanders landscape and beautiful
children made up for it. Wondering constantly about
armistice. Fearful it might not come off. No news
since leaving Havre.

"The Long, Long Trail," at dusk, around a K. of C.
wagon, with ceaseless rumble of guns as accompaniment
to rendition on mouth-organ. 30 men around performer,
with winking rise and fall of lights of cigarettes only
evidence they breathe. Their thoughts far from muddy
roadside, and business to which hands are set. Singing
softly, as if afraid to frighten haunting memories. Then
a rustle, as of leaves falling, louder, louder—the weary
tramp of marching men. Brusque commands. Dull
clanking of accoutrements, as sprawling group bestirs
itself. Shuffling of feet as they fall in on the road.
Another command—and only sound left on night air,
the heavy crunch of feet pounding in unison, slowly
growing fainter around a bend—the relief "going up."

Through Roubaix in dark, arriving Lille at 9, chilled
and hungry. Not much dinner. Hun had thoughtfully

destroyed lighting plant and waterworks, but did fairly well by selves at Hotel Bellevue.

Mon., 11th.—To office of British I.O. Lament of C——, Scotland Yard, that whole damn town was suspect. At 10:30 orderly interrupted with news G.H.Q. was on wire. Capt. J——, I.O., went out. Back in moment, saying nothing. One subaltern couldn't stand it: "Is it true, sir? Have they signed? Is the war over?" J—— looked blank. "Ah, yes—it will be—at 11 . . . but we mustn't let it interfere with our work, must we?" Business of rustling through papers. C—— blew up in good American disgust. "Hell, you damned fool, you're out of a job and don't know it!" Swept papers on floor. General handshaking, etc., and out to street.

No excitement at first. Flags began to appear. Apathetic faces, but eyes bright. Chauffeur reported not allowed to pay for lunch. That about all. Any city block at home could show more in way of celebration than whole town of Lille. Disappointed in selves. Wanted to be tremendously moved—and weren't.

N—— out to visit some cotton factories belonging to his firm. Found them stripped of machinery. Other factories, not only stripped, but not even walls standing. Met Englishman—hidden in town since '14. Nervous wreck.

Recognized nowhere as Americans. From caps, taken for *Belges*. People never even seen French soldiers. Didn't know red trousers no longer worn. Never heard of *bleu d'horizon*.

Left Lille and N—— at 3, reaching Courtrai in cold dreary rain. Got lost. Heavier rain and colder. Swell night for celebration! Every crossroad mined by

Boche. Some blown up by Royal Engineers, leaving
ugly crater, some merely marked with twig or stick.
Very dark and roads slippery., Unpleasant, expecting
any moment to hear Gabriel sound off. Ironic possibility
of being blown up night war ended. Finally slid off
crown of road onto mine. For some reason, failed to
go off. "Sait Tout's" only comment: *"C'est pas in-
téressant!"*
. Bawled out by Scotch troops for traveling with lights.
Told them war was over. "Aye," was answer, in tone
infinitely hopeless. "We've heard that before."

Lost again, and blew tire. Road blocked with huge
crater. Found selves in hamlet of Grandéglise. Simple,
kindly people, full of stories about Hun. Surprisingly
well informed as to American effort, thanks to leaflets
dropped by our planes. Said that Germans, from first
scoffing at our "bluff," had gone other way, and themselves spread wild tales about million planes, etc., coming. One squad of skilled advertising men would have
been worth more, at the right time, than several army
corps.

German rubber shortage—trucks without tires. Also,
oil shortage. Could tell Boche motors long way off,
from racket they made. Plainly weak on material.

Shared bed with chauffeur in small room with two
Northumberland Fusileers. Latter made some crack
about American tardiness in getting into war. Chauffeur spat vigorously: "Yeah, an' damn lucky for youse
guys the Canucks held 'em off till we got here."
Whereat, conversation languished.

Tues., 12th.—Allowed privilege of taking five year
old son of landlady out to yard to answer call of Nature.
Sweet little lad. Didn't guess reason for interest in
him, but mother did.

Good people refused payment for lodging, insisting we were liberators, etc. Left present for small boy, instead—more than they would have charged. So everybody happy.

Population of place 1100, but tasted war in full measure. Many young men taken away as civilian prisoners, and 25 young girls. The mine, whose crater had caused our halt, had gone off while party of villagers were working on road day previous—8 killed, 7 seriously injured. Fritz has certainly made war in gentlemanly way. Wonders plaintively why he's not more popular!

Usual difficulties with tires. Chauffeur haughtily repulsed proffers of assistance. Only tools in his bright lexicon, hammer and cold chisel—with emphasis on hammer. Got away at 11, taking stray *Belge* as passenger, who hadn't seen home or family since '14.

Arrived Mons at noon. Visited château and Boche observation tower, swaying crazily in wind—symbolic! Lunched well—pancakes with *sugar!* No lack of that during occupation. Waiter one of 43 condemned with Edith Cavell. Had face Henner might have painted—ascetic in every lineament. Just finished long term in German prison. Assured us, proudly, that he, too, had served *la patrie*.

Discovered chocolate candy—1 fr. 50. the *piece*. Group of dejected Boche prisoners being led through town, with small boy at head, carrying Belgian flag, shouting gleefully: *Nach Paris!* Canadians everywhere. Saw one with Old Glory in tunic. Grinned at usual question: "Me? Hell, I was a brakeman on the Erie." Many Yanks in Canadian uniform—some say as many as 10%. Canadians certainly *un*-English.

Many yarns about taking of Mons. On ridge of hills, just outside town, where British first met Germans in

'14, British battery just going into action when news of armistice arrived. Which reminds me, armistice signed 11th hour, 11th day, of 11th month. Hadn't thought of that!

Bitter rivalry between Canadians and Imperials for distinction of taking Mons. Said latter actually laid down barrage to prevent Colonials from getting there first. Must have been bum barrage.

Sad incidents—loss of 5 officers, 60 men from Canadian battalion in last hour of war. Things droll— British r.r. gun kept firing all day at 10 minute intervals, despite frantic flashes from German wireless, first in German, then in French and English, that war was over. Great to-do. Phones between corps, division and brigade all humming before gun located. Many isolated detachments like that—kept on hours after time was called.

Small but significant tragedy. Canadian soldier had dinner and skipped without settling. Tragedy in fact that people, after cruel years under Hun, idealized Allies. Welcomed them as liberators, nothing short of demigods. Disillusionment, though inevitable, none the less bitter!

Also things best forgotten, like Boche straggler, strangled by populace in public square. Little room for mercy in Belgian hearts these days. Jerry knows why.

Left Mons at 2. Went two blocks—flat tire. Two more miles—another flat. More hammer work, rim ruined, and back to Mons. Only bright spot, "Sait Tout," who, after being asked thousand times if we were *Belges*, came out of coma and replied courteously: *"Mais non, madame—Russes."*

For climax of day, stood by roadside in gloaming, and watched regiment after regiment, flags flying and bands playing—British army on return to Mons. And Princess Pats, *en route* to Coblentz, in blank file, with fading light gleaming dully on packs and rifles, and men singing "Over There."

Weary *repatriées*, pushing pitiful little carts and baby carriages over long miles back to what was left of homes, not too tired for smile and husky "Vive!"

Got billet from Town Cdt. British officer passed us on hotel stairs, with girl. *Femme de chambre* shrugged shoulders cynically. "*V'là*—it has already begun. Rather—it has recommenced." Asked if many girls had discovered Boche a man beneath uniform. "Many, *m'sieu? Toutes!*" Most yarns about poor violated damsels of *les pays envahis*, tosh. Why violate when there are so many willing?

Wed., 13th.—Chauffeur tinkered with car all A.M. Left at noon, after another meal with pastry—first in nearly year. Curious that we should find it in "bleeding Belgium."

Spent hours hunting bridge over canal about as wide as hair-ribbon, but all *sauté*. Finally solved problem by going through instead of over. Arrived Quesnoy 4:30. From there to hamlet of Commingies, "Sait Tout's" home. All agog with good news. *V—— est revenu!*"

Necessitous, a feast for his friends, *les Américains*. Only difficulty, finding something to eat. *Les sales costauds* carried off everything. But "Sait Tout" had brought precious loaf of white bread. Must eat of that. Protested, but in vain. Bit of ham found somewhere, and wine. Butter, too, from God knows where. Ate, every mouthful choking, while these kindly souls, literally starving for four years, asked questions of world outside, and told stories of *la canaille*.

Found woman in mourning for husband for over year. Able to tell her we'd seen him two days past, full of health. Story of French aviator who reached village, sick, hungry and exhausted—and wouldn't let them conceal him, because of what punishment would be if detected. Went staggering off into darkness—to die alone in fields.

Germans may have been right or wrong, and war forced on them as claimed. Don't know or care. But something wrong in any system that can produce such animals as have worn the eagles. German has sung devil's mass, and if his conscience is clear, he is mad.

Very anxious to find real "atrocity." Nearest thing to it was story of little boy, killed by German soldier. Petered out on investigation. Appeared that sentry, hearing noise in dark, called "halt." Figure ran away, and after calling "halt" again, fired. Went all to pieces when he found what he'd done, and sent to hospital. Irony in case, and typical Germanism—authorities fined boy's father and imprisoned him for having allowed lad out after curfew.

On to Valenciennes, 30 kilos, hoping to find lodging. Found only shattered, uninhabited town. Asked M.P. if there was hotel. His reply classic: had heard of "Hôtel de Villa" but not sure it was open.

Visited Town Major, who said there wasn't bed in place. Recommended Denain, 12 kilos off. House with beds there. Took on Irish gunner captain, in same fix. Bitterly cold. After hour's freezing ride, found selves at St. Amand—40 kilos wrong direction!

En route, met *poilu*, loaded down with usual junk. Coming from Lille, afoot, bound for Valenciennes.

Been to Lille *en perm*. Found his wife gone to Valenciennes. Immediately set out after her. Sad to think of what he found when he reached Valenciennes!

Back to Valenciennes, this time to H.Q. 4th Canadian division, and pleaded for lodging. Busy as hell, moving, but courtesy itself. Packed us off to "officers' club." Found it ruined château, minus everything but walls. Some 16 Britishers already stretched out on floor, and joined them. Had an address at last! All night, Irish gunner kept turning over: "God's truth, 'tis cold!"

Thur., 14th.—Awoke early. Frequent explosions toward Front. Rumor that hostilities were resumed. One young English subaltern expressed himself as satisfied—Hun not properly licked, etc. Howled down! Learned it was only Engineers, removing débris of bridges, etc. Hard to believe. Sounded exactly like quiet sector in morning strafe.

Usual diddling with car, and back to pick up "Sait Tout." Still center of admiring throng. Further hospitality. *"Boule"* of local cheese exhumed—more precious than gold, more awful than gas attack. Also mud-covered bottle of champagne. Much clinking of glasses, toasts, and more stories. One of old man who found 7 Boches in cellar, borrowed rifle from British, and dispatched them all himself. Battle fought in and around town. Civilians cheering the British on. Many casualties, but no deterrent effect: sudden death had ceased to shock.

Left at noon. Le Quesnoy, Le Cateau, Maubeuge, Cambrai—what was left of it. Bapaume and Albert—describable only in past tense. Irony in crossing what had been No Man's Land for four years at 60 m.p.h. For miles, shell-holes overlapping. Neither tree nor

habitation to be seen. Only sign of life, star-shells and
rockets continually lighting sky. Probably set off in
celebration by jubilant members of isolated salvage
camps. During hour or more, saw only three human
beings—old men in what had been Albert. "We lived
there," their simple explanation. "And now—we cannot even find where our houses stood."

Arrived Amiens, thoroughly frozen, at 7:30. Usual
punctures. Stopped for dinner and numerous cognacs
in vain effort to stop shivering. Chauffeur got out hammer and chisel. Ready at 11. Decided to push through
for Havre.

Fri., 15th.—Chauffeur's head soon nodding. Presently fell asleep at wheel. Took over. Superb machine
and pleasure to drive, despite discovery that among
other things, invaluable chauffeur had burned out brakes.
No one astir on roads, so got lost frequently.

Traveling entirely on hope—no more spares, no tubes,
no repair material. But reached Rouen at 4. Knocked
up gas depot, got gas, and pushed on. Hard driving,
with some rugged mountain country, and no brakes.
Nearly backed car into ravine. Reached level about
five. Bang! Another tire.

All for discretion and return to Rouen. But
chauffeur had date with girl in Havre and all for pushing on. Got out hammer and contrived a miracle.

During operations, peasant came up out of cold gray
dawn, looked us over, and despite earnest entreaties
for coffee, went on his way. "Sait Tout" shrugged
shoulders. "What would you expect from a damned,
lousy Norman?"

Reached Havre, 8:30. Letters from home with news
of flu plague. S—— expecting imminent dissolution.

Generous advice to remarry, sake of children, etc. Too tired even to be depressed. Took hot bath and turned in.

Sat., 16th.—C—— worrying about large army of occupation over here for couple of years. Not likely. Great need in U.S. is labor. Some say troops to go home at rate of 500,000 a month. Sure to go fast. Natives don't want us. Do everything to expedite matters.

Afternoon of luxurious idleness. To B.I.O. Everybody wangling to get home. Back to office and worked up iliad of last few days. General conclusions—about five divisions could hold Dutch border against defeatists.

Sun., 17th.—Wrote Guaranty Trust to buy French bonds, after prodigious figuring on ability to pay for them.*

S—— ordered to Dunkerque. Scared I may go to China. Dined with gang at G.T. Renigged on party and back to billet. Decided to go to Paris. Now the Kaiser's out, got to get some pants.

Mon., 18th.—Left on 9:10 with C——. Lunched Garnier's (fr. 27) Thrilled with Paris. First snow. Crowds on streets—women in furs. Met B——. On way home.

To pension. *Quel accueil!* Refugiées so interested in news from Belgium and north. Able to tell quite a bit, some of it, in case of Ostende and Mons, comfort-

*The custody charge on those bonds now almost equals the income from them—in dollars. A splendid investment!

ing. Dear old Mme. F—— wanted to know how little white house with green blinds, around corner from Place in Courtrai, had fared. Went through Courtrai at night, 40 m.p.h. Not able to tell much.

Paris at night—bright with *lights*, full of taxis and lovely females in furs and silks. Hard to believe, sipping chocolate in Mirabeau, that world's greatest war *finie*.

Saw B——, all in a flutter. Been doing canteen work with French. Found war "just too interesting." Ooo, la! la! Also W——, Capt. A.S., expecting orders. And A——, leaving to-night for Brest—and home. Thing getting on nerves!

Tues., 19th.—Cold. More people en route for home. Dined with C—— and J—— at Henri's. *Beaucoup* champagne. To Casino de Paris and shady dive. More champagne. Grippy—bad headache and full of virtue. Slipped away with woman, equally fed up, and walked home.

Wed., 20th.—Very cold. Loafed around. Visited Invalides. Tourist grafting begun already. Saw M——. Dismal prospects of G2 activity. Wondering how to get out. Lonesome afternoon wandering around. To Mirabeau, with J——. Lovely women. Dined, after futile protests, at Paillard's. Can't lift mortgage living this way! To Theatre Albert. Missed last métro. Walked home.

Thur., 21st.—Fine sleep. Cordiality of folk at pension. Charming G——. Search for bedding roll. Trouble with baggage. Damn French methods! Left at 5. Wangled seat and dinner place—much palaver and a couple of francs. Arrived Havre at 10. No trams. Damn French again. Walked to billet. Curious feeling of getting "home." How quickly one gets attached to a place.

Fri., 22nd.—Read papers, etc. Took bath. To B. I.O.—completely demoralized. Wangled oil stove— smoke, smell and no heat. Some comfort in warm underwear and decent breeches.

Sat., 23rd.—Worked on stove—*ne marche pas.* Dreadful prospects of being alone in Havre. Read improving books, and tried to write—nothing came. N—— and B—— in. Universal *cafard.*

Sun., 24th.—Sent in formal application for immediate discharge. Probably chucked in fire and answer: "Soon as can be spared," etc. Lonesome office. To B. I.O.—worse. Killing time. Walk and tea with N—— and B——. Tea supposed to be "cup that cheers." Found it wash-out.

C—— ordered to Paris. I hold bag. Promotion, perhaps, but just so much harder to get out of God damned army. Sign up for property and usual *paperasserie.**

Main job from now on, chasing Bolsheviks. If nothing else avails, go Bolshevik myself. Hallucinations already.

Letter from home, with description of B——, asleep, his little uniform buttoned over his pyjamas. So long since I stood watching in wonder the life which had come out of me—its beauty, innocence, wistful helplessness. Give much to watch it now.†

*Paper work: "red tape."

†A long way, now, from beauty or innocence—and the helplessness, all papa's!

Poor C——, under surveillance, because when charged
with being German-American, replies hotly and proudly
she's not—she's *German!* All very fine, but she ought
to know what *Kultur* really is. Few minutes with ladies
of Mons or Lille would be enlightening.

Apparently only people not promoted, those who came
over last year as casuals, and in line ever since. T——,
acting C.O. of battery in —th Field, and still 2nd Lt.
It's staffs and *en arrière* that get boosts, and in U.S. No
complaints, personally. Haven't done anything to get
promoted for.

Of bunch that came over together, S——never left
Tours. C——, Port Officer, B.S.4. K——still teaching
school. G——, G1, First Army. A——, nothing in
way of action beyond being stung on nose by bee.
W—— only one with any glory.

Yarn from home about W—— W—— being twice
offered Legion of Honor. And Croix de Guerre "many
times." Somebody kidding somebody.

Present prospects—to be in charge here, until later
and undefined date, when I go to Paris to help manage Peace Conference. Keeping courage up with
faith I'll be home in time for opening of golf season!

"God's truth, 'tis cold," as Irish gunner man said.
Toes and fingers *glacé*, and breath steaming. Delightful
spot, this, to spend winter. Every inhabitant has running nose.

Mon., 25th.—Puttered around office. Lunch at Club.
British in Transient Officers' Mess—never speak to each
other. No sound but rattle of crockery. Mere shyness.
Delighted when somebody cracks ice. Played rôle by
suggesting *en haut voix* U.S. demand at Peace Confer-

ence would be Gibraltar. All rose and took it—hook, line and sinker.

Banquet by French Intelligence. DeB——, leR——, "Sait Tout," M. le Commissaire Spéciale Adjoint, and C——. Also chap from B.C.R. Sort of show only French can stage.

"Sait Tout" and DeB—— just decorated by Belgians. Disgracefully ribald about it. Idea of Belgians decorating French—*insupportable!* Planning retaliation—notification to list of prominent Belges—*sousnommés élu, etc*— *sous-maîtresse, sans plaquet,* etc. *Ordre de Soleil Couchant*—upper Uganda! Much champagne—set up by "house." Home at 3, *bien allumé.*

Tues., 26th.—Long days. Nothing to do. Routine paper-work and desperate effort to find occupation for men. Order from Base H.Q. "send home available men." Promptly forwarded list entire office!

A——	Spanish	Clerk and interpreter
A——	Italian	Clerk & interpreter
B——	French	Hospital orderly
B——	**Dutch**	Stenographer
B——	French	Garage manager
B——	Canadian	Miner
C——	Italian	Mgr. movie theater
C——	Russian	Clerk
D——	Austrian	Hotel manager
D——	American	Scrap-metal salesman
D——	American	Student
F——	American	Motorman
F——	American	Bond salesman
F——	American	Salesman
G——	American	Music publisher
H——	French	Butler
H——	American	Banker
H——	American	Wholesale lumber
H——	Belgian	Accountant

K——	American	Investigator
K——	Armenian	Rancher
K——	Dutch	Diamond setter
M——	Roumanian	Chef
P——	English	Traveling salesman
P——	American	Reporter
R——	French	Bookkeeper
R——	American	Lecturer—newspaper owner
R——	French	Handy man
S——	American	Insurance broker
S——	Dutch	Interpreter
S——	French	Embassy clerk, Paris
T——	American	College professor
V——	Italian	Waiter
W——	American	Student
L——	French	Drug store mgr.

Remarkable aggregation. Carefully picked and trained. Seldom in uniform, but excellent discipline and behavior. Contrast with Base troops—like most of S.O.S., rather slack. Occasional formation, with squads east and west, just as reminder.

Officially and on surface, our work just what it was before armistice. Same controls, reports, etc. But no spirit in bones. Only short time before carcase declared officially dead—smelling already.

Could go home to-morrow and no wheel in A.E.F. stop turning. But still "indispensable"—the old *blague*. G2 crumbling fast. Hope to head west by Feb. 1. Hair thin and beginning to gray. Nose red. Posture bad. Liver worse. Morals—gone. Otherwise O.K.

Hate boots, puttees, wrapped leggings, riding breeches, flannel shirts, choke collars, overseas cap (special hate) and Sam B. belt. And W—— probably broken-hearted never got chance to wear them. *C'est la vie.*

Persistence wins! C—— finally ordered back to regiment.

Wed., 27th.—To bank with C——, and took over G2 account. To G.T. for dinner given by B.I.O. in C——'s honor. Wines well chosen. Dancing in street and other foolishness. But home at 12, fairly sober.

Letter from S——: "Why this talk of going home? Don't you realize that just when we are in full swing on demobilization, the wily Hun will rally his sleeping host for one more effort? Despite your hopes, Dep. Ass't Chief of Staff G2 tells me somebody has to go to Nice for winter, and you're probably it. G—— has orders to return to States. I don't think of such things any more. It softens the brain!"

Thur., 28th.—Soggy brain. Worried at idleness of men. Delightful place to spend winter. Few towns drearier than Havre on rainy day. Charming country, France—but could do with improvements in way of paving and sewers. Oh, for white-tiled bathroom and hot running water!

I.P.'s gave Thanksgiving banquet. M—— (en civile, chef Bellevue-Stratford), C. in C. "Cooked in six languages and five kitchens." Pumpkin pie—poem—contributed by "Y" ladies. Rolls by French baker from white flour wangled from Q.M. Champagne presented by restaurant proprietor, toothless old gent, who after numerous cognacs, put on ancient decorations and gave address of gratification that his "poor establishment scene of such gathering of noble Allies," etc.

Diffidence at first. But shoulder bars soon forgotten. Strange gathering. Harvard graduate in chevrons listening to Polish miner. California newspaper owner discussing Romain Rolland's "Life of Beethoven" with ex-waiter. College professor being bawled out for bad language by Armenian sheep-herder. The new America.

U.S. no longer mere geographic term. Nation at last.
Caste and origin forgotten. Too bad rough, frank fraternity of *la vie militaire* can't last.

Hat off to Yank. Independent, freer than any man
world yet seen, but with respect for self and purpose that
makes one glad to salute him as *man* in response to his
salute to *insignia*. Great fellow!

Speeches, of course. Early withdrawal of officers.
Many touching evidences of good will. Menu card
autographed to "our commander and friend." And for
benediction, half whispered "God bless him" from
A——, little Italian. Brought home enormity of being
officer. No greater satisfaction than knowledge of men's
loyalty. Something indescribably beautiful in blind, unwavering faith of men for leader.

Fri., 29th.—C——C—— *f . . . le camp.* R.R. station control closed. Final death G2 S.O.S. near. Lunch
with N——. British attitude toward King—see no difference in ours toward President. Great point of Wilson's picture tacked up in office.

Dreary day. Inspection service records, etc.,
Paperasse—chief activity of office. Dossier of Mr.
D——. Red Cross from B.I.O. Dirty dog! Apparently made specialty of English girls. Called on
him. Told him to take 9:05 to-morrow and save expense of boarding him in jail. Wanted to know who
the hell *I* was. Told him I was his conscience. Hope
the swine takes hint and clears out. Quieter.

Phone from Paris. 2 more I.P.'s to go.

Some time in March, when everybody's saying what
a hell of a place N'York is to live in, hope to blow in
on wintry blast and tell world there's no spot in heaven
to touch it.

Thoughts of S——. Can see her yet, standing in doorway that last ghastly morning. So strong—and so tender. Much water under bridge since then.

Sat., 30th.—Great problem—how to occupy men. Afternoon signing odd documents, and trying to think up something for I.P.'s to do. Bored with people and things. Going slowly nuts. Everybody the same way. Even P—— biting his finger nails.

December, 1918

Sun., 1st.—Absolutely *rien à faire*. Wonder how long I can last. Killed couple of hours trying to make stove work. Spilled oil, etc. Row with madame. Lights out. Cheery. Noisy *Belges* in next room. Forged pass for one of them to go to Paris.

Dined with N——. *Allumé*. To Yvonne's. Debate on *les sauvages Américains*. All agreed we were *"mals instruits."* Bell rang for customers. Disappeared into side room. Droll picture of self—chastely reading *Lit. Digest* in harlot's bedroom! On other side of door, two compatriots, rather drunk, getting rid of surplus wealth. Yanks grew loud and profane, one proclaiming loudly he had 700 fr. and could buy any God damned thing in the place, etc., with much U.S. small town smut directed at ladies present. Prompt resentment on part of ladies. Not what he thought they were. Had they been, would have smiled sweetly, sold him bad champagne till thoroughly *sou*, and then emptied pockets. That's what copy-book version of whore always does. Instead, Yvonne told them to clear out, with French too choice to be wasted. Then, new voice—Australian: "I say, you mustn't ever say things like that, you know —to a woman!" "She's nothing but a God damned tart"—American answer. Then Digger again: "Oh, but she's ever so much more than that, really. And besides—she's a woman."

Yvonne finally got Americans out. Aussie followed.

As he passed room in which I was cached, she said: "There's another American in there." National pride got bump in nose at Australian's answer—very curt: "Thanks, I'm a bit fed up on Americans."

Even in *maisons de tolérance*, *"qu'il est gentil"* better reference than *"qu'il est riche."*

Mon., 2nd.—Puttered around office. More paper work. Much excitement—8 men leaving. To Base Adjutant, sweating over service records. Regret loss of F——, Harvard graduate and perfect Sergeant Major. Bismarck was right: Any boob can be field marshal, but takes brains and character to be non-com.

Letter from H——. Still at Libourne—"instructing." "Some day somebody must answer for my internment here."

Tues., 3rd.—Wet drizzle—and *pas de beurre.* More struggle with service records. Very bored. Smoking too much. Entirely satisfied with *two* service stripes as recompense for having helped make world safe for democracy or whatever it is safe for. Hope to get home soon. Only danger, getting into "claims" or something like that. Those birds will have work for their grandchildren's children.

Mind on fact children ought to be learning some other language. Prefer French or Spanish, but easier to get exposed to Swedish. European culture so much deeper and broader than ours. Everybody knows at least one extra tongue. Anxious to get back and take education of youngsters in hand.*

*So far, have learned nothing but English—and not much of that.

Read "spy" story in *S.E.P.* Good God! Storybook spy usually suave, cultured, with high ideals and silk hat. In real life best timber found among young women with looks, moral adaptability and no convictions. Based on principle that man, however discreet among men, falls for first Delilah he meets. Yvonne D——, good example. More info. from her than any ten I.P.'s.

Singular establishment, her "Pension de Famille." There to-night to get straight dope on B——. Early, business not yet started, and found her abed, reading. Absorbed cognac and bickered with her. Charming person. At intervals, cook in to join us—large and eminently respectable, with baby somewhere *en arrière*. Hellenic display of person. Conversation on T.S.F., Red Cross dogs, love, marriage and abortion, and racial characteristics. Great candor, but singularly chaste—like anatomy to a surgeon. Perpetual celebration of death of shame.

Poor gulls of males, buying atrocious champagne at 35 fr. for hostesses—who slip into next room and give it to sewer. Stuff cost Yvonne 7 fr. *Les affaires sont les affaires.* Pathetic, the loneliness of foolish men for elegance of female companionship. Purr like great tomcats under cajoleries of damsels cold as oysters.

Wed., 4th.—Dazed before service records. Lunch with Britishers. Their resentment and mistrust of Wilson. Hard-headed practicality of English. Lack of imagination. Tragedy of the war. Come out where they went in. Same old fear of change.

Dined with N——. Bunch of Americans—just over —buying Pommard at 14 fr. for stray women. *Qu'ils sont les poires!* To show given by Australian "Wattle Birds." Very good.

Thur., 5th.—More paper work. Lunch at Club with usual crowd. Letter from S——, telling of bogus armistice celebration. What a contrast between way she saw war's end, and mine—Mons, only sound, rhythmic slosh of feet in mud; only illumination, a gleam, now and then, on a rifle-barrel.

These Britishers grieve me. So many virtues, but so mistrustful of their imaginations. Won't let ideals soar. All notions of future based too solidly on past. Fine fellows and good pals, but realms of dreams they know not of.

Eight more men ordered away. One new one arrived—venereal patient! Busy with paper work. Dinner with B—— and mellow on Bourgogne.

Fri., 6th.—To Paris, 9:05, with B——. Arrived in time to see departure of King of Belgians. Nice looking chap, manifestly popular with mob—more than can be said for most Belges. Called on W——. Found him busy wangling for home. L—— F—— came in. Called some general at G.H.Q. and said he wanted to go home right away!

At Ciro's ran into P—— H——, quite tight and much taken with pretty "Y" girl. Learned K—— still at Ft. Sill with —th Field. Lot of fellows there. All on to Casino. Supposed to be theater, but really Working Girls' Exchange. Swarm of more or less passable females strolling over place, making nightly bread. Took seat on lounge in *promenoir*, and instantly approached. Replied that I had wife, large family, and no francs. Furthermore, been in France long time, and by training, if not temperament, become callé. Contrary to notions of W.C.T.U. writers on Paris night life, this intrigued her, accepted cigarette, and began dis-

course on things in general. At curtain, asked perfunc-
torily if nothing could be arranged, and at my regrets,
wished me *bon voyage.* Replied: *"Bonne chance"*—
v'là tout.

Took chance on P——'s vague promise of extra bed
at Brighton. Found cot in room with strange gang and
turned in.

Sat., 7th.—Awoke to find T——, D——, and others
from home! Chat with T——, gist of it that if Maj.
W—— had ever seen action his own men would have
made him hell of insurance risk.

Bumped into Rev. W——, who severed himself from
large and clinging bishop to lunch *en deux.* Religious
discussion, in which, after being properly prayed over,
observed that his was form of petrified fungus, certain
to smell badly if warmed. Pleasant time had by all.

Saw D—— R——. Just promoted. Justly proud
of it, and understood why when I learned of life on
destroyers. If whole U.S. navy like him, fortunate indeed. Charming fellow. Only one flaw in seeing him
—possession of orders home. Very envious.

To Elysée Palace. Saw M—— and B——, about to
get orders; and R——, already with them. Damn!

In evening to Yale banquet at Palais d'Orsay.
Nearly 300 there. Ten from one class. All in high
spirits, even to applauding speaker who said "Yale spirit
won war!"

After elaborate arrangements to meet S——, he arrived very drunk. Spent rest of evening trying to avoid
him. No luck. Very rough and noisy.

Saw J—— M——, much disgruntled that war had
gone into receivership before he got here. Couldn't be
solaced, poor sap!

Sun., 8th.—Saw lot of fellows at Edouard VII.
K—— just back from prison in Bochieland. Slightly
balmy. G—— T——, great old fellow, amazing for
youth and charm, but my liver never could hold out
against his.

Lunched at Prunier's with crowd, getting tighter.
Then to Footit's bar. Grand experience meeting.
Many men with orders for home. F—— already got
his. Wish *I* could find some general at G.H.Q.!
Everybody heartily sick of army. B——, A.W.O.L.
Wired C.O. offering to match whether he go home or
to jail. Everybody's respectful attitude toward army
authority. Fear of consequences. Feeling of home-
sickness, loneliness, general futility of life.

Got B—— T—— out of million dollar office in
Meurice, where he's helping Hoover economize, for dinner. Nice chap, thoughtful, charming simplicity of
ways. Declines to camouflage self with uniform. Few
have courage for that. Talked politics.

Learned of chap wanting to get in G2 and stay in
France! Day of miracles not yet over! To bed with
high hopes.

Mon., 9th.—M—— and others, after much wangling,
off for visit to ex-Front. Declined invitation to join
them. Seen enough smashed buildings.

Saw D——. About as much charm as fat and half-
witted *escargot*.

To H.Q., G2, and sprang great idea about substitute.
Fell flat. "Done too well" and more such rot. Vague
blah about getting "Most important post in A.E.F.,"
and promotion. Extreme value due to intimate and
cordial relations established with French and British—
and more tosh. Meditate suicide.

Lunch chez Prunier—delightful shrine consecrated to good things that come out of sea—with B—— and B.I.O., Paris. Oysters, lobster, *coquille* St. Jacques, Barsac, Corton, *les crepes*. Succulent place!

Reading "Joan and Peter." Great book. Wells once tried to write story of happy marriage and muffed it. In this, didn't try, and did.

Met C—— and to Meurice Bar. Thence to Crillon. Saw B——, M——, and others. Disgusted with grafting frivolity of Peace Commission atmosphere. Drink and women—nothing else seems to matter.

Tues., 10th.—Left flat after difficulties with amorous chambermaid. Ran into J—— B——. Lunched with him and brother, *aspirant* in French Army, and altogether charming. Been through Foreign Legion, acquiring *médaille militaire* and couple of *blessures* en route. Mutual enthusiasm for French. His conclusion that not to love them, with tolerance for many shortcomings, wrote a man off. No gentler, kindlier, or more courteous and agreeable people ever graced crusty old earth.

Saw C—— at Crillon. Flippancy rather shocking. Man pointed out as "dangerous Socialist"—Lincoln Steffens! What rot. Don't know opinions, and probably wouldn't share them if I did. But one who has thought as he has on problems of human relations, certainly entitled to more respect than shown by tagging him "tainted." Not my notion of what war was fought for.

Met B—— at *rapide*. Poor devil—expected to meet wife, but she failed to show. Got wire, last day of leave, saying she was coming. Nice girl! Arrived

Havre at 10, and usual hike to hole in wall called "home."

Wed., 11th.—Back in the mud and muck—the knuckle-bone of France. To think people actually once spent *vacations* in this God damned land!

My rage at *les huiles* shared by B.I.O.'s 100%. Need for counter-espionage all gone. In its place, powers have set up bogie of Bolshevism. Disruptive influences under that head can't be controlled by fiat, "controls," and policemen. Only way to counteract bad propaganda is by good government. Growth of radical ideas can't be prevented. Silly, if not immoral, to try it.

Thought an elusive thing—and explosive when compressed. Nobody more dangerous than imbeciles in place of authority. Humor stimulated by reading grave report on inflammatory resolutions adopted by obscure C.G.T. group in Dijon. Yesterday, read same ideas, dropping from lips of British premier.

Presumption of enormously complicated movements of thought being dismissed by well-fed intellectual vacuum in two or three lines of official tosh.

Much twaddle prevailing about Bolshevist peril. Can't keep people healthy by locking doors against germs. Got to give them good food and plenty of exercise. Then germs whistle for job. If this mysterious Russian malady going to wreck world, then something seriously wrong with world, and ought to set about finding what it is. Not best of all possible worlds, by long shot. And not essential that all steps toward improvement be left to omniscience of comfortable. Man underneath not unreasonable in asking voice in arrangements for future. After all, he did the fighting.

To G.H.Q.'s request for list of G2 men who could

be spared. Col. W—— answers: "So far from sparing men, new personnel being added." Christ almighty—what *for?*

Time to abolish censorship. Necessary in war. Not now. On contrary, nothing more needed now than free thought and free speech. The opinion even of that shrewd old tyrant, Clemenceau. Droll to see Americans getting more Prussian than Prussians ever were.

Feel like waving red flag, myself. So many police-minded people—think like the century plant flowers.

Letter from S——, with cheering assurance relayed from new A.C. of S., G2, that "when Peace Conference terminates, things will be easier." Meanwhile—no chance. *Merde!*

Talk with Belgians at billet. Information about landlord: spiritualist—maybe worse. Maxim of La Rochefoucauld illustrated: "We hate nobody so much as our benefactors." Complete dislike of Belges for hosts, the French.

Thur., 12th.—Col. W—— turned down request for release: Despair!

Grand dinner at G.T. celebrating departure of N—— for Dieppe. Sad—my best pal here. Champagne ad lib. To Yvonne's to cry on shoulder. Rolled into careening bed about 3, exceeding tight.

Fri., 13th.—Life not poetry. Spiritual skies overcast, and stomach unhappy. Report at office M—— C—— arrived from Southampton. Found her at Moderne. Stunning in her "Y" uniform. Wanted to kiss her, but reflected she hadn't been here long enough to be used to Gallic ways. Took her to St. Addresse and *plage.* Miracle—no rain. Met M—— F——.

Sweet as flower, and so wistfully gentle. Learned of divorce. What an S.O.B. that fellow is!

Most of afternoon with M——. Heart full of joy, but stomach still in undulations and head rattling like nut with dried kernel. Got "Y" secretary's consent to dine with me, with instructions not to drink anything, and to be "very discreet." Droll—being sent out with me under set of rules. "Y" fellow been here only week. Doesn't know *I* made the rules!

Took her to G.T., in heart of *consigné* district. M—— scared "Y" people might find her there—it was on her list of places not to go to. Wished some "Y" fellow would put his nose in door. If he had, would have pinched him!

M—— and gang left at 8. Sad to see her go. Breath of home, but leaving bad case of *cafard* behind. So very long since I've talked to girl from home.

Restless as hell. Smoking too damned many cigarettes.

Sat., 14th.—Another personnel qualification card to fill out. Makes it even million! Called on P——, new **B.I.O.** Only captain, but how brass hats salute him! Indian Civil Servant, drawing much water *avant* and *après la guerre.* Saw Capt. B——, U.S.N., Port Officer. Charming man, amused at frantic search for "Bolsheviks."

Disgusted with imbecile work and idiot reports. Only gleam in day was picking up Australian, exceedingly drunk. Tried to get name, so I could steer him home. All he'd say was: "I'm sect'ry—*sect'ry,* y' understand, as the God damned English say, of th' Austrilian Bise Depot, blime me."

Annoying to have youths, just over, getting back and

into long pants while we linger on, as D—— says, "till last cork is pulled."

Sad at departure of N—— and P——. Good fellows, both, and as disgusted with life as I am. Feel that work of British Intelligence is done, and civil life needs them. Have comfort, however, of knowing discharge can't long be delayed. P——'s university asking for him urgently, and N——'s cotton firm. Sure to get priority.

Letter from D——:

"All my men working hard trying to wear out the seat of their pants. It's a mad war, my masters, now that we're no longer troubled by constant promotions and spies and things. As to homebound pennant, which should be attached to mainmast or *biroute*, I do not hear it flapping in the breeze. No prospect save endless Bordeaux. It is my melancholy pleasure to lie drunk with returning casuals. You will find me an old, erotic man, with purple face, Bull Durham dewlap and legs that look as if they had been turned upside down. I have a Bordeaux temper and that Kentucky feeling in the mornings."

Sun., 15th.—L'Union Sacrée, etc.—all shot. Used to think if nations could only meet each other personally, most cause for strife would vanish. Here we are—and national differences only intensified. Can't separate individual from country. Little personal frictions magnified into national quarrels. Too bad. Hope it's merely fruit of present abnormal situation. As it stands, French dislike English, English dislike Americans, and all join in detesting Belges. A cockeyed world!

This busy twiddling of thumbs in helpless inaction makes reason totter on throne. To be busiest and most essential man in A.E.F., bad enough. To be idlest and least important, and still linger on . . . presently go mad and bite!

How many more *brisques* before I taste cream again? Might of course flatten feet a little flatter, and get into Class D. In which case probably hospitalized and kept here forever. "*T'en fais pas, mon p'tit gars—ça colle.*"

Letter from family, worrying about clothes. Do they want me to come home in overseas whipcord, D. Haig leather-lined breeches, cap à l'Anglais, and bellows pockets? Rather more *tous qu'y a de chic* hereabouts to be bit shabby, issue tunic, etc. Shined, pressed, latest thing outfits from Barclay of Boulogne, apt to be on scented young men who fit battle of Paris these twenty bloody months.

Letter from S——: "For Christ's sake, you're in this sleuth business. Got some dope about the return trip. I've gotten to talking to myself and seeing things."

Managed to kill morning cooking breakfast and polishing boots. Hate quarters, service, meals and fellow man. No mail. Nothing to do. Dined with N—— and B——. 2 Chartreuses too much for me. Amazingly tight. Must be getting old. N—— off with girl. B—— and I in pursuit. Shadowed to Plat d'Argent. Encountered B——, English I.P., there. Enormous and complicated explanations. British military discipline shaken. Comical Red Cross fellow—very full. Home at 12, more than a little ill.

Mon., 16th.—Informed landlady her bread bad, butter worse, and coffee simply *atroce.* Replied with supreme indifference that *en Amérique* things were doubtless better. French well content when glorious Allies are again *chez eux*.

Nothing at office. Intolerable camouflage before men. Got proofs of photographs. Good God! Have I looked like *that* all these *months?* Grounds now for immediate dismissal from service on grounds of idiocy.

To tea given by Miss F——. Remarkable woman, packed with energy. Niece of Kitchener. Been in U.S. lecturing on munitions manufacture. Good conversation. English readiness to talk on interesting topics, and inelasticity of mind in thinking about them. Among those present—woman of Orange Irish gentry; country parson; Irish staff captain, up on horses, dogs and liquor; Indian official plastered with decorations; and Australian woman, running officers' club, very outspoken and masterful, with accent to shame Bow Bells. One topic significant. Parson lamented disappearance of old country squire and landed estates. Coming of small holdings—fenced off in barbed wire, e.g., disappearance of fox hunting. With it charm of rural England. Loud lament and sad. Suggested that dreadful squalor of Bloomsbury even more *triste*. All agreed, but in acquiescence of despair. Their view, that of comfortable people the world over. The park and the manor, and to hell with Bloomsbury.

Difference between them and French—latter will exhibit more interest in rights of man, but former, colder in principle, will be first to put up fences. Frenchman a better talker, and more subtle, but becomes so enamored of fine ideas, frequently forgets all thought of action.

Room in which tea was held—charming. Cretonne covers, open fire, books on shelves, etc.—*home*. Characteristically English.

Nothing less charming than French house. Paradox that artistic French dwell in homes shocking to æsthetic nerves of amœba. Mine, for instance. Street door opens with key that would sink ship. Large sign on landing, worked in colored chalks and framed in tinsel— "*Essuyez vos pieds.*" The Smell—unforgettable. Room half filled by enormous bed, with red velvet canopy. Mantel, covered with tassels, surmounted by mirror, also in canopy. Electric light cord, covered with twisted red paper, terminating in pink and gilt paper shade. On walls, two large slabs of tree-trunk, with cunningly contrived photos of Swiss mountains inserted. In one corner, picture of Buffalo Bill. In another, huge portrait of proprietor as youth. In between, large engraving of scenes in Flood. A turn to window for gaze upon "garden," and despair complete. Wet waste of mud and cinders, flanked by patches of disconsolate verdure, struggling to grow in rigorous grasp of rocks, cemented together. The one persistent tree drips soddenly. On the street . . . brass lunged pedlars. Never seem to sell anything, but never discouraged. Much prefer racket of "L." At least it means something.

Dined with N——. Both abysmally bored. Can't take to drink—already have. So reduced to merely gnawing fingers.

Tues., 17th.—Office, doing, as British say, "damn all." But fluttering clouds of pay rolls, service records, reports on subversive movements, etc., unabated.

Lunch with Lt. R——, I.O., London. Much footless crabbing. Story of Elsie Janis. Started with row between her and Mitzi Hajos. Said latter wouldn't get by on Broadway if people knew she was Austrian. Mitzi's comeback: Elsie wouldn't go so big if people knew her real name—Birbauer. Story reached long ears of B.I. Elsie jugged at Southampton. *"Feuillée à corps,"* etc. Terrible stew. Mamma B's rage. Released through efforts of G—— M——, American I.O., and old friend. Affair hushed up.

R——, interesting chap. Spent some time in Russia, spoke language, and knew many of prominence, from Trotzky to Jack Reed. Confirmed impression Bolshevism most dangerous thing in world to-day, but far from wholly bad. Certain that good or bad, not to be handled by mere passive efforts at repression. Only thing to save us—education and good government.

More or less acute symptoms of malady probable in England before long. England needs shakeup. Supporting fine flower of culture in dung-heap of drink-sodden ignorance. Beautiful on top, but soggy with booze below. If present system continues, or if, under pretense of change, mere puttering "reforms," British Empire doomed to certain and comparatively prompt extinction. In simple economic arithmetic, can't stand against U.S., with bigger population, more resources, and people educated and sober. Sentimental attachment of colonies weakening. In education, democratic government, and freedom of thought, closer to us than to mother country.

Liberal English realize cleaning-up process needed, and number of ancient ideas that must go in dustbin. But conservative, like brother in every land, seems to think a little juggling here and there going to take place of clean sweep required.

Greatest asset of British Empire, temperament of Englishman. Amazing how much he will stand for in way of class rule and government of privilege. Needs surgical operation—not castor oil.

Awful to think of fat-witted politicians, in Washington and London, determining destinies of world, deciding what alien people should think, without ever having stirred out of own little parish, or speaking any tongue but their own. Opposed to them the Bolsheviks, traveled, educated, full of positive, definite notions of human progress, experts at propaganda—could make monkey of our average statesman on any topic.

Usual way of dismissing Russia—glib remark about "people that can't govern selves." Smug indifference. But must be something more there than meets eye. Can't reconcile Lenine, who's forgotten more history and economics than most of our public men could learn, in what seems like such folly. Completely baffled.

Wed., 18th.—Lunch with L——, new B.I.O. Amiable schoolmaster, thoughtful, and with perfect understanding of what Britain faces. Saw Gen. Sackville-West. "Haw"—and monocle.

Afternoon on muck of pay rolls, and such. Dined alone on *plage*. Cold and windy, developing into real norther. Weather atrocious. Mugginess gets to soul. Fed up and then some. Nothing but change of scene, climate and occupation any good. And years before able to sustain sight of uniform without relapse.

Clump—clump—clump . . . party of German prisoners plodding through mud. Probably find life even less enjoyable than we do. But as weary guard said, at least have consolation of plenty of work.

Thur., 19th.—Nothing to report. Terrific efforts with stove—no results but smoke.

Fri., 20th.—Incipient sore throat. Got photos—and

shaved off mustache! Lunch with Britishers—can't
stand sight of treacle pudding. To office for in-
terminable afternoon of *rien à faire*. Disgusted with
new face—wish I'd kept mustache. Very cold. Dined
La Corniche. Didn't get place by stove, so had two
bottles St. Estephe, and shot of cognac. If this damned
weather gets worse I'll be in psychopathic ward. Reading "Joan and Peter."

Sat., 21st.—Had uniform pressed. In bed till return,
thus killing morning. Lunched with F—— and wife—
cold, hard, bright—straight from Mayfair novel. To
N——'s billet and talk till midnight. Good fellow,
yearning to get back to cotton-spinning.

Sun., 22nd.—Wire from Paris, asking full name.
Wonder what *that* means? Lunch with Britishers and
Capt. T——, Education Officer. Plans for occupying
soldiers' time while waiting repatriation. Cold, rainy
day. Wind howling like seven devils. Dined at Club
with F—— and Maj. P——, straight out of Kipling.
Talk of India till small hours.

Result of "Joan and Peter"—thoughts on education.
Lack of that, imagination, and capacity for co-
operation made madness of war possible. Without education, no rebuilding of muddled world, and wars again,
increasingly unpleasant.

So few men really educated, able to see over barriers
of creed, country, opinions. Like four-footed animals,
grub along, eyes on ground, enormously pained at bumping into others doing same thing. If human life to survive, heads got to come up—i.e., *education*. Not just
puttering with Greek grammar, academic, fragmentary
"literature," stodgy history. Not "practical," either—

penmanship and double entry bookkeeping. Got to teach young something of world, something definite, coherent, and their relation to it. Got to make them political-minded. Know economics as something more than formulæ.

Keen to tackle specific problem—education of my own. Every parent probably feels that way. Eager, plastic minds tempt and flatter, with illusion of our power. But not as plastic as they seem. Miracle of character, odd twists of inheritance, instinct, bob up to confound and puzzle. But much can be done—more than we have done.

Dreadful waste of impressionable years. Left to watchdog attention of servants, half-contemptuous incomprehension of stiff-minded teachers, to weary, bored, underpaid mechanisms of secondary schools. Tragic. Probably talk down to children. They think more than we appreciate. With their minds clutching so eagerly for ideas, understanding, we give beads, bright-colored yarn, games beneath intellectual interest of kitten.

Too much turning over of children to uninterested incompetents. Too little personal influence—mysterious aura defying courses, systems, formulæ. Not enough *frankness.* Dodge questions about sex, about God—try pitifully to pose as omniscient. Put them off or invent silly little substitutes. Give them outworn tools we've discarded. Urge courage—and give example of cowardice. Marvel that children should ever respect parents—probably don't, often. Tricked, evaded, condescended to, unreasonably ordered about, simplest things confused—why the hell *should* they respect us?

Their interrogations at strangeness of life, these days, answered with "daddy's killing Germans." So easy to dispose of tiring subjects. Whatever daddy does is right: therefore Germans forever wrong and bad. Perplexing world of to-morrow not going to solve difficulties by such easy distribution of rightness and wrongness.

Tossed about, our dogmas shambles, we turn over same old stuff to young, with smile and idiotic pretense that despite cracks and thumb-marks, as sound as ever. Hypocrisy of education appalling. Children, presently, going to see through it. Going to object being taught things we don't believe.

Our insincerity. Burn ourselves on sex—and answer child's questions with hokum about stork. Start him off with double mind—trying to believe fable, obliged, increasingly, to recognize fact.

Ambitions for my own—sane, balanced, idealism. Sympathy for other peoples, other creeds. Liberal, but with firm creed of their own. Able to use hands, and respectful of manual labor. Democratic in lives, aristocratic in ideals. But neither wise enough, nor they plastic enough, for more than shadowy approximation of hopes. Still—a target to shoot at.

The world changing. Got to change with it. No use lamenting security that's gone. A clean slate, now, such as man hasn't known for centuries. Got to write on it without heeding grimaces of ghosts.

Mon., 23rd.—Off, 9:05, to gay Paree, for merry Yuletide. Invaluable H——! Found myself alone in compartment, *mirabile dictu!* Explanation—card hung on door: *"Réservé pour le Mission Militaire Américaine."*

News of M—— C—— from stray "Y" girl. Tea at Ritz—very pleasant. Dined with R—— and L——. Much talk of going home. No hope myself.

To Olympia and Hôtel de Louvre—A.E.F. officers only. Awakened by commotion in hall. Manager of hotel, saying harsh words to American Major. Latter pleading for less noise. Pretty "Y" girl behind him, pulling on clothes. Major's explanations: "Just showing lady his room." Didn't seem to get away with it.

Tues., 24th.—Tried to see Col. W——, no luck. Talk with R——. Everybody sore, but hopeless. Lunched with M——, S——, etc. "Getting home"— *the* topic: Back to H.Q. Hanging around—hopes lower than ever. To Crillon. Got C—— (Maj. O——, excess baggage) and to LaRue's for marvelous dinner—settlement of war wager. Vintage wines, etc. Then round of dives. Rather *ennuyé*. Home at 3— mellow.

Wed., 25th.—Up at noon. Heart-warming Xmas cable from C——s. Saw M——, *deuxième classe!* To Meurice. Melancholy drink with L——. Not much Christmas, but better than last. Offer of berth with Ray Stannard Baker in press section of Peace Commission. Dubious.

Dinner *intime* at Foyot's, guest of J—— B——, Sec'y to Hurley of Shipping Board. Latter really *big* man. Vision and grasp of world. Sees far and broadly. Faculty of getting to point of things quickly. Imagination stirred.

J—— B—— did ordering. Maître d'hôtel almost in tears. Called for "claret," but at *sommelier's* blank face, left choice to him. Latter brought vintage stuff in decanters. J—— protested. Couldn't get away with anything like that—insisted on seeing *bottle!* *Sommelier* purple and not seen again. *Oh, les Américains! Qu'ils sont sauvages!*

Thur., 26th.—Still pulling wires. All so far attached to jokers. Saw Maj. H——, aide to Gen. C——, G2. Took me to B——, Sec'y to Col. House. Offered job as information collector. Liberal spirit fighting for attention. Need for men to make dumb lips of masses articulate. But fed up with *experiences*. Homesick as hell. Besides, family to support *chez moi*. And children more interesting than Dantzig corridor. Decided for home—and doubted decision. Amazing! Never dreamed of seeing two sides to *that* question.

Rumors from home of Labor Party forming. Bound to come. Progressives the forerunner. But build on Personality. World ripe now, as not before in our time, for new things. What's happened in Russia symptomatic of what in one form or another, going to happen all over world, U.S. included. Due for one of those upheavals of common man that come every so often.

Took H—— to dinner. Too broke to cast Château Quelque chose at 20 fr. before American water-drinkers. Ordered fine old Pinard. *Sommelier* startled, but H—— content. To next *poire* that asks *boisson*, doubtless reply with nonchalance of true connoisseur: "Pinard, I think."

Oh, these God damned women! Not good for man to live alone. Season of furs, silk stockings, red cheeks, bright eyes. After year playing tedious and unsatisfactory imitation of St. Anthony, prospect of further bouts with angels all too round and fleshly, not intriguing. Yearn for armistice.

Fri., 27th.—Called on H——, bright and early. Checkmate! Advised to be "patient." Hell! To Ave. M. Caught Col. C—— on wing. Suave and evasive. "Do all he could," "Just as soon as possible," etc. But hypnotized him. Talked him into corner. Finally dictated memo. Knowing gent's habits, secured copy from stenog.

Back to H.Q. after lunch. Found memo had died. Action "one of these days." G.O. authorizing step not known, etc. Hunted through Army Reg. and G.O. file, found something that fitted, typed nice letter to A.G. requesting issuance of orders for immediate return to U.S., had it taken into Col. C—— with bunch of correspondence—and it came out *signed!* Glory be to God! Back to hotel—complete nervous wreck. But headed West!!!

Sat., 28th.—Saw **H——**, trying Courier Service wangle. No luck. Tried **B——** on same thing, for Shipping Board. Small hope. And **J——**, none. Everybody trying same thing. Not less than hundred thousand officers willing and anxious to be couriers and carry dispatches to U.S. Saw **W——** and wired **S——**, at Tours.

Dined with **M——**. She a little melancholy. Half regretful myself at thought of leaving. Perverse creatures we are!

Sun., 29th.—To Elysée Palace. No one there. To Rue Bassano. Bicker with **S——**, **W——**, and others. To Versailles with **B——** and Monsieur **C——**, scholarly Franco-Græco-Serb.

B——'s experience. Joined up with N.Y. outfit—black. Proved political affair. No discipline. Black captain over him. Junior officers not backed up by Col. **H——**, prominent political figure. Landed in France, and turned over to French as best way of disposal. Latter put them in line, and kept them there—

for same reason. Comic incidents. B—— out on patrol.
Own men began shooting. Called for carrier pigeons.
Evanouis! "Boss, somebody done ate 'em!" B—— cer-
tainly had worst war I've heard of.

To Rue de l'Université for dinner. Smitten with
C—— D——. Exquisite musician. Sad to think of
seeing her no more. Much to be said for Mormon idea.

Mon., 30th.—After terrific job, shipped bedding roll,
etc., to U.S.

Met B——, busy wangling, like *tout le monde.* To
personnel office. Fixed up rating card, etc. Saw
C——. Long face and doubts as to my getting away.
Spoke of Rents, Requisitions and Claims. Very low.
Picked up Australian, out since '14, and homesick. Talk
of blue skies and warm sun. To Olympia. Great
change in public morals. Few women on deck. Not
much like year ago.

Tues., 31st.—To Crillon. Eleven o'clock rising,
cocktails, etc. Hell of life. Complete demoralization
of everybody around Peace Conference. High ideals
in discard, frivolity in place. Cynical laugh for drool
about importance of occasion. From stem to gudgeon,
nothing but lark. And for this so many gave lives. It
sickens, rather. Creatures of mire, we rise to heights,
but can't hold the pose.

Talked to S—— at Tours. Orders not arrived. Worried. Saw B——. Nothing stirring on courier game.
To Crillon. Saw S——. A card! Trying to attach
himself to some Peace Conference job. No luck, so took
red document seals, embossed them with eagle from uniform button, doped up some "orders," pasted on seals,
and off to see Europe!

Hard to have gay time in Paris when broke. But compensation in all virtue, and poverty effective counter-irritant to vice.

Dined with D—— L——. In "Y." Won't let him go home, so won't work. Spends time showing soldiers on leave around town. Tale of three doughboys—Eiffel Tower, etc., and—to save money—lunch at Duval's. Profuse thanks—and display of pocketful of francs, with: "Say, mister, where's this here now Maxim's?"

To Palais de Glace. Watched boxing and M—— and H—— serving hot dogs to 3000 hungry *militaires*. Better New Year's "revel" than anything at Ciro's or Folie Bergère.

Strolled about. Near Opéra, American officers, drunk and disgusting, furnishing spectacle for American privates, sober and disapproving. Tempted by uncommonly lovely wench, and decided, about 2:30, to retire in good order. Whereupon real work of night began—with decoration in Grand Order of Boobs.

Heard girl crying. Found young officer beating her up with broken umbrella. Interfered, suggesting actions not altogether chic. Injured dignity on his part, and threats to place me in arrest! Very drunk, so piloted him to hotel. Had lost key and forgotten room. Tried most of rooms in Red Cross hotel. About four, young man decided it was not his hotel. Tried most of hotels in neighborhood. Finally located right one—up on Champs Elysées. Nothing for it but tote him along. Many stops for embraces, giving of card, and details of fine old Southern family. Also many kicks in pants and bad words. Finally laid away just as sun coming up on 1919. To bed cursing self for not turning him into clink in first place.

January, 1919

Wed., 1st.—Up at noon. Lunch at Pyramides. Met P—— R——. Same place we met before—he en route to Front and certain of getting killed.

To Crillon. Everybody in stew over Lansing. Took 5 o'clock for Havre. Pathetic young *poilu*, just out of hospital, minus leg. Chased out of compartment— *simples soldats* not allowed in *première classe*. Arrived in rainstorm. No transportation, of course. Got to hand it to French. Who but they would have stayed in this God damned country as long as they have! But cold can't chill spirit now—"Awaiting orders home!" Though not easy in mind till on ship, with water between me and France.

Gods growing easy. New G.O. revoking restrictions on canteens selling chocolate, etc. Whole office spending accumulated savings on candy!

Thur., 2nd.—Many letters. Also Xmas package. And mess of "reports." Lunch with L——, Australian, and young Englishman. Latter, according to Australian, typical—sports, women, drink—not much else.

Saw Port Officer, *re* getting home from Havre. Agreed, but not cheering. Gave up scheme.

Heard from Tours that request from Col. C——, for orders sending me home, been received. So far so good. But request forwarded to G.H.Q. Can't understand

301

that, except that I.O.'s nominally S.O.S., take orders from Chaumont.

Process of turning over to M——. Signing reams of vouchers, etc. Worried over possible hitches. Fear reassignment. But hope for land of free by Feb. 1.

Story from home of B——'s crimes and punishment. Thought that perhaps punishment should be for elders. Child's natural passion for burning and cutting. Instead of teaching use of fire and edged tools, merely forbid them. Too much education *de post facto*. No hell deep enough for rogue who nicks well-honed edge. Better, wholesome shame of that, than fear and evasion of parental fiat.

Fri., 3rd.—Turned over G2 accounts to M——. Getting affairs in order. Phone call from Paris—orders come to proceed to B.S.5! Terrific excitement. Nervous as cat. So many things to do. M—— well content, having wangled trip to Belgium. Mind in chaos. Absolutely rattled! Dined alone La Corniche. Home to frenzied inefficient packing. Even joy of purpose hardly enough to balance ennui of *packing*.

Sat., 4th.—Peaches for breakfast. To office, cleaning up. Nervous. Lunch at Transient Officers' Mess, with P—— and L——, hopeless idealist, even to extent of advocating intermarriage with blacks. P——, Indian official, in utter horror, not comprehending idealist mind. L——'s gift of books. To paymaster, filling out forms.

Hurry call from Gen. B——, C.O. Base. To Base H.Q. and cooled heels till 5. Loathsome aide! Then terrific row over suspected irregularity of transfer as I.O. Gen. B——, still fighting Piutes, wanted to know where orders were. Told him they came by phone. Intimated I'd fabricated them. Tried to explain A.G. special order *re* G2, but old bird knew no orders later than '61. Bawled out, threatened with arrest if I "said another word," and chased out of office. The God damned "military mind." Raging at silly injustice, but helpless.

To office, burning wires to Paris. Telegram at 6, relieving me as I.O. What to do? Dined with M—— and L——, a bottle of Corton soothing and strengthening soul. To Signal Corps office. Second wire at 9:10, with orders for Paris. Laid both on Adjutant's desk. Court martial or what—*je m'en fou.* Resolved to beat it.

Farewells to Britishers. Warmed at friendliness. Almost like Limoges. Saddened. L——'s pathetic plea for England. "She'll need friends in the years to come."

Sun., 5th.—To 9:05, fearing hand of M.P. on shoulder any moment. P—— down to see me off. Touched. Autographed "Joan & Peter" for him—the New Testament for the devil!

Compartment with offensively jovial "Y" men—newcomers. Quick journey, thinking alternately of home and possibilities of detention, court martial, etc. Arrived Paris 1:30. Amiable Red Cross lad helped with baggage.

To Crillon. Saw F—— and spilled story of Gen. B——. To Continental. Amazing change over last year. So populous and gay, and *ascenseur* running both ways. To Choiseul and got M—— C—— for dinner. To bed at 11. Hard to sleep.

Mon., 6th.—To Elysée Palace. Saw W—— L——.

Got letter to Capt. G——, at Brest. (Written on U.S.
Embassy stationery!) Saw J—— S——. Joke on
B——. His wangling a complete washout. Stuck in
Angers. Harvard jibes at Yale "democracy."

To H.Q., winding up, and bank, closing out account.
Back to Montaigne. Eleventh hour scare over settle-
ment of contingency accounts. Running for train, with
Sgt. Major on heels—slight mistake showing me owing
Uncle Sam 1969 fr. My God!

Cheering good-bys of office. To Gare Montparnasse.
Hard to get seat. *Système D!* Picked up flier, Lt.
M——, and dined with him. Left 8:18. Woman with
baby and *poilu* husband. Gave her seat till 3. Then to
woman with three *gosses*—one very like B——. Children's hobnails on iron floor of corridor. Guard complained at noise. Father talked back. Threats of being
put off, arrest, imprisonment, etc. Petty tyranny of
les fonctionnaires. Pathos of poor people. So timid.
Always getting it in neck. Got seat at 5.

Tues., 7th.—Arrived Brest 9:30. Saw T——
W——. To Casual Officer's camp, ahead of crowd.
Saw Capt. W——, presented G2 order and got permission to sleep *en ville.* To I.O. Wangling O.K. so far.
Glad when it will be over. Several weeks, maybe.
Lunched wretchedly Hôtel des Voyageurs, with W——.
To *gare* in fruitless search for trunk. Called on
Capt. G——, presenting W——'s letter. No effect
perceptible, though pleasant. Sure I'd get off in
less than week. Wandered around town, not feeling too well. Dined alone at "Y" hotel. No desire to talk. To icy room and bed. Never saw room-
mate. Glad when this hurdle is jumped. Still nervous.

Wed., 8th.—Located trunk. Notice to report registration desk. Alarmed, but proved nothing. Rumor of imminent departures. To I.O. Wrote official letters. Lunch with Capt. G——, at Officers' Club. Good fellow. Universal detestation of regular army. Story of Gen. H——, Base C.O. Poor damned casual, on way to boat, failed to salute him. Called back and put at bottom of sailing list—three weeks more of Brest.

Interesting talk with F——, examining surgeon. Theory of heat as cure for gonorrhœa. This year certainly been all to good for doctors. Learned a lot.

Back to room. *Rien à faire.* Hard to realize actually en route for *home!* Loafed away afternoon, with frequent visits to Bulletin Board, hoping to see name posted. Oppressed by Brest. Dreary—all movies and shows closed account of flu. Very cold and rainy.

Thur., 9th.—Breakfast with "Y" fellow. To hotels, hunting J—— B——. Ran into F—— B——. Lunch with him at Moderne. Saw D——. Assurances of "luck" at escaping Camp Pont Nezon. Luck, hell! It was damned hard work!

Nameless fear of nameless nothing. Anxious for water 'twixt me and France. Vague, dreadful presentiments. To H.Q. Casuals, and got qualification card. Located B——, in company of Sgt. R——. Illustration of difference between civilian and military point of view. To Bulletin Board all evening. At 11, list for *S.S. Canada* put up. Not on it and rather glad. Home and to bed, glad another day gone.

Fri., 10th.—New bedfellow. Saw Capt. G——. Assurance I'm on *G. Washington*, but counting no chickens. Rumor she'll be held for President. Usual visit to Bulletin Board.

To B——'s room. Amorous chambermaids, ripe for plucking. Oh, me, oh, my! Hard to be Sir Galahad. Sore throat. Fear of sickness interfering with getaway. Nervous. Still hoping for G. *Washington*, but fearful of slip. Wangled bread for B. Baruch and party. Latter pained at not having private car. Poor fish—B—— got him only sleeping car on road.

Saw J—— at 4. Assurances of *tout va bien*, but still fearful. Hail and snowstorm. To room—played out. New bunkie, ranker, aide to Gen. C——. Typical. New list to be up at 8—but wasn't. To bed at 9—shot to pieces. Feverish sleep and wild dreams. If I get the flu *now*—Christ!

Sat., 11th.—Up at 6. Hasty breakfast and to Casual H.Q. Glory! My name on list. Got sailing card. Enormous relief. Physical exam—crabs, cooties and clap. Scared to death, but O.K. Thank God, didn't take temperature! Changed money to good old dollars. Sent cable. Teeth chattering, but happy.

To R——'s flat for lunch. Charming company. Got car with Maj. H——, and to dock. Aboard ship at 4. Luck held—got assigned to room, found trunk, etc. Enormous feeling of relief—almost safe!

Good dinner. Movie show. Luxury—feeling of sublime contentment. Then usual line-up, and picked as berthing space officer. Drool about "duties" by Navy egg, regular and hard boiled. Usual R.O.T.C. drip. Wonder where the hell he thought we'd been this past year.

Last minute rumor of 42 men to be taken off ship.

Panic! Everybody ducking for cover. Ship amazingly hard place to hide in!

Sun., 12th.—Down for watch on G deck at 5. Chaos —men jammed in triple-tier bunks, etc. Weary hours. Not allowed to "read, sit down, or smoke." Four hour watch. Backache. Constant clangor hobnailed boots on iron ladders.

Passed up lunch. Fitful dozing till 4. Dreams of S—— and children. Wandering around, arranging reliefs, etc. No place to sit down except stateroom, and choice company there. Those not morons, foul-mouthed swine. On watch again at 8. Broke regulations and saved reason with Jacobs' "Night Watchman."

Mon., 13th.—Fairly rough sea. Bunkies laid out— much worse sick than well. Found good company with officers —th Div. Slow passage of time. Boat drill —silly farce.

Maj. H——, flier, charming fellow. Planning flight across Atlantic, but admits feet getting cold. On duty at 12. My post close to popular G.I. can—"1, for the use of." Short arm inspection between vomits. Doctor sicker than patients. Droll but pathetic. Hard, having to chase poor devils on deck. Cheerfulness of Amex soldiers. Their cleanliness. Superiority to officers.

Time changed—to our loss. Off at 4. Talk with Doc O'H—— widely traveled vaudeville actor, enlisted in Navy. Fried chicken for dinner, with orchestra accompaniment. Also movie show, with best seats reserved for Navy—splendid interservice entente as result. Can't see, though, that Navy reserve much better treated than Army.

Tues., 14th.—On watch at 4. Resent imbecile job, but habit of obedience strong. Rough ocean. Not sea-sick, exactly—but not enjoying ride. Very light break-fast. Talk with old Engineer Major—choice epithets for regular army. "Y" man—wounded . . . and de-lighted.

Maj. H—— looking at waves, made formal renounce-ment of plan to fly across Atlantic. Ocean broader than he'd thought it was.

Concert and Charlie Chaplin—military comedy, with expert audience. Tried to play shuffle-board, marked "for U.S. soldiers and sailors." Navy padlock on it, and wouldn't give us key. Complaints from soldiers of sail-ors swiping souvenirs. Likely to have a private war be-fore ship docks.

Good dinner. Best meals in months, but miss Burgundy.

Wed., 15th.—Chat with Lt. Col., M.C. The "God damned regulars" again. Same in French army. Famous surgeon, serving as hospital orderly.

Alarms, fake boat drills, formations all over place. And hours staring into space. Sea just rough enough to make land seem like nice place to be. Afternoon do-ing nothing down in G1. Back to cabin. Tried to sleep, but filthy tongues of mates prevented. Such ani-mals! Concert in evening by band, —th Inf., and good movie. Music and shows all over ship.

Thur., 16th.—Due for watch at 4, but went A.W.O.L. Slight spice of risk to offset ennui. Fed up with job, ride and bunkies. Longing for liberty.

Extremely rough, with gale blowing. Losing speed. Probably not in till Wed. To concert. Played *Berceuse* from "Jocelyn." Thoughts of S——. Red Cross girl and Gen. C——, *très intime*—talking "French" to keep me from hearing! Naughty, naughty! *Les oreilles vous écoutent!*

Ports closed. No sleep. Low at prospect of 1600 miles yet to go. Not half there yet. First edition of "Hatchet" out. On watch. Ventilation terrible, with G.I. can overflowing. Stuck to post till 11, retiring in good order.

Fri., 17th.—Imbecile racket of bunkies. Old pig, H——, using precious Poulbot drawing to wrap up false teeth. Delivered short address, with words not in dictionary.

Cold, with snow and gale. Few females aboard *pas jolies*, but nobody particular—supply less than demand. Lonesome as hell, but cheered with thought that army days are numbered. Probably arrive Tuesday P.M.

On watch at 12. Boring and uncomfortable. Uncomplaining doughboys—contrast with officers. Walk on deck with H——, and *porto* in cabin. Punk service on ship. Rotten discipline of colored personnel. Small credit to navy. But probably considered O.K. for army. Heigho—four more days!

Sat., 18th.—Lovely day, with fairly smooth sea. Went A.W.O.L. for breakfast. On deck all A.M. No chairs, so stood up. Rumor abroad that demobilization halted. Incredible—but everyone worrying. Refuse to believe it.

316 miles to-day. Hopes improving. Meals getting worse. Tried to read. Impossible with intruding dreams of home. Reveries of past—fantasies of future. Planning so many things.

Sun., 19th.—Hours staring at gray waste of wind and water. Talk with H——, on most interesting of all topics—religion. To room and learned that bunkies, as result of bawling out to H——, had decided I was old regular. Played up by mumbling something about "third hitch"* and let out some more mule-skinner stuff. Marked increase in respect shown. Comic!

A—— to sick bay with flu. Rest of cabin scared stiff. Movie show: "Man without a Country." Ribald hilarity of expert and critical audience.

Mon., 20th.—Usual morning service down in G1 hole. To cabin, still playing hard-guy old timer to bunkies. More *blague* about being ranker, staying in service, etc. Too droll.

Ship paused to let down mine sweepers. Cheerful thought. Roommates certainly fine fellows. H——'s latest: swiped silver sugar bowl for souvenir. "Officer and gentleman"—hell!

Tempted to go A.W.O.L. again, but discipline ground too deep. *Afraid!* And disgusted with self for being so.

Tues., 21st.—Docked 9:30. Usual *paperasse*, physical exam, etc. Orders not to wear Sam Browne belts. Cheered with thought that hour or so would see us free. Then—orders for Camp Meade, and no leaves allowed.

Long wait for Red Cross car, and finally to Yale-Princeton Club. Saw crowd of fellows there. Impossible to realize that to-day not year ago. Wonderful bath and lunch. And grand parade, with H—— up

*Enlistment.

5th Ave., wearing S.B. belts! Overwhelmed with beauty
of women.

To H——'s office. Oppressive heat of buildings.
Telephoned S——. Thrilled to hear her *voice*. Out to
Mt. Vernon for dinner party. Talked self dry—found
myself all wrong on everything. J—— called me "pro-
German." My God—such fire-eaters! We certainly
saw show from different seats. No more talk for me!

Wed., 22nd.—To town. Got H—— and to Hoboken,
getting mileage, baggage, etc. Annoyed by "passes."
Silly rot. Decided to leave 3:25. Decided not to. Decided I've lost all power of decision. Strolled around
with H——, still swanking belts and hoping to meet
M.P., but no luck. Fearful of length of sentence in
Camp Meade. Two months, some say. . Horrible idea!
Wonder if I'll ever really be free again? Probably
not. Poverty will take place of uniform.

Dined delightfully at Gotham with J——, and to
spy-play, "Three Faces East." Stage-spies got to be
made up: no drama in real ones. To bed in daze. To-
morrow I see my own true love!

Thur., 23rd.—S——arrived 9:20. What a picture—
lovely. Feeling of being boy and girl again. But such
a brief moment. Rushed off to Penna. R.R. station for
few short moments in waiting room, before leaving for
Baltimore. Tantalizing!

The Pullman—such service! And the diner! *Ma foi*,
but they do themselves well, these Americans! Arrived
Baltimore 3:30. Wait for tram, and then jitney to
Camp Meade. Got there at 5. Pouring rain and sea
of mud—worse than France. Fears of tardiness un-
founded. Shuffled to and fro. Supreme indifference

of *les fonctionnaires*. Got lost. *Musette* busted
(thoughts of Southampton). Soaked, tired and angry.
Finally got billet. Good mess and quarters, but best of
all, assurance that couple of days would see me out. Old
fear of possible hitches, but mild. Contented and comfortable.

Fri., 24th.—Awoke to bugles. Thoughts of Souge.
To personnel office. Lt. Col. B——, S.O.B., first grade.
Official greeting to U.S.: "Your belt's twisted." And
trying to use his pen: "This is *my* desk—do they act
like that in France?". And being helpful: "If you
haven't sense enough to fill out a form, you'll be here a
month."

Got through, somehow, by noon. Then to lightning
physical exam. Droll question by psychopathic doctor:
"Glad to be out of army?" One fellow hesitated, and
doctor said: "Hold him for further examination."
Ought to hold him for life!

Through at 2. Nothing more till to-morrow.
Tempted to go in town—but saved money and stayed.
Impossible to grasp fact that long race nearly run.
Whiled away afternoon, reading, shining shoes, etc.
Unendurable heat of rooms. And tireless bugles.

C—— and two more from *G. Washington* arrive.
Rancorous at treatment. Much worse than anything in
France. C——'s plaint: "Good God, what have *we*
done to be ridden? Treat us like lousy bums!" Ordered
to remove insignia, ripped off wound stripe, too.
F——'s comment: "Silly—nobody'll know he had one."
But as C—— said, who would care?

Sat., 25th.—To personnel office. Got order of discharge at 9:30. Then to finance office—clear across

camp—to make out mileage and final pay. And another long hike, toting bags, to disbursing officer. Army system—make everything as hard as possible. Meditated staying to give Col. B—— one good kick in teeth,* but in to Baltimore instead, catching 12:15 for N.Y. Free man at last—and in a daze!

Couple of doughboys on 42nd St., talking to cop. Saw me and came over. Snappy salutes. "Lieutenant, could you direct us to a prophylactic station? That God damned flatfoot never heard of such a thing." Tragic —all the good work wasted. Sort of symbolic of the whole bloody war.

Caught 6:41 for Mt. Vernon. Seat with ex.-A.E.F. Didn't expect to be met with band, but thought it thick to have div. insignia ripped off. "Treated worse than Huns." God damned regular army, silver-striped S.O.B.'s, etc.

Didn't listen. *Je m'en fou* 100%. *That* war's done with.

*McG—— obeyed the impulse, nearly sending Col. B—— to morgue before bystanders intervened. Too bad the ceremonies weren't private!

Glossary

abri, a dug-out.

A.C. of S., Acting Chief of Staff.

A.D.C., Aide-de-Camp. A young man of pleasant address acting as private secretary to a general.

affichage, promulgation of laws by posting on the bulletin board of the town hall (*mairie*).

A.G., Adjutant General.

alerte, the warning signal. Given in various ways, such as banging on an empty shell case, suspended from a tree. This had a marked resemblance to the sounds given off by a railroad eating-house before the advent of dining cars. The *alerte* in Paris, against air raids, was given by sirens and the firemen, blowing their horns.

allumé, slightly and pleasantly intoxicated.

Archies, anti-aircraft guns. Very unpopular with concealed batteries. It was their habit to dash up like a fire-engine, shoot a few rounds of their perfectly useless firecrackers, and decamp just before the enemy, having located the battery, responded with H.E.

Arrival, a shell coming on its way from the enemy. The larger variety announced their coming with a peculiarly unpleasant whistle. The smaller merely announced and went off simultaneously: whence the name "whiz-bang."

A.S.C., Army Service Corps (British).

au feu, the Front.

A.W., the Articles of War.

A.W.O.L., absent without official leave.

Bat' d'Af., African Discipline Battalions: military penal units. Legend had it that these incorrigibles were offered the privilege of

315

service in the Trench Mortars—the "Suicide Club"; and that all accepted joyously. Hence the title: "Les Joyeux," and "Les Zéphyrs."

B.C., Battery Commander.

B.E.F., British Expeditionary Force.

"benzined," said of an officer brought before a Board of Inquiry and retired, reduced in rank, or transferred to innocuous desuetude.

berloque, the recall: blown by the Paris firemen at the conclusion of an air raid.

Big Bertha, the German long-range gun that bombarded Paris.

B.I.O., British Intelligence Office (or Officers).

blague, according to Professor Feuillerat, *blague* is the satirical, jesting pretense of not taking seriously what one actually respects —hiding the most sincere convictions under an appearance of cynicism, ridiculing what in one's heart one considers sacred, steeling oneself against emotion and tenderness. *Blague* is certainly the most characteristic of French traits, and the most difficult for a foreigner to comprehend.

blessés, wounded men.

blessures, wounds.

en boîte, in the hoosegow—jailed.

brasserie, combination beer-saloon and restaurant.

brisques, chevrons, indicative of service, rank (in a non-commissioned officer), or wounds.

B.S., Base Section. In another sense: "hot air" (very free translation).

B.S.R., *Bureau de Service de Renseignement:* French military intelligence.

bubble & squeak, an English pudding, peculiarly flat.

bunk fatigue, doing nothing—resting.

bust, reduction in rank.

C.A.C., Coast Artillery Corps.

cafard, le, the blues: a malady from which no one was immune.

callé, sophisticated.

"ça marche," "that's all right."

camion, truck.

casual, a man not assigned to a unit.

C.G.T., *Confédération Générale du Travail:* French Federation of Labor.

C. in C. Commander-in-Chief.

cingalis, caterpillar treads used on the 155 G.P.F.

clairon, trumpet.

C.O., Commanding Officer (American).

C. of S., Chief of Staff.

consigné, forbidden.

copain, comrade (French).

costaud, term of reproach (French).

C.R., crossroad.

cushy job, a sinecure (English).

dactylo, French for "stenog."

défaitisme, political policy of rapprochement with Germany.

défaitiste, un, might be rendered roughly in our vernacular, as a "quitter."

au Delà, God: the Beyond.

Departure, a shell on its way toward the enemy; sounds exactly like the tearing of strong silk.

deuil, mourning: grief.

Diggers, Australians.

dog-robber, officers' orderly-servant: "striker."

Dungarees, blue denim over-alls.

enfilade fire, by moving guns forward and firing as far as possible on a line parallel with the enemy trenches, greater use was made of a shell's oval pattern of burst.

en repos, out of the line for what was called a "rest."

Ersatz, substitute (German).

Etat major, staff.

F.A., Field Artillery.

fade, flat, stale and unprofitable.

F.A.D.R., Field Artillery Drill Regulations.

fantassin, infantryman.

Feldlazaret, Field hospital (German).

filer, to beat it: get away in a hurry.

Flic, a French detective: corresponds to our "dick."

Je m'en fou, usually printed *je m'en f*. . . (I don't give a damn). Before the war never used in any but the vulgarest circles. Nice people expressed the idea with *"je m'en moque,"* though under strong provocation they might descend to *"je m'en fiche."* The etymology of *je m'en f* . . . is obscure but indelicate.

Foyer du Soldat, French equivalent of Y.M.C.A.

funk hole, a shelter against shrapnel.

G2, Second (Military Information) Section of the General Staff.

gaffe, a blunder.

galloné, "braided": refers to sleeve indication of rank.

G.C.M., General Court Martial: for more serious offenses than the Summary Court Martial.

G.H.Q., Headquarters— American.

G.I. can, galvanized iron can.

G.O., General Order, as distinct from division, regimental and other orders.

goldfish, ration issue of canned salmon.

gosse, a youngster.

155 G.P.F., 155 milimeter long-range gun, designed by Col. Filleux of the French Army.

G.Q.G., *Grand Quartier Général:* French Headquarters.

gros légumes, the higher-ups.

Guard House Lawyer, unofficial interpreter of the A.W. and Army Reg.

c'est la guerre, the explanation for everything.

H.E., high explosive.

huiles, les, the higher-ups.

Intendance, Quartermaster Corps (French).

I.O., Intelligence Office (or Officer).

I.P., Intelligence Police (or Policeman).

issue, clothes, rations or supplies provided by the government.

Jerry, Yank designation of the Germans.

Joyeux, les. See "Bat' d'Af."

jusqu'auboutiste, bitter ender.

Keystone War, Border Service, 1917.

K.P., Kitchen Police: the cook's helpers — peeling potatoes, washing dishes, etc. Man-power usually supplied from ranks of minor offenders against discipline.

Limey, Britisher: derived from ancient British custom of serving out lime juice on their ships as a preventive of scurvy.

L. of C., Lines of Communication (British) : corresponding to our term S.O.S.

Lopin, little patch of ground, all one's own: the Frenchman's idea of heaven on earth.

O.C., Officer Commanding (British).

O.D., olive drab: i.e., the American uniform.

O.P., observation post.

O.R.C., Officers' Reserve Corps.

maisons de tolérance, regulated houses of prostitution.

Manège, riding hall.

maquereau, a pimp.

M.C., Medical corps.

médaille de charrion, identification tag.

merde, called the *"mot de Schönbrunn,"* since Napoleon found it the only word adequately expressive of his feelings toward the Austrian proposals after Wagram. Translatable, but not printable.

Monsieur le Bureau, officialdom.

M.P., Military Police.

musette, small traveling bag, slung over shoulder: usually seen with a loaf of bread sticking out one end, and a bottle of wine out of the other.

N.G., National Guard.

panne, trouble: applied specifically to automobiles.

paperasserie, paper work: red tape.

Parigot, a Parisian.

perm, short for *permission:* leave.

pip squeaks, small caliber guns.

piston, captain (French slang).

planton, orderly (French).

plucked, originally, said of cadets flunked out of West Point. Applied to any failure to pass a test.

poilu, literally, "the bearded one." The French private soldier. An anachronism, since the great bulk of the soldiers were beardless.

poire, what we would call a "sucker."

Poireau, decoration awarded *pour la mérite d'agriculture.* Used in a derisive sense of any military decoration which had lost significance through over-distribution.

potato masher, German hand grenade.

Q.M., Quartermaster Corps.

réformé, discharged from the army for disability, and returned to civil life.

Réveillon, the night before Christmas: celebrated by the Parisian like our New Year's Eve.

réverbères, street lights.

rien à faire, nothing to do.

rien à signaler, favorite expression of the *communiqués:* no news to-day.

Rosalie, French slang for their bayonet: also called "Josephine."

R.O.T.C., Reserve Officers' Training Camp.

S.C.D., Surgeon's Certificate of Disability. Often a polite form of "benzining."

Service de Bois, Lumber and Forestry Department of the French Quartermaster Corps.

short arm inspection, examination for venereal disease.

singe, "monkey meat." The French army ration of canned beef. That is, it was *supposed* to be beef.

S.O.L., completely out of luck. (Free translation.)

sommelier, waiter charged with service of wine.

S.O.S., Service of Supply. Originally called Service of the Rear, but changed because "the rear" is synonymous with the latrines, and those in it were sensitive.

square-head, Prussian, specifically; Germans in general.

Strafe, German word meaning "hate"; later, slang for bombardment.

supprimé, abolished.

Système D, any method of circumventing rules and regulations.

T.B., throw-back. Officer withdrawn from the line for inefficiency.

tenu, uniform: "get-up."

tenu de fantaisie, uniform not strictly regulation.

T.M., Town Major: officer (usually a Second Lieutenant) in charge of billeting.

Toubib, Medico (French).

T.S.F., *Télégraphie sans Fils:* radio.

U.K., the United Kingdom:
Great Britain.

washout, total loss (English).

whiz-bang, small caliber shell.

V.C., Victoria Cross. One of
the few medals that meant
something.

"Y", Young Men's Christian
Association.

W.A.A.C., Woman's Army
Auxiliary Corps (British).

Ziz Zig, numerous Anglo-
Saxon equivalents.